Goliath's Mountain

Rita Klundt

WESTBOW
PRESS®
A DIVISION OF THOMAS NELSON
& ZONDERVAN

Copyright © 2017 Rita Klundt.

All rights reserved. No part of this book may be used or reproduced by any means, graphic, electronic, or mechanical, including photocopying, recording, taping or by any information storage retrieval system without the written permission of the author except in the case of brief quotations embodied in critical articles and reviews.

Scripture taken from the New King James Version®. Copyright © 1982 by Thomas Nelson. Used by permission. All rights reserved.

WestBow Press books may be ordered through booksellers or by contacting:

WestBow Press
A Division of Thomas Nelson & Zondervan
1663 Liberty Drive
Bloomington, IN 47403
www.westbowpress.com
1 (866) 928-1240

Because of the dynamic nature of the Internet, any web addresses or links contained in this book may have changed since publication and may no longer be valid. The views expressed in this work are solely those of the author and do not necessarily reflect the views of the publisher, and the publisher hereby disclaims any responsibility for them.

ISBN: 978-1-5127-9419-9 (sc)
ISBN: 978-1-5127-9418-2 (hc)
ISBN: 978-1-5127-9420-5 (e)

Library of Congress Control Number: 2017910995

Print information available on the last page.

WestBow Press rev. date: 09/25/2017

With love, for Howard and Ellene

ACKNOWLEDGEMENTS

I've laughed, cried, and lost sleep over the events and people on these pages, but I haven't done it alone. "Thank you" isn't enough, but it's where I must start for Rob, Paula, and Aimee, who encouraged, and trusted me to tell *our* story.

Jan, Rhonda, and Kevin offer proof that giants aren't quite so daunting with brothers and sisters on your side.

Some great people from Liberty Baptist Church have been my friends, counselors, and confidants. They are my second family, and a precious gift.

My generous friends, Rishma and Anita, read my first draft and used their red ink with enthusiasm and kindness.

I'm grateful for my Word Weavers friends, from the Land of Lincoln, for sandwiching ample praise around their constructive critique.

Dr. Timothy Najpaver was more than my pastor. He was a teacher, encourager, and friend. I'm a better writer and person for having spent time with him.

And there is Roger. He knew this would be a long and messy journey when he committed to walk with me. On occasion, he carried me. His presence makes my past more than just another sad story.

> Jesus said, "I have told you these things, so that in me
> you may have peace. In this world you will have trouble.
> But take heart! I have overcome the world" John 16:33 (NIV).

INTRODUCTION

My former pastor and friend, Dr. Timothy Najpaver, was a good listener, until he started hearing excuses.

I wished, for a moment, that I hadn't shared the urge I felt to write my story. If I couldn't fathom every potential repercussion of allowing strangers to see the ugly side of my life, how could Tim? My initial intention was to put facts on paper, in story form, for my children. The truth about their father was something they needed to know and remember. Strangers might misunderstand or judge. Tim couldn't possibly know what it was like to face that sort of stigma and scrutiny. He wouldn't be the one asking Rob, Paula, and Aimee to face it again.

"Tim, I appreciate your support, and I want to be obedient to God's will, but what if telling our story wakes some sleeping giant? The last thing I need in my life right now is another goliath."

"God wants all of you," Tim reminded me. "He can use a single mistake, more so than the sum of our successes. He can find a way to turn a scar into a thing of beauty and a past into a passion."

Some of his best sermons, as far as I'm concerned, weren't delivered from a pulpit or a stage.

I started writing, partly to satisfy a need to place a checkmark on my mental to-do list, but mostly because I felt God wanted me to. Sometimes the words flowed, and sometimes I struggled. Sometimes I cried, but nearly as often, I laughed out loud. My grandchildren would read these words one day. I wanted them to see their grandfather in more than old photographs. The writing stalled at the intersection of my telling a story and a loved one's legacy.

Tim asked about my progress. "When are you going to let me read this book you're working on?"

Whether or not he saw through my excuses to the real reason I had put aside the manuscript, I don't know.

Tim's advice, "Write your story, and let the Lord work out the details."

A few weeks later, I was invited to share part of my story at a ladies' conference. It wasn't as difficult as I thought it would be to say Jack's name, and talk about suicide, without tears and a tissue. Several of the women gave positive feedback about my message, and one expressed how my talk helped her understand what her daughter had been going through. She said, "I wish I'd heard that ten years ago. You should write a book."

Could seeing my scar help someone else to heal? I thought of Tim's advice. I needed to finish writing my story, and let the Lord work out the details.

One day, Tim and I were talking about the theme of my manuscript, and my life. We shared a fondness for the biblical account of David and Goliath. We talked about how faith is meant to be demonstrated, first in the little things. He reminded me that David started by picking up one stone. I tried arguing the differences between me and David, the shepherd boy who became a king, but Tim was much more competitive than me, and smarter. I played checkers. He played chess.

"You experienced a Goliath-like beating and survived," Tim said. "You've lived in the foothills of Goliath's mountain. Folks who are there, need to be reminded that God doesn't live under a steeple. He's in the foothills with them."

"But Tim…I'm not…"

"Just pick up the next stone, Rita."

Within a month of that conversation, I had written the hardest chapter of this book, and Tim was diagnosed with the cancer that took his life. I wish he had written a memoir.

So, this is my story. I call it *Goliath's Mountain*.

1

THE TRAP

"Mrs. Curtis didn't pray this morning when the preacher told us to."

Somehow, even as a four-year-old, I knew that statement was powerful enough to start a lively Sunday dinner conversation.

Mommy asked, "How do you know?"

"She had her eyes wide open."

That was the first time I remember stepping, mouth first, into a very uncomfortable trap. The smirk on Jan's face suggested my big sister felt superior in having never been caught in such a predicament. She made no attempt to feign compassion or hide her immense delight in watching me squirm.

My statement opened, carried, and closed our table conversation. As she served fried chicken, mashed potatoes, gravy, and green beans, Mommy presided over a stern but brief lesson about tattling. She included examples and case studies. When she left her place at the table to retrieve the banana pudding, Daddy began a lesson I would have titled *Prayer 101*. I supposed he thought it more important to pray, than to refrain from tattling. Ninety percent of everything I know about prayer, I learned that afternoon.

I think Mrs. Curtis had a family, but I never met them. She rode with us to church every Sunday and regularly offered insight into the lives of other church members, but kept her own life a mystery.

If Mrs. Curtis were alive today, she would probably still be wearing one of her few flowery print dresses with a skinny belt separating a button-up top and a full-skirted bottom. She might still be drowning in cheap perfume. One would hope to see a pair of pantyhose replacing those thigh-high nylon stockings that always slipped down to her ankles by the time church was over.

Based on adult conversations around me, I believed her to be a critical and unhappy woman, but for some reason she liked me. When other children would receive a scowl of disapproval, I would get half a smile that said, "I'll have to tell your daddy if you do that again." She often told me I was pretty as she stroked my hair. Mrs. Curtis made me believe, not that she would tell my daddy, but that I was pretty.

It was puzzling. She was so pleasant to me, yet I never heard her thank anyone for the weekly rides to and from church, or offer a compliment to anyone other than me.

I imagined she must have numerous almost-empty candy dishes scattered around her home, because she always offered Jan and me hard candy. The little treats were so sticky with age, we were seldom able to separate them entirely from their wrappers. The bits of paper never hurt us. It was the amount of lint picked up from the bottom of her deep pocketbook that was scary. Jan politely said "No, thank you" or pretended not to hear her offers. I looked forward to the sweets and never refused.

Most Sundays were the same. I liked the singing, but a feeling of extreme fatigue would overcome me after three to five minutes of a sermon. I typically sized up the possibility of resting on Mommy's lap, and if the prospect looked dim for any reason, I would scoot toward Mrs. Curtis and stretch out on the pew close to her, using hymnals for a pillow. I wanted to, but couldn't imagine how I could rest my head on her lap. She was a very round woman.

Mrs. Curtis didn't appear to be suffering from physical illness or pain. Hers must have been an emotional pain. My parents wouldn't speak of it, which only fed my curiosity about what had made her so sad and cranky. *Was it the death of a loved one? Had she been betrayed? Was she forced to surrender a dream?* I wondered if she was just tired from a struggle and what that struggle might have been.

Loneliness can soil our spirits and steal our joy, but who or what had been taken from her?

I was only four, but knew that people didn't act that way unless they'd been wounded. In a million years I could not have imagined what might make me feel what Mrs. Curtis felt.

There is a little girl, not much older than I was when I tattled on Mrs. Curtis. She sits with her family on the pew in front of me nearly every Sunday. I love the way her shiny brown hair frames her innocent five-year-old face. On a recent Sunday, the congregation stood as the pastor led the benediction, and my eyes focused on the bow at the back of her head.

Bless this precious child, I prayed, *keep her safe. Let her make friends as she starts school, and let her be happy.* For some reason she turned around and lifted her head. Her eyes met mine as if to say, *Busted! Your eyes are wide open!*

After the pastor's amen, I touched her hair and told her, "You sure look pretty today."

I hadn't thought about Mrs. Curtis in years, but at that moment I could almost feel nylon stockings wrinkling around my ankles.

Mrs. Curtis was the first person who intrigued me with her secrets—with the lingering presence of a private story censored as too harsh for innocent ears.

Jack was the second.

His family had started attending our church. So, when I saw him in a school hallway, I did what I'd been taught.

"Hi. It's Jack, isn't it?"

He only nodded, which wasn't enough of a response by my standards. I had no idea he wasn't a talker when I asked, "What was so important that you had to leave during a prayer?"

"How do you know I left during a prayer?"

Awkward. He thinks I'm the pew police, I thought. It hurt to be fifteen and still tripping, mouth first, into painful traps. Then his childlike grin made it all better.

It was clear that Jack wasn't going to tell the "good girl" from Sunday school why he was sneaking out of church. I redirected.

"So you moved to Illinois from Kentucky? My parents are from Kentucky. What part of Kentucky?"

"I don't know. They're your parents. What part of Kentucky are they from?"

"You know what I meant!"

Weeks would pass before I managed to craft a question for which he would have to give me a direct answer. School let out for the summer, and we saw each other only on Sundays.

"Are you having a good summer?" I asked.

"Are you?"

"Wait. I asked you first."

"I start a job next week."

"Hey! You answered one of my questions."

"Did I?"

His use of questions would have been maddening, except that I found it playful and engaging. Sure, he was withholding some things. But he had me hooked. We established a friendship with minimal conversation, and what I lacked in quick-thinking banter, I made up for with patience.

I expected his story was similar to mine. Unlike Mrs. Curtis, he'd only had fifteen birthdays. Too young to have lost a loved one or suffered betrayal. Too smart to have let go of a dream. Too confident to have given in to a struggle—and too handsome to be lonely.

But then why did he keep secrets? I thought Jack was like that candy Mrs. Curtis pulled from the bottom of her pocketbook. Sweet, and worth the trouble of peeling off a sticky wrapper.

2

THE QUEEN AND THE PRINCE

Jack was present on most Sunday mornings, but his disinterest in church concerned me. I assumed he'd submitted to parental expectations, but he managed to slip outside during class or the worship hour.

"You missed your dad's solo. Can you sing like him?"

"What? You like that kind of music?"

"I do when your dad sings it. He has a beautiful baritone voice. Was he trained professionally?"

"That depends. Do you call forcing our entire household to listen to Frank Sinatra and Dean Martin for hours *professional training*?"

"Haven't you noticed the way little old ladies pull tissues from their purses before his first note?" I asked. "Surely you've noticed that by his final chorus, they're passing tissues to the other old ladies?"

Jack looked down during those solos and usually doodled on a Sunday school flyer or church bulletin, pretending not to hear his father sing. It bothered me—but not enough to pray about it.

Members of my family were present every Sunday unless we had a fever *and* were declared by a medical doctor to be contagious, which happened once or twice. The only other acceptable excuse was if an out-of-state family member died or was buried on a Saturday night, and we couldn't make it back to Illinois by Sunday. That never happened. If it had, we would have worshipped with the grieving congregation of the dead relative on Sunday morning and then skipped bathroom stops during the six-and-a-half-hour drive to central Illinois in order to be in our usual pew for the evening hour of worship.

I rarely missed a Bible study or fun church activity. In fact, I was active in planning many events, sang in the youth choir, attended camps, and loved missions activities and projects.

As a member of the Girls Auxiliary, an organization sponsored by my church, I accepted a leadership role and worked to earn the organization's title of "Queen" by memorizing Bible verses, doing service projects, and completing learning activities. The coronation ceremony, held in front of the entire congregation, ended with my GA leader placing a gold-painted and glittery cardboard crown on my head.

My energetic style of leadership was appreciated by most adults, but during a youth meeting Jack responded to one of my suggestions with "Yes Queen" and a mocking bow. The other kids chuckled. During the rest of the meeting, my input was given with less enthusiasm. Jack read my feelings. As we left the room, he attempted to apologize.

"The one time I speak up at one of these things, and I say something stupid like that," he said.

Pride caused me to deny any insult.

Over the next few months he would look my way more often, and I looked back. He had yet to capture my thoughts when he wasn't around, but if he was in the room, I was distracted. A trip to the Six Flags theme park was coming up, and I noticed he had not signed up.

"You should go. It'll be lots of fun."

I judged his lack of response as a lack of interest, not expecting he would wake up with dew still on the grass for a church-sponsored activity. He construed my invitation as a request for a date.

We boarded the church bus, mob style. I strategized for a window seat near the back. The seat just behind the back tires is a rougher ride, but the wheel well makes a great foot rest for short legs that would otherwise dangle.

Surrounded by friends, I didn't see a need to arrange who would be sitting next to me for this three-hour bus ride. I plopped into my seat, and before I knew it, Jack was sitting next to me. Conversation went on all around him—typical high-school stuff—and he said *maybe* three words in a total of three sentences. If I'm correct, all three words were answers to questions of mine.

I thought, for Jack, it must have been a long, slow ride to St. Louis. I thought wrong.

Later in the day, he corrected my thinking, "Just because I'm not talking doesn't mean I'm not enjoying myself and the company I'm with."

Except for a few dating couples, it was mob style again as we disembarked and raced toward the park entrance, and then toward the rides. Joining a line for the rides did require some strategy if one wanted to avoid the sweatiest and smelliest boy, and there was one in every line.

The roller coasters were the most popular, but then there was a simple ride. We entered a large, enclosed, cylinder type space. The floor and walls were covered with scratchy carpeting. We were instructed to spread out evenly and stand with our backs snug against the wall. No belts or handlebar restraints. *How exciting could this be?*

Once the door closed, the cylinder began to spin. It turned slowly at first. Then I noticed it took more and more effort to separate my head and limbs from the carpeted wall. The floor began to drop as we spun faster. We were pressed to the wall, and held in place by nothing but increasing centrifugal force.

I tested my strength against the force. I lost, but it was so much fun trying to climb the wall. Then the revolutions began to slow, and I was at least two feet below the rest of the crowd. This experiment would cost me my pride and a little bit of skin. I tried to climb back up the wall, but centrifugal force was no longer a source of entertainment or my helper.

With one arm barely able, I reached out for the person next to me. They squeezed my hand, which did nothing for my safety, but did make me feel more secure.

My heart was pounding as I pushed through the crowd toward

the exit and a breath of fresh air. I was a little embarrassed to have let this silly ride get the best of me. The only lingering physical pain was a slight carpet burn on my elbows and throbbing fingers on my right hand.

Jack had been my rescuer. His grip was still tight enough to cause my knuckles to turn white and the tips of my fingers blue.

"You can let go of my hand now."

He loosened his grip and gave my fingers a brisk rub to help return the circulation. During the next hour or so I complained about my bruised knuckles, not because I needed medical attention, but because I was enjoying Jack's attention.

I quit complaining after he offered to buy my lunch.

"That's so generous," I said. "But I have my own money."

"Oh, you do? When you asked me to come, I thought you wanted someone to pay your way?"

"No! I'm not in the habit of asking guys for a date. You thought this was a date?"

I wasn't in the habit of going on dates at all. I'd only had one official boyfriend, and fewer than five official dates—unless it qualified as a date when a boy had his father drive him to pick you up for church roller-skating parties. Then, it would be seven.

Jack reached over my food tray, and I noticed an unusually thick wallet, especially for a teenager.

"We're together," he said. I let him pay.

"You have money left over after buying my lunch. If you reimburse me for my park admission ticket, we'll call it a date."

Thank goodness he laughed. I already felt greedy for getting the large drink and fries. Theme park prices!

We spent the rest of the day together, rotating between rides out in the hot sun and shows in air-conditioned theaters. Without speaking a word, he looked at me in one of those darkened theaters and asked permission to hold my injured hand. Later, he told me that several attempts to do so had gone unnoticed.

None of us rushed to board the bus for the trip home. Chaperones and teenagers were tired and dragging their feet. Jack and I were dragging our feet too, but for a different reason. We were sorry to have the day come to an end. He followed me to our previous seat.

The chatter began once the bus was on the freeway, but Jack and I sat silently and listened to exciting tales of roller-coaster rides and soaking wet adventures. The ride home seemed to take half the time. I hugged the window less, and he sat closer to the middle. For most of the trip, his forearm rested over my shoulders while his fingertips unknowingly played with the nerve endings of my upper right arm.

We sat with each other during church the next week and every week after. I kept asking questions, even though my original ones had not been answered.

"Why don't you ever bring your Bible?"

"We're supposed to bring a Bible?"

The next week, he carried a Bible. A thank you for my suggestion would have been nice, but who needs words when actions speak so sweetly? During the sermon, I picked up his new looking Bible and opened it to find Jack's distinctive left-handed writing in the margins, and verses underlined. Since he was not in the habit of bringing his Bible to church, it meant he studied it at home. This guy had more than a gorgeous smile and wads of cash.

I wanted Jack to be my boyfriend, but I was pretty sure he wouldn't ask, and there was something in our way—the unanswered questions. Those I had asked and those Jack had not asked. If he was interested in dating me, shouldn't he want to know certain things?

I found myself praying for a person more than for food, good grades, and a steady babysitting job.

Sometimes God says yes. Sometimes he says no. Lots of times he wants me to wait. Often, God clearly says to do something first.

"Jack. Do you mind if I ask you a personal question?"

"How personal?" Of course, he would answer with a question.

"Are you a Christian?"

His smile was building with what I thought would be another of his question answers.

"I'm serious. Don't laugh," I said.

"Yes, I'm a Christian."

"Good."

He had probably been truthful, but I wasn't satisfied with the quick, multiple-choice answer. If I wanted the full essay, I would need to be specific in the way I phrased my question.

Ever since first grade, when my six-year-old school mates made me the joke of the week for admitting my "new best friend" was Jesus, and he "lived in my heart," I'd avoided saying the name of Jesus out loud. Somehow, my entire first grade class had fallen for the whole *Santa down the chimney* thing, and couldn't accept hearing the truth from another first-grader. Our teacher refused to back me up. None of my classmates wanted to hear about Jesus' death on a cross or that they were sinners. Maybe they couldn't trust another first-grader with that truth either, or maybe they needed to hear the story from the beginning, and I was allowed too little time during Show and Tell.

Unless I was in church, I avoided saying the name Jesus. Saying the name changed things, and that made me, and the people around me, uncomfortable.

If I wanted to know what Jack believed about Jesus, I would have to practice saying the name *Jesus* aloud. Waiting for Jack to stand up in church and tell his story would take, as Grandma used to say, "a lifetime of Sundays." Maybe things were different since I had graduated from the halls of grade school.

With a friend to my left and another walking in front of me, I muttered, "Jesus. Jesus. Jesus."

"Rita! Are you swearing?"

"No. Just testing."

I prayed for courage as we walked to our next class, and suggested to Jesus how he could arrange for me to get Jack's essay answer. I think He laughed, but I know He heard me.

The leaves on the trees were starting to turn, and the Illinois humidity had left the state. It looked like fall but still felt like the best part of summer. My favorite time of year. That could have been the reason I decided to walk home from school rather than take the bus. Then again, Jack walked that way to work after school.

Our high school sat on a big hill with a scattering of trees that provided shade and nice homes for a community of squirrels. By the time I said good-bye to friends and stopped at my locker, Jack was headed down the hill, half a football field ahead of me. So I ran.

Then, because the legs on my five-foot-two-inches weren't enough to catch up to all six-foot-two of Jack, I yelled.

"Hey, Jack!"

I stopped for breath. He kept walking.

"Hey, Jack!"

Good, he turned around. From twenty yards away, I knew it had been a good decision not to take the bus.

After that day, Jack and I walked down our hill five days a week. Rain. Mud. Cold and windy. We didn't care. I walked with him as far as the grocery store where he worked, then continued walking toward home, thinking about Jack and talking to Jesus. Jesus always had a suggestion or a question for me to ponder.

That was in the days when most families had one, or maybe two, telephones wired to a wall, and few teenagers had the luxury of a private phone conversation. The only private conversations between Jack and I took place on that hill. As time between the final school bell and the start of his shift at the grocery store permitted, we would stop to talk, face-to-face, under a tree. I wouldn't trade one of those ten minute talks for a month's worth of private texting, even if I could.

One afternoon we were caught up in a discussion—perhaps about a particularly cranky teacher, or who would win the next political election, or maybe what kind of car we would buy if we had the money. We could have simply been, as Grandma would say, "sweet talking" when the conversation was abruptly interrupted by a squirrel's pantry of nuts falling on us and around us.

No injuries, so we brushed the leaves and debris from our hair and shoulders to go on with our conversation. We had rested our backs against the trunk of that tree for only a moment, when a whole family of busy brown squirrels scurried down as if we weren't there. They flocked to recover their stash of nuts, and before we could move out of their way, they scurried back home, along the same path.

Our first kiss was beneath that tree.

"Why do you call her Ginny?" I asked.

Jack didn't seem to mind my questions as conversation starters, until that one.

"Because it's her name."

His answer loaded at least a half-dozen more questions that I didn't feel permission to ask. "She's my stepmom."

"I'm sorry. I had no idea."

"Hearing me call her Ginny didn't give you a clue?"

"But Joe calls her Mom."

"He does. Doesn't he."

Jack followed up with an essay answer the next day. Unprompted.

I learned that his father, John, had left his mother, Margaret, when Jack was about five years old. John took the kids from Wisconsin to Kentucky, where they moved in with a woman named Ginny and her children. Joe was a toddler when they moved to Kentucky and the only one of John's children to call Ginny "Mom."

According to Jack, Joe and Ginny bonded quickly and easily. Joe was the baby of the family, almost as quiet and shy as Jack. Joe teased Ginny and made her laugh. Jack got along with her, but they never developed a tight relationship.

In hindsight, Jack understood how his belief that Ginny was the reason he couldn't be with his mother restrained him from reaching out to her, and Ginny hadn't put much effort into nurturing a bond.

"I learned how to take care of myself. I didn't need a mother the way Joe did."

That was less than I wanted to know, but all Jack was ready to share. Over the next few weeks, he listened as I rambled. I told stories from my childhood, barely noticing that the usual friendly exchange of similar or contrasting family stories was missing. I was doing all the storytelling.

He heard about how, when I was five, Jan convinced me that I was adopted. I told him about having pneumonia and other childhood illnesses—measles, mumps, chicken pox, mononucleosis, and more. We realized we went to the same doctor's office, which provided more material. Jack was a perfect audience, asking his questions occasionally and keeping his eyes on the teller.

Talking to him, I learned where the phrase "a touching story" came from. After I narrated a particularly funny or sad event, Jack would reach out and touch my arm or shoulder. I'd never confided in anyone about how much my parents argued. Jack took my hand.

"They argue over the silliest things. I used to wish they would get a divorce so the arguing would stop, but I know they love each other."

"How do you know?"

"It's gross. You should see them. Dad puts his hands on Mom. It embarrasses her and us kids, too. I guess it's better than the bickering."

Jack stroked my hair, and I got goose bumps. I didn't know that could happen. It certainly never happened when Mrs. Curtis stroked my hair. And she told me I was pretty!

If he liked that story, I should tell him about having to repeat freshman biology.

"It wasn't totally my fault. My lab partner was cute, and it was hard to concentrate when he flirted."

No touch. No stroke, so I shifted my strategy.

"From the time I was a little girl, I wanted to be a nurse, but you need biology for that. I'll probably work in a preschool."

"You remind me of my sister, Bernie," Jack said. "She's a nurse."

"I do?"

Bernie had dark hair like me, but she was tall, stunning, and had a beautiful smile. Jack thought the world of her.

"You do. She cares about people. She's the strongest and smartest person I know."

That may have been the finest compliment Jack ever gave me, but my sixteenth birthday had been days earlier, and I wasn't looking for compliments on my strength or intelligence.

The unintended blow to my ego caused a flashback to all my school pictures since the third grade. Bad haircuts and disastrous perms on the night before picture day are a rite of passage for any schoolgirl, but my overbite was severe enough to draw the attention of bullies. How could Jack think I was pretty, let alone beautiful like Bernie?

I would rather he touched me. I felt like a Cinderella when he touched me.

Soon, the walks after school weren't enough. Jack started to walk me home after church. He had been a most-Sunday-mornings kind of Christian, but by now, he was a two-time-a week regular. I begged, but he still declined each of Mom's invitations to join us for Sunday dinner.

Jack started filling in some blanks—not so much from his childhood, but with what was going on in his life on any particular day.

He found school difficult and thought he was not as smart as other kids, even though he earned decent grades. A bad report card would bring unwanted attention both at school and at home. He had severe test anxiety. Math came easy, but subjects requiring much reading were stressful for him. He dreaded reading aloud. Dyslexia wasn't something understood or in our vocabulary then. Years later, a magazine article would describe Jack's problem and give a reason for his academic struggles, but by then, he had adapted.

I didn't know how to take some of his revelations. "I wake up to my own alarm. No one has to yell or shake me. No one has to help me remember my homework. I do my own laundry, and now that I have a job, I pay for my own lunch, buy my own clothes, and pay rent."

Was he taking pride in his independence, or lamenting the unreasonable expectations of the adults in his world?

"You pay rent? You're only sixteen!"

"Yeah."

"That's crazy! Parents don't charge rent to their own children. It's not right!"

"Who says?"

Jack had a way of causing me to question what had always made sense to me. "Not everyone comes from a perfect family like yours."

"You know my family isn't perfect."

"I used to be Dad's favorite. Before Ginny. She cooks, but other than that, she doesn't lift a finger."

"Well, I'm no one's favorite, and you've heard my parents bicker. My life isn't exactly perfection."

The more I conceded to the differences between our family dynamics, the more Jack began to defend Ginny. He complained about his stepmother, hinting she was to blame for the bulk of their family's problems—without actually disclosing many problems—then sprang to her defense when I spoke the truth about her. I never understood that.

"She's a good woman. She puts up with a lot, between my dad and everything else."

When a topic led to uncomfortable thoughts of his home life, Jack was fine with the silence. Sometimes he would take my hand as we walked, and that was my cue to be quiet and give directing our conversation a rest.

I enjoyed the hand-holding, but the silence was torture.

"You'd be good at sports," I suggested.

"Oh, I get it. You want to know why I'm not on some sort of team. I'm too thin for football."

"But there's basketball, baseball, wrestling, and track. You'd be good at any of those."

Coaches agreed, and encouraged. Jack loved to run and he could hit a ball, but if it required practice time outside the parameters of a school day, he claimed not to be interested. We never talked about him and sports again.

He shared pieces of his childhood, one impression or statement at a time. Jack's stories were rare, incomplete, and never enough to fully satisfy my curiosity. The more time passed, the less my need to know competed with my need to be close to him. That's when I generalized.

"So do they have VBS in Kentucky?"

"VBS?"

"You *know*. Vacation Bible School."

"We had that."

I couldn't let Jack leave me hanging. "Well, did you go?"

"Ginny took us every summer."

Jack and I had heard the very same Bible stories at VBS. Stories that taught us important life lessons. He tried to mimic his favorite teacher's thick Kentucky drawl, but he had too much Wisconsin left over to do it well. VBS lessons were reinforced with activities and games. Both of us memorized verses that would serve us well in later years. I liked the music and stories about missionaries the most, and his favorite was outdoor recreation. We both looked forward to snack time, and both of us remembered painting bricks and calling them "bookends."

We agreed. VBS was a good time. Jack's soft-spoken and confident enthusiasm surprised me. "When I have kids, they will go to VBS every summer."

I pictured a little boy who looked like Jack on the last night of a VBS—Parents' Night. He was on a stage with a group of other children, in the back row and barely seen. I imagined a little girl in the front row and near the microphone. She looked like me. I couldn't help wondering if, someday, his kids might be *our* kids.

Over the next week or so, when other subjects of conversation sank, we went back to our VBS days. Jack finally answered my question about his Christianity with a brief, but satisfying, essay. He had been faced with the most important decision of his life on a Thursday morning in a little Baptist church. That VBS teacher, the one with the lovely Southern accent, led him in a prayer that changed his life. Jack believed, because Ginny took him to VBS.

One would expect Jack to reciprocate with some interest in what qualified me to consider myself "Christian." But no. If he cared, he didn't let me know. Moments of silence came and went. There were ample opportunities for me to blurt it out, or casually tell him about the day I made the decision to follow Jesus, but I wanted him to care enough to ask.

3

FAST CARS AND DANGEROUS SPORTS

Jack's dad, John, had a "souped up" car. I never bothered to find out what criteria gave it that status, but there was nothing soupy about that Impala. It was solid, fast, and could go from a dead stop to pressing my upper torso deep into the seat cushion before I could swallow twice.

It was John's toy, and a front seat ride was considered a privilege. He refused to allow Jack, or any of his children, the keys. Ginny didn't drive, so they only had the one car.

Dad let me practice driving in his little two-seater sports car. It was used, but British made, and cool—very cool. He taught me to drive a stick shift. We went to parking lots where he *made* me do donuts on wet pavement, but not until he had demonstrated the proper technique multiple times.

"You need to know how handle a car. You need to lose control in order to learn how to regain control." Dad said it, and when I quoted him at the dinner table while reporting on my driving lesson, Mom almost lost control.

He had that car only a short time. "Something" went wrong with the transmission before I'd mastered shifting gears on steep hills. Too bad. I liked that car.

And then there was Mom's work car. "Something" happened to it as well. It was a late model, but family-like, and practical.

During a heavy rain, our basement flooded. Water ran from

the street, down our driveway, and under the garage door. It only happened a few times before something had to be done. The solution was to build our driveway higher than the street, creating a drop-off into the garage. Entering the garage required a slow, controlled descent, because there were metal shelves against the forward wall, and Dad parked his motorcycle in front of those shelves.

Backing out, over the four inch bump, was only possible with a little extra pressure on the accelerator. I was still driving under a permit when I suggested to Mom that I back her car out of the garage while she went to grab her purse. She agreed. I buckled my belt, adjusted the mirrors, and started the car. With it in gear, I pressed the gas pedal to the same level as I had done before, just enough to back over the bump.

One problem. The car was in the wrong gear—drive instead of reverse. Mom's car lunged forward, raising Dad's motorcycle two to three feet off the ground. One of the handlebars ended up through the shelves and inside the plastered wall. Those were some solid shelves, and that was some solid plaster.

The motorcycle dangled there for two hours before Dad got home.

Mom's reaction: "You're gonna be the one to tell your dad!"

My thoughts: *I may as well, I'm gonna die anyway.*

I cried and speculated about the damage and cost of repairs. This was unlike any mess I'd made to date. It couldn't be cleaned or covered up.

Dad came home, and before he could get his lunch bucket to the kitchen, I was apologizing for the terrible thing I'd done.

All he said was, "That's what insurance is for."

His motorcycle was unscathed, except for a few scratches and twisted handlebars. The car was dented and needed some touching up to the paint. The shelves were totaled, and most of the tools stored on them were damaged.

Dad actually gave me a hug instead of a punishment, and never brought it up again, not even once. If I married, I thought, it would need to be to a man like my dad. I messed up a lot.

I'd heard it said we fall in love with someone, not for who they are or even what we think they'll become, but for how they make us feel. And Jack, like no one before him, made me feel beautiful, smart, and like I had a bright future.

This could be love. It felt like the kind of love fairytales are made of, but I'm no Cinderella. We haven't even been on a real date. We're only sixteen. People fall in and out of love.

I thought myself smart, disciplined, and mature not to let daydreams influence my choices. Lust is a feeling. Love is a choice, or so I'd been taught. I wasn't ready to choose.

I got a part-time job, working in the boys department at JC Penney. It gave Jack and me something more in common, and more reason to talk. We compared savings accounts. For someone so private, Jack kept me updated. Our finances confused me. It didn't make sense that he had enough for a down payment on a car, and I had only enough to make one payment and buy my first tank of gas.

My first car was a guys' kind of car. When I pulled up next to another car and tapped the gas pedal, I was the center of attention. Boys looked twice. Not at me, but at my red Pontiac Ventura, loaded with every available option.

John beat Jack to the curb where I had parked in front of their house.

"Isn't this the car your dad just traded in?" he asked.

"It missed our driveway."

Jack was slow to react, and it wasn't much of a reaction. "When did this happen?"

"Dad took me to the dealership when he got home from work. I guess he's driven by the car lot every day this week, and regretted letting it go. He loves this car, but he needs a six passenger."

"So he just went and bought back the car for you?"

"No. Well, he helped with the down payment, but the loan is in my name. It'll help me build credit."

John went back into the house. Jack and I went for a ride.

"You should've heard Dad's song and dance at supper," I said, not allowing opportunity for Jack to indicate interest. "When Mom got home from work, he had some explaining to do."

"He didn't talk to your mom first?"

"I know. I can't believe it. She wasn't mad. Dad kept telling her what a great deal he got, that it would be safe and dependable, and that he knew 'the previous owner.' It has the smell of new leather, low miles, and Dad waxed it twice before he traded it in!"

I exhausted his effort to absorb my excitement, then apologized for bragging.

Jack still didn't have a car. Parking space was limited at his house, and he knew there was no point in bringing up the subject. I offered to let him drive on our first "official" date.

"No. That's okay. You drive."

If being seen with a girl behind the wheel injured his ego, he didn't let it show or change our relationship. School rules limited parking permits to certain students, and I wasn't one of them, so we still had our weekday walks home. Most of our dates were group dates with our church youth group. A few movies, some bowling, skating, or an occasional football game, but none of our dates were too memorable.

Most of the time, it was a burger and shake, then watching TV with brothers and sisters as chaperones. When other options seemed mundane, Jack helped me keep my Pontiac washed and waxed. It gave me a chance to swoon over his biceps, which he pretended not to flex for my enjoyment.

I knew girls who had been taken advantage of in cars parked in dark alleys, so the first time Jack suggested we go to a popular "parking" place, I gave him a lengthy discourse on the dangers of physical intimacy outside the boundaries of marriage. My surprise was diluted with some disappointment when he agreed. Sure, I wanted to be the kind of girl a guy wants to marry, but I didn't want to be a girl so easily resisted.

Soon after, upon my suggestion, we drove to the top of a big hill overlooking the river and the city lights on the other side. People drove from miles around for this view. Jack had never seen the Illinois River from this vantage point. One long look, and he had seen all he wanted.

"Did we come up here just for the view?" he asked.

We both knew the answer. He leaned in and kissed me. It wasn't like in the movies. I was nervous. I knew we shouldn't be there. "Just kissing. That's all."

Another disappointment, not with the kissing, but that I was once again so easily resisted. From that night on we looked for reasons to be alone. We walked slower, and even found a couple of spots where the church, or the school between my house and his, cast a dark shadow and made trips between his house and mine last a bit longer than necessary.

Our parents had a general idea of how long our walks should be, so when one of our afternoons turned to evening and Jack still wasn't home, Mom got a call from Ginny. Jack and I were coming in the front door when the phone rang. Mom was using her telephone voice.

"They just walked in. They're alright. One of us will drive Jack home."

Mom's telephone voice got real after she said "Goodbye" to Ginny.

"Where have you two been? Ginny is worried sick. She said you left almost two hours ago! Howard. Give Jack a ride home."

Dad was whistling when he returned. I was holing up in my room, so I didn't see the look on his face, but it seemed all was well.

The next day, when I asked Jack about his ride home, he had nothing to say. The next week, when I turned into a familiar shadowed corner of the schoolyard, Jack kept walking. He refused my sultry invitation, or even to look back and answer me.

I ran to catch up with him. "Maybe we should talk about this."

But Jack was not in the mood to talk. *Tomorrow*, I told myself. *We can talk about what we're doing tomorrow.*

Several tomorrows came and went.

I didn't appreciate or understand all the reasons behind all the rules when I was sixteen. I did desire to avoid shame. And another thing. My shame would be my parent's shame. And yet another thing. Fear. According to some friends, my virginity wasn't a lot to lose, but I was afraid to lose it.

A friend of mine had been physically intimate with her boyfriend several times. We weren't close—I suspect because she knew I would caution her against the "evils of premarital sex." She let an intimate secret slip into a casual small group conversation, and I wasn't able to hide my surprise. The group looked at me. Their expressions said they thought I had no right to be shocked.

"We only kiss," I protested.

My closest friends believed me, but a couple of girls laughed, and hinted that I was either a liar or too dumb to know about such things.

A friend of Jack's also teased me. I had a stinging answer to his rudeness, but I walked away.

Jack talked me through the tears. "You did the right thing. You can't dignify those comments with a response. They can think what they want to think. You're not too young to understand. You understand better than they do."

"But they laughed at me. Who knows what they say about me—to my friends!"

Jack was quiet for several minutes as we walked hand in hand. Then he said, "So we may as well go all the way, if everyone thinks we already have."

I considered it.

It couldn't have been more than a week later when Jack and I were alone at his house. It was the first time that had happened. Jack denied orchestrating events, but he had that way of expecting me to tweeze the truth through his smile. I never once minded that he took advantage of my naïveté.

When the kissing started, my brain began to buzz and my stomach (or was it my heart?) began to swirl. He offered his hand and guided me across the room, but when we got to the foot of the stairs I let go.

"I can't."

"You can't what?"

"I can't do this."

"Do what?"

"Do this." I pointed up the stairs. His next kiss landed on my forehead as he turned to walk toward the sofa on the other side of the room.

"I would never hurt you, Rita."

"I know."

"We don't have to do anything you don't want to do."

"You've got that right!" I illustrated a defensive move my dad had taught me.

Jack laughed. "Rita. Rita. Never let the enemy know where you hide your weapon."

He wrestled me to the sofa. I didn't put up much of a fight. I saw no reason to keep secrets or my defenses between us.

We heard a loud muffler come around the corner. I ignored it, but Jack imagined John in the driver's seat and Ginny opening the passenger door. Then we heard two car doors close, and voices. False alarm. It was the neighbors. Jack laughed, loud. I didn't.

"That's not funny, Jack. We could have been caught."

"Doing what? We weren't doing anything wrong."

"We almost did."

I slipped on my shoes and walked out the door, but not so fast that Jack couldn't easily catch up. He still had a look of relief at not getting caught with a girl in the house. I was embarrassed. *What if the neighbors saw us?*

"Jack. We can't let that happen again. I'm serious. We both know better. This isn't a game."

"But you play it so well. You're my favorite sport."

"Promise me? We won't get that close again."

"I promise." He took my hand.

I caught Jack's cue. He cared about me. I was his favorite sport.

Within a day or two, he handed me a ring. No ceremony, but I supposed it was official.

"No strings attached?" I asked.

"No strings attached. You keep teasing, and when I can no longer resist, I'll ask for the ring back."

"Okay."

The ring was made of heavy gold with a unique cat's-eye stone.

I wrapped it with angora yarn to make it fit the ring finger of my left hand, and unless my hands were under water, I wore it all the time.

A girl whose face I recognized from school came to my register at JC Penney one evening. She noticed my ring finger.

"That's a cool ring. My ex-boyfriend has a ring just like it."

"What's his name?"

"John."

"My boyfriend's name is Jack."

Days later, I wondered if our boyfriends could be one and the same. Jack described his former girlfriend when I told him about the chance meeting. It didn't change my feeling for him when he admitted how, over the past couple of years, he had used his "dual identity" to his advantage with girls who might sit next to each other in a literature or geometry class. That explained some of the odd looks I got from other students when they heard me use his nickname, and why he never corrected anyone when they called him "John."

The ring was a distraction, almost a nuisance for all the changing of the angora yarn, but it gave me status. I didn't feel the need to ask him so many questions, but I did have one. It bugged me.

"Jack. When did you break up with her?"

He gave me a lopsided grin. "The Monday after Six Flags."

4

DAVID AND CINDERELLA

"What's your favorite book?"

With Jack, starting a conversation was work. I was beginning to think he tolerated my talking for the sake of a few kisses at the end of a date. Our kisses were becoming more passionate, and I would be less than honest if I didn't admit to looking forward to when the kissing would start. Whatever the topic or story, it lost its fizz when Jack interrupted mid-sentence with a kiss.

"Jaaack. My mom and dad are upstairs." It's hard to be taken seriously when you're whispering. "What's your favorite book?"

"You know I don't read much."

"So that means you don't have a favorite book?"

"Okay. David and Goliath."

"Really? David and Goliath? The Bible story, David and Goliath? Like in the skinny little book with the gold binding?"

"Yep."

He scooted away. Not far, but enough that I could have put a stack of books between us. And he sulked. That's what he did when he didn't get his way, or when he was thinking something he didn't want to say to me. He'd done it before. Date over. Not even a kiss would make him smile. I knew the look, so I stood, turned, and offered my hand for him to get off the sofa.

He held on, refusing to budge.

Then he said, "*You* tell me. What's *your* favorite book?" He gave me a tug, and I landed on his lap. Sitting on Jack's lap was a bad idea.

"Mom and Dad are upstairs!"

"I know."

"My favorite is *The Diary* of Anne Frank."

"Diary of who?"

"Never mind. You don't want to talk about books."

"I don't want to talk."

We kissed. And we kissed again. Dad's footsteps went unnoticed until he was on the bottom step. My guess was that his throat clearing noises were intended as a warning.

Date over. For good.

I think Jack was afraid of my dad. I know I was.

It wasn't so bad that Jack didn't get to hear my book report on *The Diary of Anne Frank*. I'm not even sure it was my favorite book, but it was the kind of book to spark conversation, and it happened to have been the last book I had been assigned to read.

My final thought before falling asleep that night was that I saw Anne Frank as an example of hope. Jack wouldn't have seen beyond the evil and brutality. Maybe the story of David and Goliath was his favorite, and maybe his mother read those Little Golden Books to him when he was small. I decided not to ask.

I woke up before the alarm clock, thinking of Cinderella—the Little Golden Book version. Mom read it so often when we were little I had memorized nearly every page. We also had a nice collection of children's Bible stories. I shouldn't have teased Jack, because David and Goliath was my favorite in that category. Again, I had memorized most of the pages.

We spent the next morning riding our bikes on hills and bumpy trails. I was surprised by how much I enjoyed just being with Jack, and no talking. I wondered if he enjoyed the time with me, and no kissing. Again, I didn't ask. I trusted his contemplative look, and his occasional smile when he glanced my way.

I was the one, per usual, to provide the opening statement when we stopped to rest. We were sitting on opposite sides of a picnic table, drinking colas and sharing a bag of potato chips. A memory from my childhood had entertained me during the last mile or two of our ride, and I was anxious to share. Maybe, I thought, if I tell him what it felt like for me to be six years old, he would let me in on what it was like to be him. I told Jack about *David and Cinderella*:

Dad worked the second shift a lot back in those early days, and we were a one-car family. Taking him to work in the afternoon wasn't a big deal for Mom. She was a housewife. Picking him up at night however, meant dragging sleepy kids along. Mom read to us to keep us awake until it was time to go get Dad. She knew how to read a good story. I could usually keep my eyes open until she started the car.

I thought about the night we had read both of my favorite stories just before leaving to pick up Dad, and were still talking about David and Goliath when he got in the car. In a past-my-bedtime stupor, I blended the two story lines, and it came out something like, "So, David and Cinderella lived happily ever after on Goliath's Mountain."

I may as well have sent an engraved invitation for Dad to preach a sermon. He didn't account for my sleepiness when he asked, "Where did you hear that story?"

"Mom."

Mom explained. Dad continued with his sermon anyway.

We heard how important it is to understand the difference between reality and fairytales. He preached to a congregation of four. Jan, myself, and two-year-old Rhonda listened from the back seat as Mom drove home.

Somewhere in the middle of his sermon Dad called out a string of fairytale characters, and the person of Santa Claus was exposed as a fraud. He must have considered the potential impact of what he had just said, because he paused. The streetlights helped Jan and me to see Mom glaring at him.

"*What did you just say?*" she scolded.

He turned around and looked at all three of us girls to declare that Goliath was real, but there was no such person as Prince Charming or a fairy godmother.

"You need to know the difference between truth and fairytales.

You need to be able to recognize a goliath when you see one. And believe me, there are goliaths out there."

Mom did not explain or confirm the truth about Santa, but Jan and I knew. We did our best to protect Rhonda's innocence. Until Rhonda and Kevin (our youngest sibling) were of an appropriate age, if the name Santa was mentioned, it was accompanied by a look instructing Jan and me to tread softly. We kept the game going. It was the right thing to do.

The message of Dad's sermon was nearly lost in the lateness of the hour, but after that night, when Mom read us a Bible story she read it straight from her Bible, the King James Version. She occasionally did some paraphrasing, but we always knew the difference between the truths in God's Word and a make-believe story.

I was probably the only first grader in my school who could define the terms fiction, nonfiction, biography, and autobiography. I was six when I gave up the dream of being swept off my feet by a prince. The most I hoped for on Goliath's Mountain was charming—if a giant didn't get me first.

On those late nights when we went to pick up Dad after his evening shift at the factory, I would stare out the car window and watch through the streetlights and shadows for a goliath.

I knew he was out there. My dad wouldn't lie.

Jack had listened through the entire telling of my story. No interruptions, no touching or attempts to hurry me along. My plan was working. Jack had remembered something from his childhood:

Ginny convinced John, after a few years of living in Illinois, they needed a family vacation. John wasn't keen on the idea, but for the sake of family peace, and quiet for himself, he agreed to pack the luggage, three kids, and Ginny in the car, and go to Kentucky. At every rest area, gas station, and restaurant along the way John noticed a different attractive female. Ginny, Debbie, Jack, and Joe knew he noticed the women, because John couldn't manage to keep his thoughts to himself.

The kids observed Ginny's aggravation, and John's delight at watching it build. They wondered how many times she would listen to John comment on a woman's "pretty hair," "long legs," "cute shape," or "tight sweater" before she reacted.

It was a long day in the car, but John and the boys were entertained. Ginny and Debbie couldn't have their hair messed with the windows down, and the air conditioner wasn't set high enough, or low enough, to please them. They made it to Kentucky without blowing a tire, or anyone's temper.

On the way home, Ginny noticed a woman, about her age, but trying to appear much younger. "Look at her," she said. "That woman isn't fooling anyone."

John couldn't let that comment stand, and he loved having the punch line. "Oh. I suppose it's fine for you women to size up each other, but it's not okay for me."

Further observations that day were pretend whispered toward the boys in the back seat, which aggravated Ginny even more.

As they neared home, Ginny asked John to stop at a grocery store to pick up a few items. She handed him a list and sent him in. On his way out of the store, John's head turned toward a woman wearing a short skirt and high-heeled shoes. Ginny asked the boys, "What's your dad going to say about that one?"

John got in the car, and of course, he commented on the woman's physical appearance, using the precise wording the boys said he would. Ginny didn't scold or complain. John drove out of the parking lot, driving by the woman for one final look. Ginny rolled down her window, stuck her head out, and called to the object of her husband's attention, "Hey! My husband thinks you have a nice ....!"

Jack added the moral to his story, "... and that's why you'll never hear my dad, me, or Joe make a lewd comment about a woman."

His story made me want to hear more, but it was time for the date to be over.

5

DIRTY DISHES AND OTHER MESSES

John's oldest two children, Bernie and Bill, had married and moved out before Jack and I started dating. All of Ginny's children, except for her youngest, Debbie, were married as well. Debbie was a couple years older than Jack. On the day there were only three teenagers (Debbie, Jack, and Joe) to do physical labor around the house, a new rotation of household chores was created.

Debbie, Jack, and Joe were not happy about the new rules, but Ginny had a plan, and John had spoken it into effect.

One of them would set the table and help Ginny cook, one would do the dishes, and the other would have the night off. Seemed reasonable.

Jack was clearing the table when I rang the doorbell. Debbie let me in on her way out. I checked my watch and the large clock on their living room wall. I was on time.

"Smells good. What did you have?" I walked toward the kitchen.

"Supper."

"Jaaack. Well, whatever it was, must have been good. No crumbs left." I checked my watch again. "We need to get going. Everyone's meeting at six."

Jack kept clearing dishes. "I can't go."

"You can't go? But on the phone you said . . ."

"I can't go. I've got to wash dishes."

"But it's your night off?"

"Debbie went to a friend's house *to study*."

"But it's your night off."

"Not anymore."

I took off his ring and put it on the window sill. That angora wool was a beast when it got wet.

"What are you doing?" he asked.

"Dishes."

"No. You should go. You can still make it."

"I'd rather help you."

He washed. I dried. Joe fled to his room. John read the newspaper and Ginny worked a crossword.

We were putting the last of the pots and pans away when the doorbell rang.

John invited Debbie's best friend, Sandy, to come in.

"Is Debbie home?"

"No. She's supposed to be at your house. *Studying for a big exam?*"

It took a few unintelligible verbal noises before Debbie's friend came up with, "Ooooh. She must be with *another* Sandy."

Jack was aware of only one friend named Sandy, but Debbie did have a boyfriend. I didn't want to miss any drama, so I stood in the doorway between the kitchen and living room as I dried the last pan. John went back to his newspaper, and Ginny resumed her crossword. John chuckled, but neither spoke.

Jack and I finished in the kitchen, he grabbed his ring and we walked out of the house without a word. Whatever it was that we were supposed to do that evening was well underway without us, so we went for a drive and Jack talked.

On the evenings when Joe was to do the dishes, he would suffer from fatigue and somehow fall asleep while standing at the kitchen sink. If that didn't relieve him of his duty, his lack of concern for detail when either washing or rinsing would. Dishes seemed to break when Joe was at the sink. Bubbles of soap rose to the top of John's water glass on one occasion. Jack was often required to supervise and assist.

When it was her night to wash dishes, Debbie would sit at the kitchen table with one ear glued to the telephone while the boys prepared dinner. She supervised the necessity of every pan and utensil used for cooking and setting the table. On those nights, Debbie would always seem to be craving simple foods and would insist her stepbrothers begin cleanup while the cooking was still in progress—advice she never followed when she was the cook. She was known to leave the biggest messes on the stove, the counters, and the floor.

According to Jack, having his name on the family calendar next to the word "dishes" seemed to bring out the gourmet in both Debbie and Ginny—full-course gourmet, requiring many pans and complicated utensils. In Debbie's defense, she did enjoy cooking, and there were few complaints about her meals—that is, until it was time to clear crumbs from the dirty dishes.

Extra homework or a final exam were never a good enough excuse for Jack to be relieved of dishwashing duty, but Ginny thought nothing of reassigning chores to excuse Debbie for a date, a phone call, stomach cramps, or to "study with a friend."

Jack was angry, yet he was able to laugh and make me laugh with his telling of their nightly routine.

I shared my own signature "dishes" story:

Jan would have been about ten and I would have been seven when our four-year-old sister, Rhonda, started picking out tunes on the piano. She kept Mom and Dad entertained with a new song every other day or so. Jan and I had been taking piano lessons for about a year, and we weren't that bad. We weren't that good either. Rhonda would listen to what we were attempting to play and mimic the melody, only without the frequent hesitations to search for notes.

By the time she was five, Rhonda was playing four-part harmonies. They called it "playing by ear." I never liked that phrase. I had ears. She had something else, somewhere between her ears and fingers. Whatever it was, Jan and I didn't have it. Jan calculated her talent right away and gave up with her lessons.

I was a little less inclined to do the math, a lot more stubborn, and somewhat more available to sit with young Rhonda while she waited before and after her lessons. Sitting on our piano teacher's front porch while Rhonda played inside, I was embarrassed that everyone could hear her playing at my level of competence, if not better than me, but I never missed an opportunity to brag that she was my little sister.

Other students joined me on the porch while they either waited for ride home, or for their turn at the musical scales and exercises. A week seldom passed when I didn't hear another student or parent comment about the little girl whose feet couldn't touch the pedals. I wasn't the only one my age to be intimidated to take a place on the bench after Rhonda.

Her talent would end up affecting the division of household chores. We seldom used the good dishes, if we even had "good" dishes. And the glasses we used most often were painted aluminum or some other kind of metal. They were sturdy, stackable, and unbreakable. Our everyday dishes were melamine. Not even fire could easily destroy them. I sat one near a gas flame on the stove once, but the charred edge made it no less suitable for our weekday meals.

I don't remember Mom complaining about washing dishes until she started working outside our home. Jan was about twelve by that time, and I was nine. Both of us were capable of housework, but it wasn't something we did. Dad tired of Mom's complaints and decided to lighten her load and end her drudgery. I didn't jump at this opportunity to serve, and neither did Jan, but Dad insisted Mom get out of the kitchen and leave the dirty dishes to us.

Our brother, Kevin, was exempt, initially because he was only a toddler, and then later, because of some Y chromosome thing. Jan and I suggested use of a dishwashing rotation several times, but Dad thought it best for us to work together and get the job done faster. It didn't work. Jan and I would find a way to aggravate each other, making kitchen duty miserable for the entire household.

Rhonda was old enough to help, but while at least one person was still eating—usually Mom, Rhonda would discreetly make her way to the piano. Jan and I would try to slip away, but not even homework was an adequate excuse. When Jan or I complained because our third worker was absent, we heard, "Rhonda is practicing piano."

I protested once or twice. "Wait a minute! Who really needs

the practice? Can't Rhonda already play better than us? Are we the only two who see what's really happening here? Should I start taking trumpet lessons?"

My arguments had no effect until five years later, when Dad bought an automatic dishwasher.

Jack liked my story. He agreed that as middle children, we'd both been under indulged and overlooked.

Neither of us said it out loud, but other than a few dirty dishes, our family stories had little in common. I'd seen firsthand how John allowed Ginny to show favoritism toward her children. Jack had accepted his place in their family's hierarchy. I felt he had given in, when I would have rebelled.

Without offering specific circumstances, Jack mentioned severe spankings. He told me that John would discipline his own children at the "least complaint" from Ginny, while the misdeeds committed by Ginny's kids went unreported. There was hardly ever a conflict between one of "his" and one of "hers" because, early in their blended family life, John's kids learned it was safer not to tattle. It never worked in their favor.

While I lacked personal experience with stepmothers, I had read the Cinderella story. Jack, however, blocked my stereotypical images from interfering with his status quo. Any conversation regarding his and Ginny's relationship ended with, "but Ginny's a good stepmom." He didn't need me as an advocate for his rights in their household. He didn't need me for anything, so I kept my opinion of Ginny to myself.

In an odd sort of way, it was Ginny who made Jack a charmer. She couldn't take credit for his genetically perfect smile, but he practiced his manners with her. More polite than most of his classmates, Jack's formal and genuine "Yes, ma'am" or "No, thank you, ma'am" made him a frequent teacher's pet in primary school. For such a shy boy, he was able to engage females of any age with his eyes. Thanks to Ginny, he was oblivious to his power over the opposite sex.

Jack worked to stay out of trouble in school, never stood out in any way, and was a natural at maintaining his position in the background. I'm sure, in part, because of his stepmother. Ginny also took John and the kids to church. She wasn't licensed to sit behind the wheel of the car, but she was definitely the driver.

Margaret's name was never mentioned where John or Ginny might hear, and any contact with Jack's biological mother was not allowed. Jack snooped to find her address, then slipped a card into the mailbox. Margaret responded with a nice letter requesting a visit. Ginny was the first to get the mail, and she saw it was addressed to Jack, but with Jack and me in the same room, she gave the letter to John.

John read the first few lines, his face reddened, he crumbled the pages, and his fist came back, ready to strike. It could have been my presence, or it might have been that Jack, several pounds lighter and an inch taller, was ready to offer a respectable defense, but John abruptly gained composure and backed down.

I picked up the letter before we walked out the front door.

"Here." I handed Jack the wrinkled pages.

"I don't want it."

"Then you take it and throw it away. If I take it, I'll want to read it."

"Read it. I don't care."

We sat in the driveway as I read the letter aloud. Margaret expressed regret, an apology for not being able to visit, and pride in her children. Twice she asked for pictures. Not one word about John or what had brought about their separation. She mentioned a boyfriend, but little else of her personal life. The letter was closed with love and a request for Jack to send her love to Bernie, Bill, and Joe. Jack pressed the wrinkled pages between his hands and his thigh, then folded the letter at its original creases and placed it in his shirt pocket.

Only one other time had I been party to such private pain.

I was in middle school at the time, and one of my friends mentioned that her father was touching her inappropriately. At that age, I didn't know what it was her dad was doing, but I knew it was wrong and dirty. I responded with shock, condemned her father's actions, and told her how I would fight and not let it happen. We continued whatever it was we were doing.

My friend wanted something that day I didn't know how to give. I did pray for her, once or twice. Now she was sixteen and had a baby boy who looked an awful lot like her dad, except the baby was adorable. I wondered if, when I was twelve, I shouldn't have used another word when I mentioned to a teacher and my parents that her dad was "creepy."

"Jack," I said. "Families have secrets. I'm sure my family has some ugly secrets. They're just hidden better than yours."

"Maybe."

I was driving and keeping my eyes on the road, failing to think of a competing secret to make us equal in Jack's eyes. I asked another question instead. "Why do you have your father and grandfather's name, and not Bill?"

"I don't have their name, I'm John Robert the Third."

"Jaaack. Give me the straight answer."

"How's this for straight? My grandparents were in the process of disowning my father for marrying my mother when Bill was born."

"Why? Didn't they like your mother?"

"She wasn't good enough."

"But then they named you?"

"Yeah. They got over it for a while."

"So what do they think about Ginny?"

"They got over her too."

Jack was talking more than usual, but I hadn't heard anything that qualified as a *big ugly secret*. And I didn't want to seem pushy or nosey, so I changed the subject.

"Did I ever tell you about the dream I used to have?"

"You dream?" Jack asked.

"Sure. Don't you?"

"Not in a long time. So what was this dream?"

"It was when I was six. I had it every night for weeks. Pretty scary. Our house was on fire, and everyone had escaped, except me. It was so real. My throat burned from the smoke. I could hear sirens in the background, but they never got louder or closer than the sound of crackling flames surrounding my bed. It was so hot, my tears evaporated before I could wipe them away."

Jack was a great listener, so I kept talking.

"Show and tell time would, I thought, be the perfect time to tell about the dream, but my first grade teacher interrupted me mid-sentence. Without apology or explanation, she redirected the class to a more cheerful topic. I tried again at recess. A friend told me she dreamed there where monsters under her bed, but she couldn't feel, smell, or hear the monsters. She didn't understand that my dream was different."

I wasn't sure what to think of Jack's response. "Is that the worst dream you've had?"

"Yeah. You've had worse?"

"Who's to say? I don't dream anymore."

Jack was done sharing (or maybe he simply paused), so I continued. This was my opportunity to tell him what I believed it was to be a Christian, and how I came to believe it. I hadn't rehearsed. This would be a test. His response would measure whether I passed or failed. Could I talk about Jesus without sounding like a fanatic or one of those hippy Jesus freaks? Maybe it was cool for some of my friends to be seen that way, but I needed acceptance. I couldn't handle being too different, or special. I asked for help in one of my quick, eyes-wide-open prayers.

Jack must have sensed I was about to tell a touching story, because he took my hand as I began to tell him about Karen, the girl who lived next door when I was six.

Karen and I played together. In the summer, we would stay outside until the mosquitoes started biting. Sometimes we would trap fireflies in a mayonnaise jar with air holes punched in the lid. Simple things like chalk for writing on the sidewalk, a ball, or a tree could keep us outside and entertained for hours. A tuna or bologna sandwich and some Kool-Aid could last an hour or longer while we rested from play. Between bites, we exchanged facts and speculations about the scary people who lived on the other side of the alley and Mr. Martin, the old bachelor who rented the small house situated on the back of our property, there was enough mystery for a series of books, television shows, movies, or all of the above.

We followed my rules when we played. Karen's requests to trade roles or give her the advantage in our games were either ignored or overruled. Mom stayed out of our disputes most of the time, but were it not for her occasional interventions, Karen would always have been the last and the least in all our games.

One day Karen and I were playing house, using some old dishes and utensils that our mothers had donated to our cause. I put together a pie made of dirt, water, and some kind of berry picked from a shrub in our yard. It must have looked yummy, because Karen took a small taste. Unbelievable! She ate dirt! Disgusting!

Whether Jan told on me, or Mom came outside because of my dancing and hilarity, I don't know, but she ran to Karen's aid, and she stopped me just as I was encouraging the second bite. I was probably threatening not to be Karen's friend if she didn't eat the whole pie. In any case, I was deservedly scolded, and our play was supervised a lot more closely over the next few days.

Karen had a learning disability and was in special education at school. She was physically clumsy, and her speech exposed a lack of skill with most things social. Her family members used one word to describe Karen's inability to keep up with other children her age. My parents warned it was a derogatory word, not to be used. Witnessing the ugliness on the faces of other children when they chided Karen with that label upset me, but she seemed undaunted by the laughs, jeers, and name-calling.

One Sunday afternoon, I was involved in a game with a group of friends, and didn't see a way for Karen to be included. Our neighborhood was home to several families with children, and our extra-sized yard was on a corner, making it a good spot for play, but that day, our yard was full of my church friends. They didn't know Karen, and I wasn't inclined to introduce them to her.

I told her to go back home, but she just stood there. She embarrassed me in front of my church friends. That mean-spirited word flew from my lips. The game continued, and Karen went back into her own yard, but not before I saw the look on her face. I knew I had inflicted pain. I couldn't have hurled a stick or stone more accurately than that one awful word, and Karen was my best friend.

"For about a week," I told Jack, "I thought of nothing but Karen and the way I had been treating her. Then on the next Sunday, I prayed silently and asked Jesus to forgive me of all my sins, especially for the way I had treated Karen. I asked him to come into my heart and be the Lord of my life."

When I finished telling Jack the story about Karen, I felt the kind of relief that comes after a dreaded, but inevitable, task has been accomplished. Jack didn't laugh, roll his eyes, or sneer at me. No funny looks or blank stares. He squeezed my hand before releasing it, then offered to buy me a strawberry sundae at the Dairy Queen. I *was* a Cinderella, and I'd found my prince.

6

NURSES DON'T WEAR MINISKIRTS

The miniskirt from the sixties was still popular in the early seventies. Mom was still believing they were a fad, but Dad's was the opinion that mattered at our house, and his girls didn't wear them. Since the eighth grade, Jan had been rolling her skirts to well above her knees the minute she was out of Dad's sight, and it worked for her.

It didn't work so well for me. I always ended up with a bulky waistband, giving me the shape of a Christmas ornament with two "ever-whites" (Jan's words) for legs. Then all the rolling and tucking would come undone sometime between my first and second hour of class. If only I had known that longer hemlines would arrive in the eighties, I would have been a trend setter.

I was seventeen, and Jack wanted to take me to a *real* restaurant. I don't recall a special occasion. It might have been a reward for all the dates that had cost him less than two dollars. We could eat free at home, but it was nice of him to offer.

I bought a new blue dress, blue angora to wrap his ring, and added some blue eye shadow to complement my mascara, blush, and bubblegum-flavored lip gloss.

"Where are you going?" Mom's eyes focused on my hemline.

"To the Chateau."

"Can you afford that?"

"Jack's paying."

Dad wasn't home, or her comment would have been directed

toward my short dress and not the expensive meal I was about to enjoy. If Dad had been home, I wouldn't have worn the dress. Mom had a harder time saying no, but she didn't make leaving easy.

"And after?"

"Jack has to be home by ten."

I could tell Jack liked the dress. The eye shadow didn't elicit the same positive response.

Jack and I had been content with bike rides, walks in the park, and television in our family living rooms, but it was nice to act and be treated like adults. The meal was lovely, the conversation sparse, and three unscheduled hours remained before Jack's curfew.

We sat in the restaurant parking lot and, from the car, watched a lake do nothing. I was getting better with our silences, but my own thoughts were seldom enough to entertain me whenever Jack was around.

"I think this is supposed to be romantic." I didn't mean to sound critical or complaining.

"Are you saying I haven't romanced you tonight?"

"No, Jack. I'm saying, waiting for this little lake to do something interesting is a waste of our time. Not even the fish are coming to the surface to check out this view."

His eyes scanned my dress, then tuned to my exposed legs. His hands followed. "I don't know. I like the view."

My own right hand landed firmly on his, not because I felt threatened or wanted him to stop, but because I needed to convince myself that I wasn't *that kind of girl*. I wished I could be that kind of girl—whatever kind of girl Jack wanted me to be—but I was afraid. A memorized list of potential consequences came to mind, and I recited them as though Jack had been absent during those lessons at church, school, and home.

I made it home two hours and forty-five minutes before Jack's curfew, and before Dad saw the blue dress.

That night I fell asleep asking permission: *Lord, will it always be this way? How about if we . . .? Why shouldn't we be able to . . .? No one has to know. Everyone says we're such a cute couple. What's the worst that could happen? Jack called me a tease. Maybe I am. Are you talking to Jack right now, or is he sound asleep?*

I was known, among my circle of friends, to be the last one talking when the lights went out. When no one else was around, Jesus listened while I presented my questions and needs. They say God never tires of hearing our prayers, but often a verse of scripture seemed to arrive me at "Amen" before I was done rambling. This verse quieted me several nights in a row: "Let no man despise your youth, but be an example to the believers in word, in conduct, in love, in spirit, in faith, in purity" (1 Timothy 4:12).

A few days passed before Jack and I spoke. I found a reason to stay after school, and he didn't wonder why I hadn't met him at his locker. He hurried down our hill without me. I think it was a Tuesday when we exited the school building at the same time. Jack didn't have to work, so he walked with me, toward home. Twenty silent minutes later, we sat on my front porch steps, and Jack was smiling, and ready to talk—but not about what mattered, only about the blue dress.

It was my idea to talk about college.

We had toyed with the idea of marriage before, without saying the word, and expressed what we thought a life together would be like, the way I expect a lot of high school kids do. But we hadn't talked about what would happen immediately after high school graduation.

Jack told me he wanted to go to college, but it was inconceivable. He had known, from the time he was six or seven, that he would need to work and support himself completely—starting on the day after he turned eighteen. I wanted to attend a four-year college in a bordering state, but I had never felt comfortable asking my parents to help with the tuition, room, and board that would be involved. I had the impression they couldn't afford it. We were in the same sort of predicament, except I knew my parents would allow me to live at home and attend junior college. That's what Jan had done, so that was my plan. Jack either had no plan, or he didn't know how to verbalize it.

He brought up my dream of becoming a nurse. Jack was my safest confidant, so I lamented to him about not having what it would take to fulfill that dream.

"I think you would make a great nurse."

Once again, Jack compared me with his sister, putting me on a pedestal only slightly shorter than hers, telling me I was smart enough. He followed, with comments about what I would look like in one of those all-white nursing dresses and joked about being the recipient of a sponge bath.

"Nurses don't wear miniskirts!" I shot back.

Before putting my dream back into its deep sleep, I wondered if his comments had been sincere. His dream, contingent on a college degree, he would not share. "What's the point?" He told me. "I'll find a factory job."

He said he would work two or three jobs if that's what it took in order to move out on his own. All the talk about our futures and the feeling of impending doom at the stroke of midnight on his eighteenth birthday turned his mood sullen and gloomy again. My mood wasn't far behind. There we were, two teenagers on the verge of some very adult decisions, feeling uncertain and a little scared.

I was disappointed in Jack for the first time. His apparent lack of ambition was a pretty good cover for his insecurity. I would not marry a man who had no ambition, and I wouldn't date him (seriously, that is) knowing he was not marriage material. With no argument or raised voices, we volleyed the idea of breaking up. I don't know who served that part of the conversation or who made the final grand slam. It doesn't matter.

I took off his ring and held it out, hoping for a little drama, but none was offered. He took the ring, the one with the cat's-eye stone, and sprang to his feet without an answer.

"So that's it?"

If he heard me, he didn't let me know. There weren't so many tears I couldn't watch him walk down the sidewalk. He was a block away when he used a baseball-like pitch to throw something. It was the ring. Growing up was not going to be as easy as I thought.

My prayer that evening went something like this:

Dear Lord. What just happened? Was that all in your plan? What brought it on? What am I going to do? If I really loved him, wouldn't

I be crying up a storm now? Maybe, just maybe, this conversation was what we needed to make both of us wake up and see how foolish our dreams are. He was a huge distraction, and there are lots of other fish in the sea, cars on the lot, weeds in the garden, and grapes on the vine. Thanks for making me feel better. Maybe he'll go back to what's-her-name and they can get married and make lots of babies together while he works three jobs to support them. No, no. I take that back. I really do hope he has a good life, but not with what's-her-name. Help me to move on. Sorry for being so selfish in my prayers lately. Do you tire of listening to my silly teenage thoughts and cleaning me up after my stupid mistakes? Okay, I know you don't, but I'm tired of having to bring them to you. Maybe I should be a missionary like Lottie Moon and go to China, or be like that brave little lady, Mildred McWhorter. I wouldn't want to live in Houston, but I'm sure Chicago has gang members who need to know about Jesus. There are plenty of single missionaries. Maybe I could do that. Yes, I could do that. Would you want me to do that? Amen.

7

CHILDISH THINGS

Breaking up wasn't so hard to do. Neither of us fell apart after our matter-of-fact separation. We acknowledged each other in passing at church and in the hallways at school. There were no regrets, and there was no drama. If it was going to end, I was grateful that it had ended quietly, with our privacy and dignity intact.

We both started dating other people. Nice people, smart people, just not the right people. Neither of those relationships amounted to more than a movie or two over the course of a couple months.

My one (and only) official boyfriend before Jack was home on leave after completing his basic training for the army. He surprised me by showing up on our doorstep to ask me for a date. Why not? I went, and we had a pleasant reunion. He asked me for one of my senior pictures during dinner, and I promised to give him one. On the way home, he hinted about a goodnight kiss. I didn't give him reason not to try. Then, with his kiss at the door, I remembered why I broke up with him. He was a smoker.

I excused myself to retrieve a picture and hurried back to the front door. With a pen in his hand he asked me to sign the back, so I did.

"I had a nice time. It was good to see you again." I thanked him for the dinner.

"Maybe I can call you once I get settled in Texas?"

"Sure. That would be nice."

I turned to go inside, pretending not to see him leaning in for another kiss.

He must have been settled within a few days, because he called. I think he sensed my lack of enthusiasm, but he called another three or four times before we came to the mutual decision to remain friends and nothing more. I asked him if he had destroyed my picture, or worse yet, posted it on a men's room wall with a nasty note. He assured me that my photo was still in his wallet.

I had just one regret. I wished I had asked for his senior picture. He sure was good-looking.

It was a happy time in my life. More grown-up decisions were on the horizon, and I was determined to enjoy the life of a juvenile for as long as possible. Note that I didn't say juvenile *delinquent*. I still avoided the four big teenage temptations—sex, smoking, drugs, and alcohol. Nothing I did would have landed me in jail or caused my family to disown me, though there were a few misadventures that, had they been discovered, would have embarrassed my church-going parents and scuffed my goodie-two-shoes reputation.

Someone in my group of friends hosted a slumber party every two or three months. Some of us were invited to spend the night in a large camper that was parked at the home of a girl who was more of an acquaintance than a friend. Within a few minutes of the party starting, she started dragging out bottles of alcohol. I should have left right away, but I didn't want to be the party pooper, so after announcing that I wouldn't be drinking, I stayed. We laughed, talked, and listened to music until the wee hours of the morning. I woke up with a horrible headache and slipped out while the other girls slept. It hurt to fully open my eyes, and my mouth felt like I'd been chewing on cotton balls.

On Monday morning, one of my friends disclosed that the cherry flavoring in my cola had not been cherry syrup, but cherry vodka. I was irate, and willing to do the right thing. "We should tell her parents." Then I learned it was her parents who had provided the liquor.

Most of my friends shared my values, but peer pressure could still persuade me to break the rules. Having one friend stay with me over the weekend while my parents were away turned into a house full of unsupervised teenagers. No one listened to the announcement that the party was over, and it was time to go home. Peer pressure wasn't the only factor in my decision to only make the announcement three or four times. I was truly enjoying myself. It turned into an all-night party.

I managed to graduate without incident and worked as many hours as I could get before starting junior college in the fall. Several of my friends attended the same school, and we were able to schedule breaks and lunches together. It was like high school, only better. The freshman level classes weren't too hard. There were a few new male friends, some flirting, and a few dates, but nothing regular and nothing serious.

I started teaching a children's class at church. I prayed when I needed something, but felt I needed little. I read my Bible just enough to review the children's stories I'd memorized years earlier. My friends didn't come to church much, and I didn't blame them. We were too old for the youth group, and adult church members either treated us like "helpers" or ignored us all together. I didn't mind.

It was an easy life. I lived in that place on Goliath's Mountain—that make-believe place between waiting for your fairytale to begin and putting away your childish things.

That year flew by. Jack and I saw each other less and less. He worked most Sunday mornings. The time or two he did come to church, he came in late and sat on the pew next to me. A little more space between us, and polite greetings made me feel rather grown-up. That was the first time I remember wanting someone to think I was something I was not—over him.

I managed to hear rumors of his latest girlfriend from time to time, and I occasionally found an excuse to go to the grocery store where he worked. He caught me wandering the aisles one day, without a cart and no intention to buy.

"Hi, Rita. Can I help you find something?"

I had no bills, only a few coins in the bottom of my purse. "Gum. I'm looking for the gum."

"It's up front, by the cash registers. Where it's always been."

A few nights later, to my absolute surprise and pleasure, he appeared at JC Penney while I was working.

"I joined the army," he said. "Before I leave for basic training, we should go out for some pizza."

Yes, I remembered his lack of ambition and the anger that had propelled that cat's eye ring, but I had no control over the indescribable feeling that came over me when he was near. Some call it butterflies.

Today, an eye doctor occupies the space where our favorite pizza place used to be. I don't know what happened to Angelo or if his real name was Angelo, but he made a really good pizza. Old black-and-white movies played on a big screen. They were either silent movies or the sound was always off. The place was known to be packed, noisy, and smoky.

Jack called it his "last supper" because the recruiter would be picking him up early the next morning. We didn't know it would really be his last supper at Angelo's, or we might not have let the smoke and noise cut our evening short.

Jack seemed distracted. He denied being nervous, and reminded me of friends, a lot less capable than he, who had already made it through basic training. I didn't recognize the look on his face or the tone of his voice when he told me why he had decided to join the army. "The GI bill will pay for college."

"Oh, so you do have ambition."

"Not really."

I needed more than a vague answer. "But you plan to go to college?"

"It's what you think I should do."

"Join the army?"

"No. Go to college. It's what the kind of girl I want to marry expects."

"What kind of girl is that?"

"Your kind."

I was in no way ready to discuss a mature commitment, but

liked where our conversation had taken us. Jack no longer seemed distracted.

We kissed.

"Are you trying to convince me to stay home?"

He was joking. *Or was he? Did he want me to convince him? I'd be willing to try. What kind of papers had he signed? Was it too late to change his mind?* Jack seemed ready to put away his childish things. *Was I?*

Two weeks went by before his first letter came. Then a quick phone call. The next letter was closed with "Love, Jack." I always wrote back and simply signed my name. I wanted to be sure. I doubted he was. If and when I knew, I would speak the words in person, not through the mail.

The edges and folds of Jack's letters were worn from going in and out of the envelopes, and the ink on the pages faded from over-reading.

I didn't question God during those days. Why would I? Happy to take advantage of his goodness, and enjoy the benefits of my youth, I prayed with a smile on my face, and always fell asleep after the "Amen." My relationship with Jack had been rescued. It was easy to love God then. God is good, I thought, *all the time.*

8

I SAID I WOULD

His skin was brown, and he had added a few pounds to his slender frame. The sleeves on his old shirt were tighter. I wished he had waited until we were alone to lift his shirt and show me the new ripples on his abdomen. I also wished I'd spent more time in the sun, and lost a few pounds during the weeks he was away.

It wasn't like Jack to brag, but when his father told him to show me his newly defined muscles, he complied and invited me to touch. How could he expect me to dismiss my blushing thoughts and carry on a living room conversation with his parents and Joe?

Somehow I managed.

John supplemented Jack's stories of running through mud and navigating obstacle courses, just enough to let it be known he missed his own good ol' days. Ginny, Joe, and I contributed little to the conversation, but we enjoyed our front-row seats for a rare moment of father-son bonding.

We had only a few days together before Jack would board a bus for more training. He was excited to be on track to be an airborne ranger, and I was excited to see him excited. This trip home had been to pack personal belongings in his old room.

Once we were alone I asked, "Why would you pay to spend all day, and most of the evening, on a hot bus with other sweaty people for the pleasure of having two days at home doing what Ginny could have done for you? It hardly seems worth it."

"You think I came home to see you, don't you?"

I had grown comfortable with Jack's indirect answers, especially the ones that came with a hug or a touch.

"I'm glad you finished basic training in one piece, and by the way, I love you too."

"Back at you." His smile said he knew how to play my game.

Between my work schedule and his work at home, we spent fewer than eight hours together before I drove him back to the bus station. Another long, hot day on a bus without air-conditioning, and a new group of fascinating strangers were the topic of his next letter.

Letters, in either direction, were answered on the same day.

His training regime was physically demanding, and he liked it. Going to bed tired and sore was part of the job. Phone conversations were only occasional and typically brief. One evening he called, but he didn't have much to say. Long pauses, and the way he spoke, made me suspicious. I had to ask twice before he told me what was wrong.

On his second jump he had injured an ankle, badly enough to force him out of airborne training. If he couldn't be airborne, it didn't seem to matter what he did. He fantasized about going AWOL (away without leave). Without a job or a bedroom to come home to, the fantasy didn't last.

He tempted me, "We should run away together."

"You can't run. Remember your ankle?"

When the call ended, I knew I was officially Jack's significant other.

I wanted to tell him "I love you" again, but couldn't throw those words out there, only to hear, "back at you." His hazel eyes and teasing grin would be ineffective over the phone.

It was obvious he was not calling or writing John and Ginny. Jack didn't tell them about his injury and not being eligible for the rangers. I did. His parents were kind to me and made sure to speak to me each week. They invited me to dinner, but it would have been uncomfortable without Jack there. My work schedule provided an acceptable excuse until one Sunday, when the only thing on my agenda was a nap.

Ginny served a nice meal on their fine china. Jack had been right. She was an exceptional cook. I enjoyed the dinner almost as much as their hospitality. John sat in the kitchen while Ginny and I washed and dried dishes. He was laughing and smiling more than usual. I saw where Jack, Bill, and Joe had learned to charm.

"I told Jack you were the girl he shouldn't let get away," he said.

Ginny smiled and scolded John for oversharing. They took turns bragging about Jack. John acknowledged, not that Jack was his favorite, but why the rest of the family might think so.

"He's a quick learner. I only had to tell him once, and he would mind. As a baby, he was early to walk and slow to talk. As a child, he was quick to walk away from a fight. Not mouthy like some of his friends. Kept him out of trouble. Jack never got into any *real* trouble."

Ginny told me about the girls.

"The girls liked Jack, and he liked them back. He saved for six months to buy his sixth-grade girlfriend a bracelet. Then he ended up giving it to another girl because she was prettier and spent time with him on the playground, practicing spelling words."

The infantry was last on Jack's list of preferred assignments, but he would be able to join the training without major adjustments. Army doctors considered all the marching to be physical therapy for his injured ankle, and his commanding officers agreed.

Each letter added another hint that we wanted our futures to be together. Each letter, a test to see if we were ready to share a deeper commitment. We knew we were young and lacked wisdom about a lot of things. The miles between us allowed room for our relationship to grow. Some conversations are best held face-to-face, so I purposefully kept my desires vague. Jack was the one teasing now, stopping short of any "forever" kind of commitment. In at least every other letter, he gave me the opportunity to back out gracefully.

You can do better than me.

I didn't know how to reply.

I'd understand if you wanted to date someone else.

I tried to ignore comments like that, but it was hard. When he called, I told him so. "Why do you say things like that in your letters? You know I don't want anyone but you."

"Just letting you know your options are still open, but not for long."

Like any girl would, I imagined several romantic and creative scenarios where he would pop the question. My answer and reaction would be the same no matter where we were or how he posed the question. *I love you, and of course, I will marry you.* Then he would stand (having come up from one knee), and we would embrace. The proposal was simple, yet beautiful, when I practiced it in front of a mirror.

A message that Jack had called and would be arriving home the next day for thirty days of leave was not a surprise. He had mentioned, more than once, the day and time his training would be complete.

It was 1974, before cell phones, and it's a wonder we communicated at all, especially that day. I didn't worry about the time of his arrival until about four-thirty in the afternoon when I had to leave for a five-to-nine shift at JC Penney.

The older ladies who worked with me took every opportunity to tease. Two of them, Lucy and Edith, worked exceptionally hard at initiating me into their secret (from men anyway) society of adult humor.

When I mentioned that Jack had not yet arrived home, it was what they needed to put some fun into an otherwise slow night. They suggested I should go ahead and start looking for a new boyfriend. Every man old enough to carry a driver's license, and able to walk through the department was critiqued for his potential. Each and every one of these men had a major flaw which either Lucy or Edith named a way to overcome.

"Rita. Look at that one. You can buy him some teeth and hair," Lucy said.

Edith was not to be outdone. She pointed discreetly. "With a shower and a clean shirt, that one would be a catch, and he paid with a gold card."

When Jack called me at work, they arranged for me to walk out of the store at 9 p.m. sharp, but not before they pressured the promise of a full report the next morning. After all my dates with Jack, they would interrogate me, hoping something would have changed. Both were widows and claimed they would like to have lived vicariously through my young love life, if I had a love life.

John and Ginny's brightly lit living room made it easy to see through the dark and their sheer curtains. I saw him in uniform for the first time. Say what you will about uniforms, but for a female on the brink, a man in uniform can cause her insides to tumble.

Jack got up to answer the door before I rang the bell. His six-foot-two frame leaned down to embrace all five-foot-two inches of me. Then came the kind of kiss I longed for, but not the kind of kiss that should have happened in front of his parents.

I expected a few minutes of small talk with his family, but Jack opened the door again to lead me back outside—no words. John suggested Ginny warm up some leftovers, spouting about how delicious their dinner had been. The ornery smile on his face let everyone know there was no need for late-night kitchen duty. The invitation was meant to tease. He knew Jack and I wanted time alone. I offered a lame excuse for our departure as Jack held the door with one hand and pulled on my elbow with the other.

His ankle was swollen and he walked with a slight limp, but he assured me he was much better, and that an ankle wrap, tightly laced combat boots, and ice every evening were indeed, the best physical therapy. We drove around for about an hour, eliminating venue after venue of entertainment, either because of Jack's injured ankle or lack of interest.

We settled for burgers and fries at a place called Steak 'n Shake. I remember shivering and asking the server if she couldn't set the thermostat on "something warmer than arctic." I don't know if I was shivering because of a cold draft or nerves from being with Jack. He was not his usual beguiling and quiet self. He talked of anything and everything without saying much, allowing his food to get tepid and unappetizing.

His arm around my shoulder was not enough to take away the chill, even after we stepped outside. The hot July sun was sitting on the horizon, but had left the blacktopped parking lot steaming and sticky. I didn't turn on the car's air-conditioning right away.

We were at the stop sign on the corner of Sheridan Road and Florence Avenue when Jack asked, "Are you warm yet?"

That was when I noticed the perspiration on Jack's forehead. He didn't look well.

"My next duty station is in Germany. I leave in twenty-eight days."

What he would say next might hurt. I braced my foot firmly on the brake. *Was he ready to end our relationship? Was an agreement to date other people going to follow this abrupt announcement? Why had he waited until now to deliver this news?*

The car wasn't in motion, but I glued my eyes to the road. I put all the stoic I owned on my face while I waited.

"Will you go with me tomorrow to pick out an engagement ring?" Jack asked.

The lump that had instantly appeared in my throat with the news about Germany began to dissolve. This question warranted an appropriate pause before a response. I put the car in park, and with a seatbelt and the console of the car between us, I was able to shift my weight to face the man who had just offered a marriage proposal. My practiced response didn't fit his question or his posture, so I improvised.

"What time?"

A quick kiss before the driver of the car behind us would start honking their horn, then I put the car in gear and we headed toward his house. I had been as vague in my answer as he had been with his question, but that didn't mean Jack would be able to avoid what should happen next.

"You'll have to ask my father for my hand in marriage, the old-fashioned way."

"Okay."

When the doorbell rang the next morning, I knew who it was and raced to be the one to answer. I was working to conceal my exuberance after sleeping, or trying to sleep, on my untold news.

Dad was in the living room. Mom was in the kitchen. I walked Jack upstairs and announced to Dad that Jack "needed to talk" to him before I turned and bounded down the stairs.

I couldn't sit still. I paced and tried to hear the conversation, but I couldn't. When after only a few minutes (the kind of minutes that seem like hours) I heard Dad laughing, I thought it safe to return upstairs.

A few questions about how Jack planned to provide for me were all that was left of the conversation. Jack communicated with Dad in a way I wasn't able. If I had been the one to either ask permission or announce our engagement, there would have been at minimum two hours of lecturing. The way Jack handled himself, and my father, was impressive—especially considering he was still a couple of weeks shy of nineteen years old.

We didn't talk much as we drove toward the jewelry store, but Jack said enough. He credited his father for instructing him on how to ask for my hand in marriage. "Don't tell him how I messed that up."

"You didn't mess it up."

"But I did. You didn't say yes."

"Yes to what question?"

"Yes, to will you marry me."

"I'm waiting for you to ask."

Jack swallowed and took a little too long to respond. I tried to lead him on with my eyes and smile, but I was never too good at that sort of thing.

"Will you let me love you forever?" he asked. "Will you be my wife?"

"Yes."

The jeweler pulled out four trays of rings and placed them on top of each other, I'm sure according to price. The old guy had probably sold a ring or two. He led us away from where we approached him and directed us toward the end of the counter where the lights were brighter. We were keenly aware of our youth and inexperience, but Jack had done some research, and John had included some advice about countering potential sales pitches. Once again, I was impressed with the man I would marry.

The top tray was filled with one carat or bigger rings. My eyes went to a particular diamond right away, the biggest on the tray. So heavy, my finger couldn't support the stone upright, and I wondered how it could even be real. I had to at least try it on—for the fun of it. When I saw the price tag, I knew it had to be real. The salesman looked at Jack as if I weren't there.

"If you like that style, I have another wedding set with a little smaller, but nice-sized diamond that will make her happy."

He put away the top tray.

I saw the ring he was talking about and reached out to it like a kid in a candy store. We had not discussed price, and I didn't want my exuberance to influence Jack to go beyond his plans and his budget, so I hesitated before I touched. I glanced his way. Jack's eyes were fixed on me. After an affirmative nod, the jeweler picked up the ring and gave it to Jack. He took my left hand and placed the ring on my third finger.

"You're sure? You will marry me?"

I used to think I could be an actress, but I gave up that daydream. Jack could have asked me twenty more times and I still wouldn't have been able, in the moment, to recall my perfect and rehearsed answer to his question.

"I said I would."

The salesman cleared his throat.

"We'll take it," Jack said.

The old guy returned the rest of the trays to the locked counter, and they completed the cash transaction. Before Jack opened my car door, I paused and asked, "Are you sure? This is happening so fast."

"I'm sure about you—and the ring."

"You know, Jack, I'm engaged to marry a man who has never told me, face-to-face, that he loves me."

"That's nothing. I just spent three months' wages on a ring for a girl who never signs her letters 'With Love.'"

That was the first, but not the last time I heard him say, "I love you."

Boy, oh boy. Did I have some news for Lucy and Edith!

9

28 DAYS

Twenty-eight days from engagement ring to returning from the honeymoon. That was all we had.

Jack, Mom, and me sat at the kitchen table and used one bridal magazine, one sheet of notebook paper, and less than an hour to plan a wedding. Time didn't allow for embossed invitations or special ordering of anything.

"Your dad and I were married right after a Sunday morning worship service." Mom hadn't necessarily offered it as a suggestion, but Jack and I liked the idea of a simple, no-frills, church wedding. Mom and Dad were still happily married nearly a quarter-century after their Sunday wedding. Why not do the same? Ours would be immediately following a Sunday evening worship service when most of our family, and many friends, would already be at the church.

I hadn't spent much time dreaming the details of a wedding day and had no standard of perfection to achieve. Wedding showers, wedding decorations, and wedding drama didn't appeal to me. Having only twenty-eight days took away the pressure and the worry that is part of most wedding celebrations. Gifts weren't even a consideration. We didn't have a house or apartment that required furnishing.

Our list didn't grow far from a cake, nuts (the good mixed ones), mints, and punch. The July 21st church bulletin would read:

You are cordially invited... A reception immediately following in the church fellowship hall.

"A few phone calls to family and friends," I said, finishing up that portion of the plan. "What else do we need?"

"A preacher would be good." Jack caught that minor detail, missed by Mom and me.

We went to the church together, hoping the pastor was in his office. He was, and we had our first premarital counseling session—on the spot, no time to waste. We confirmed the date, and the pastor shook Jack's hand. With a comment or two about this being a big step, a couple of questions about our plans, and asking if our parents supported our decision, we were in and out of his office in less than fifteen minutes.

"Maybe we should elope?" Jack said as we walked out of the church.

"What's the matter, Jack? Are you afraid he might try to talk you out of marrying me?"

"No. But he might talk you out of marrying me."

"Why would he do that?"

"Oh. I don't know."

A second of doubt prodded my conscience, but I didn't allow it to steal my good mood. If Jack had doubts, I didn't want to know. We had already admitted to being not quite nineteen-year-olds making the adult decision not to wait three years before consummating our love. We had chosen each other and were committed for the better and the worse.

The following day, our pastor gave little advice. He started with questions. Jack's favorite. Essay questions. About family, and the past. About past relationships, including our relationship with Jesus Christ. About our plans for building a life together. Jack's manner through the whole process would have made anyone want to hire him, if it had been a job interview.

We talked about handling conflict, dealing with disappointments, and managing finances, in-laws, and raising children. We didn't talk about sex.

The order of the ceremony was chosen. No rehearsal. No rehearsal dinner necessary.

The pastor put a book in a large envelope, and explained as he added worksheets, a list of discussion questions, and helpful hints for a happy marriage. "I want you to read this. Each of you on your own, then discuss it chapter by chapter."

He led in a prayer, and we were dismissed as having dutifully completed premarital counseling.

Really? A reading assignment?

We threw the packet in the back seat and drove away.

The next priority was, of course, the dress. It was hanging in the middle of a rack, as though the JC Penney store clerks thought by hiding it they could forget about the upset customer who promised never to return and to tell all her friends about their incompetent alterations lady. Too much off the hem became some poor bride's disaster, and my off-the-rack, fit-me-perfectly wedding dress bargain. Using my JC Penney discount, I paid ninety-nine dollars.

Sometime around day seven, Ginny went with us to the courthouse to get our marriage license. At that time, boys could carry a gun in the armed services and do a lot of other things with proof they were at least eighteen years of age, but until a boy turned twenty-one, a marriage license in our county required a parent's signature. The clerk didn't ask to see my identification. Maybe I had a familiar and honest face, or maybe it wasn't required?

The counter was shoulder height for me, and I could barely see what Jack and Ginny had signed, but I questioned their spelling of what would soon be my new name.

"No. That's how we've always spelled it."

I felt like a child who had interfered with adult business. In my defense, Jack had passed up numerous opportunities to correct me. Or perhaps he'd expected I might notice the return address on every one of his letters?

Ginny wanted us to drive her to a neighboring town to buy shoes for the wedding. I already had my shoes and suggested a store in our local mall, but she insisted and offered to buy us lunch. Jack and I had looked forward to a private lunch after dropping her off at home, but neither of us spoke against Ginny's request.

From our seats near the door of the shoe store, Jack and I observed while the frustrated salesman worked to find the right shade of off-white, with a two-inch heel and nonslip soles. Ginny seemed to be enjoying herself. I would have liked to offer my opinion, but to do so would have complicated and delayed her decision. My mind wandered.

I mumbled so that only Jack could hear.

"Jack. Your mother doesn't know you're getting married. You should at least call her."

"Why?"

I thought the answer was obvious, "Why does anyone tell their mother about their plans to marry?"

"We need to talk. Later."

Ginny settled on some tan sandals and a pair of black patent leather pumps. (For the wedding, she wore a pair that had been in her closet.)

Lucy and Edith offered little empathy when they heard me tell how my future mother-in-law had stolen our afternoon. They laughed, but they also convinced the store manager to allow days off work that I hadn't earned and to hold my position for me when I returned from a short notice, honeymoon vacation.

I went to Jack's house after work that night to let him finish the conversation we had started in the shoe store.

"I should tell you about my mother," Jack started. "My real mother. She isn't well."

"Oh no! What's wrong?"

"Nothing like that. She has paranoid schizophrenia."

I had heard the term, and I knew it was a kind of mental illness.

"That's why we can't invite her to the wedding?"

"She wouldn't come anyway."

"But…"

I had more questions, but Jack began to tell me about the day his mother was dragged from their home and admitted to a mental hospital. He spoke of it with no emotion. He told me about men wearing white coats, furniture being overturned, and his father instructing Bernie, Bill, and himself to remain seated and out of the way. Jack had watched his little brother being pulled from the arms of their mother.

"Joe cried for days and through the nights. It was bad."

"I can't imagine. I had no idea."

"So if you call off the wedding, I'll understand." If it were only for his voice, I might have believed that's what he wanted, but I saw his eyes.

"Call off the wedding? No. I don't want to call off the wedding."

I thought of Jack's mother the next morning, but there was no time to worry about the past when our future was only days away.

We continued to check things off the list I'd ripped from my bridal magazine. I babysat for a couple who owned a local bakery. Their gift to us was a beautiful cake. Another one of my babysitting clients was a photographer. She gave us a great deal. Our church's choir director agreed to be the soloist. Neither of us knew a florist personally, but I loved daisies, and evidently they "are always in season."

Other important players were obligated by family ties. The key men and boys in our families were the churchgoing, own-a-suit kind of guys. It only took a slight amount of pressure to get them to agree to coats and ties on a hot Sunday evening. Mom would help me decorate the church fellowship hall for the reception. Jan would stand with me as matron of honor, and Bill would be Jack's best man. I couldn't choose between two potential flower girls, so I asked them both.

Joe and Kevin would be ushers, but they had little responsibility since the majority of guests would already be seated in their usual pews.

By now, Rhonda's feet could reach both the piano and organ pedals. She had already learned the wedding march and could accompany our church music director as she sang "I Love You Truly." It wasn't a song of my choosing, but I readily accepted her suggestion, since she only had a week to prepare. Her solo turned out to be the one thing that made our wedding unique among our generation of friends, and ladies cried. Isn't that what matters?

Fourteen days after the engagement, my father walked me down the aisle and Jack and I became husband and wife.

I can't recall if there was rice, and those were the days before birdseed or bubbles, but there was a crowd of well-wishers waving as Jack drove us away from the church. We didn't drive far.

"This whole thing may not be legal," he said. Then he swooped me up from under my arms, the way one picks up a small child, and carried me through the door to our hotel room. It didn't help that I was resisting the whole threshold tradition thing, and that Jack had heard he was supposed to carry me over it, without ever having seen it demonstrated.

"We just got married. What do you mean, 'May not be legal'?"

"Ginny never has signed paperwork making her my legal guardian."

I squirmed, forcing him to set me down. "You can take me home, if you're afraid my dad will have you arrested?"

"No. What's done is done."

For the honeymoon, we planned to drive in any direction for one week, stopping where and when we felt like it. The rest of our time before Jack flew off to Germany would be spent driving back, stopping whenever the mood struck. It was Jack's idea. It was a great idea.

We never got more than fifty miles out of town. After the first night together, we learned that a honeymoon isn't about sightseeing.

We opened the packet of reading material from our premarital counseling session around day eighteen. I read aloud and Jack listened. There was a chapter about sex. Jack grabbed the book a couple of times to check that I wasn't paraphrasing to my advantage. We laughed and learned as we completed every assignment. Our happily-ever-after had finally begun.

I didn't want Jack to remember me with puffy red eyes, so I fought off tears all the way to the airport. He made sure I could recite the steps needed for me to join him in Germany. I would get my passport and update my vaccines right away. He would apply for housing, so we could celebrate our first Christmas together. The money from the sale of my car would be put aside to earn interest so we could buy another car upon returning to the States. The list was short, but we repeated it over and over, trying to pass time while waiting for his boarding call.

I studied Jack's every move until he disappeared inside the plane. The way he stood tall. The way people looked at him. I wasn't the only female watching the man in uniform. Jack never looked back. I watched and waved, not knowing he was seated on the other side of the plane.

A lady, who had been standing nearby, watched with me until the jet's contrail began to disappear. We noticed each other's tears, and she asked how long he would be gone.

"For almost three years, but I'll be joining him in a couple of months."

By the time I got to the car, my thoughts were on a second honeymoon in Europe.

That was in August of 1974. I wouldn't see my husband again until April of 1975.

My bedroom at my parents' house was cramped with wedding gifts under the bed, in the closet, and in every corner. I added a wedding band to my solitaire diamond engagement ring and had a new last name, but little other evidence indicated I was a married woman and not simply a nineteen-year-old college student.

The first letter arrived two long weeks after he left. He explained that I would be receiving the bulk of his paycheck, and he would receive just enough for everyday spending. He mentioned a waiting list for housing along with syrupy language describing how he missed me. I carried that letter with me and read it on breaks at work, every night before bed, and any other time there was no one looking over my shoulder.

We agreed to write at least twice weekly, and once I had his new address, I began to follow through on that promise. I sent extra cards and letters. When I changed the name on my driver's license, I wrote to let him know. When I deposited any amount of cash into our newly opened joint savings account, I let him know. I summarized every accomplishment that got me closer to boarding a plane headed to Germany.

After about six weeks, he called. The conversation started with him telling me he couldn't talk long. International calls were expensive, and someone else's soldier was always waiting in line for the pay phone.

His next words jolted my state of mind. "I don't think you should come to Germany."

"Why?"

"It's for your own good."

I struggled to breathe. "For my own good?"

"Yeah."

What I heard Jack saying was, *I don't want you.*

With my family in the living room just around the corner, I muffled my responses and held in the questions I was dying to ask. This first sign of trouble needed to stay between me and Jack. One of the things I knew, without having to read it in our pastor's guide to marriage, was that marital conflict is often escalated unnecessarily when in-laws get involved. Our conversation ended without him telling me he loved me, and his "I miss you too" sounded obligatory.

A couple days went by before his next letter was delivered. I cried before opening the envelope, anticipating what I might find on the pages. It was postmarked before the phone call and contained no clue as to what might have prompted it. He asked me about what needed to be done before I bought a ticket. He missed me. He couldn't stand being apart from me. He needed me. He wanted me. Sketches in the margins, were meant to amuse me.

My letter, loaded with additional postage and questions about his phone call, was already in the mail. I expected a response letter would fill in the gaps and explain what had caused his change of heart. It didn't. Neither did the next or the next.

My passport arrived. I faked excitement. I had all the necessary shots, and saving money had been easy since my life consisted of going to work, church, and school. Summer was over, and with the fall semester about to start, I followed Jack's latest instruction and registered.

Jack's letters were hot and cold. One letter would be filled with romance and desire, and the next would tell me not to come, because Germany was a terrible place.

He was in the infantry, not an airborne ranger. There was the marching and hiking. His ankles would still swell on occasion. He hated the boots. He hated the uniform. He hated the food. His unit would go to "the field" for two or three weeks at a time.

His letters from the field were more informative. I read about identifying trees and which trees were best for what purpose. He'd learned and practiced survival techniques, and he drew pictures when using words would take too long. One envelope contained nothing but a list of parks and places where he wanted to take me camping.

"Just you and me. No sergeants. No lieutenants."

He liked being outdoors, until he experienced his first German winter.

Another phone call, and this time he told me it would be a long time before we could get into government housing. Instead, we'd live off base in the town of Aschaffenburg. He had worked on a budget. We could rent a furnished apartment near the base, and I would only need to go on base to take care of occasional business, for laundry, and to shop at the commissary.

When his next letter arrived, he told me what had happened to the wife of a man he knew, along with a plea for me to stay in the States. I understood his concern even without the graphic words he'd never say to my face. I tore his letter into tiny pieces. I didn't need to read it again, and if anyone snooped, I didn't want that to be the letter they saw.

I wrote back: "I'm sorry about what happened to your friend's wife, but women are brutally raped in the U.S. every day. Only a few more weeks left in this semester. I'm having a terrible time concentrating during class for thinking of you and our honeymoon. I want to spend Christmas with you. I've been saving every dime of your check. There is nothing important I need, except you. We have money for my plane fare, money to us set up in an apartment, and about as much in our savings account. Please give me a date when you won't be in the field and can pick me up from the airport. I miss you. I want to be your wife, not your pen pal. Love, Rita."

His response consisted of one short paragraph. The first sentence was written in all capital letters, and traced over several times, giving it a bold, definite, and unforgettable message:

"DO NOT BUY A TICKET! You should register for winter classes. You need your education. Please find out what we would need to do to get our marriage annulled, and let me know. Love, Jack."

It was his handwriting, and I could almost hear his voice as I read the words aloud. I hid this letter farther under my mattress than the others. Over the next few days, I prayed no one would mention his name or ask when I would be joining him in Germany. Tears and an unsolicited, emotion-stuffed confession would have burdened them. No one asked, and muffled tears in the privacy of my room were enough release to keep me from mental breakdown.

His request echoed in my thoughts. *Annulled!* He wanted to discard me. The guy who asked my father for my hand in marriage without fear, who supposedly joined the army in order to keep me in his life, who laughed at my jokes and said he loved me, had now made it my sole responsibility to tell family and friends that our farce of a marriage was over.

I was a big girl now. A big girl who had tried being a woman and failed. I'd made a mess of my life, and I couldn't tell a soul. As far as anyone knew, I was remaining in the States to save money. Pride supported my pretense. This must be my fault, but what had I done?

A friend sensed trouble. She wondered if a rumor that had circulated months earlier had been true. "You would have told me if you were pregnant. Wouldn't you?"

"You know I would!"

"Anyone who knows you well knows it isn't so."

A story had circulated that our wedding was a rushed affair because I had been pregnant. When that rumor would have died for lack of evidence, another story was crafted to explain away the first rumor.

"No, I wasn't pregnant, and no, I haven't had a miscarriage."

"I didn't believe it," my friend said. "But you've been so down lately, I was beginning to wonder."

"I just miss Jack. That's all."

I wanted to confide in my friend. She was one to be trusted, but something made me want to protect Jack in all this. He had a secret, and until I knew what it was, it was my secret too.

I struggled with the deceit, especially with my close friends and family. Living with such a lie required barriers and withholding from people I loved and people who loved me. The counsel of someone older or wiser might have helped, but what if their answer was to oblige Jack with an annulment? Maybe he had messed up, but I still loved him. I couldn't admit the truth until I knew what the truth was.

Whatever was happening between us, I didn't understand. I only knew it was bad and out of my control. My imagination played a variety of scenarios every night before I cried or prayed myself to sleep. He could be having an affair—the obvious. Illicit drugs were prevalent in his unit. I knew, because he wrote about it. There was also alcohol, but I didn't believe alcohol would affect Jack this way. He wrote about friends and even sent me pictures where he looked fine. Maybe he was under a tremendous amount of stress?

I wondered what part of everything he wrote was a lie. I'd heard about men who told their wives they were in one place far away, when they were actually closer to home, living a secret life, but some of his letters had been mailed using German postage stamps and had Aschaffenburg postmarks. No place was so awful my imagination couldn't take me there.

Could he be in jail? Could he be the one who had hurt his friend's wife? I answered my own thoughts—aloud, "No. That couldn't be. Jack would never . . ."

I was married to a man I didn't know, and I couldn't finish that sentence.

The packet we'd read on our honeymoon remained on my

nightstand, under my Bible. I read it again, cover to cover, this time opening my Bible to read all the references. I found answers to other questions, but not mine. We had committed, during our premarital counseling session, to talk to our pastor before considering divorce. I underlined the telephone number on the inside cover—just in case.

God, what did I miss? What did I do other than commit to love someone? Jack repeated the same vows. Is this some sort of test? How could he express concern for my education and talk about an annulment in the same sentence? Does he love me? Did he ever love me? If he didn't, was any part of those twenty-eight days true? Please make him come to his senses. Please.

It was one of those nights when I thought my questioning might tire God, but a Bible verse came to mind: "We are hard-pressed on every side, yet not crushed; we are perplexed, but not in despair" (2 Corinthians 4:8). This time, I said *"Amen"* before I fell asleep.

With a little rebellious irony, I registered for the next semester, but only one class. It was a German language course.

10

THORNS IN HIS ROSES

Christmas 1974. I wondered who was celebrating the holiday with Jack. He was living single, in a men's barracks, and I was a married woman, living with my parents, opening presents around the tree like every other December 25. Jack made sure my present arrived in time for Christmas, but an expensive trinket tucked into a beautifully wrapped package was not how I'd expected Christmas to look that year.

The phone didn't ring until the day after Christmas. Long wait times for pay phones was an acceptable excuse, even though I thought his overdone apology suggested he was keeping something from me. The weeks between the fall 1974 and the winter 1975 semesters were hard. Jack's letters continued as though it had been decided he would finish his time in Germany while I waited at home. He never commented after I told him about registering for the German course, and nothing more was said about an annulment.

German was a challenge. I'd taken two years of Spanish in high school, and I could read it, but was lost when it came to understanding anyone other than my slow-talking classmates. I was too inhibited to roll my Rs in the classroom. What made me think I would be any better with German? This class was a pumped-up version of high school. According to the syllabus, we would be covering, in one semester, what high school students would study over the entire year. No matter how great I sounded in the car or the shower, my inhibitions took over when it came to speaking German in front of my instructor or my classmates.

Even so, learning German gave me hope. The numbers, names of the months, some simple phrases, and important vocabulary kept my anticipation of traveling to Germany alive. Cultural tidbits helped keep me motivated and provided some cushion for my grade.

Studying for only one class allowed me to work more hours and take a position in human resources as a receptionist/file clerk/phone operator. My paycheck was bigger than what I could earn on the sales floor, and I had less time to worry about relationship problems.

The tone of Jack's letters continued to be anything from romantic and hopeful to foreboding and depressing. I may have been young, but I wasn't ignorant. He must have met someone in Germany, but wasn't man enough to let me know. What other explanation could there be? But if that were so, why would he bother answering any of my letters, and how could I be so easily manipulated by the sound of his voice?

I didn't allow myself to be angry with him. With no proof, I wanted to be angry with myself for believing Jack loved me in the first place. More than that, I wanted to be angry with God for not answering my prayers. But anger is a funny thing. When you let it surface, other people can see there is a problem, and I wasn't ready for that.

I had faith in God's promises, including the one to work things out (Romans 8:28), but I wasn't sure if I was feeling "the call according to his purpose," which is a condition of that promise. I doubted that God's good was good enough. I tore into that verse like the contract it was meant to be, and I found no loopholes.

Faith isn't much without doubt, and I had plenty of doubt.

My first big step of faith in this situation was a determination not to give up on my marriage, or Jack, until I was in Germany to see for myself what was going on. As soon as I finished the semester, I would go.

I resolved to stop nagging. Instead of trying to get Jack to agree I should come to Germany, I wrote longer letters about family, friends, work, church, and local news. I asked how he was doing, without prying, and I wrote how much I loved him and missed him. Over the next couple of months I noticed his letters were longer, more informative, and more consistently affectionate.

His Valentine's Day card arrived a day late, but his tardiness was immediately forgiven when I read his personal, handwritten note. Clearly, he had been missing me.

I went to a travel agent the next day and bought a one-way ticket to Frankfurt, West Germany. As I put the first class stamp on the envelope that held my response to his Valentine's Day card and a copy of my flight itinerary, I prayed. He would have about a month, in the field or not, to prepare for my arrival.

I held my breath every time the phone rang. When Jack finally did call, around four in the morning, I jumped from bed to answer before anyone else stirred. I didn't know how ugly the conversation might be. My name was on the flight manifest of a plane heading to Germany, and nothing he could say would cause me to miss that flight.

Despite my fear, it was so good to hear his voice.

His words were good too. "My leave was approved. I'll meet you at the airport."

"I leave on April 1st. April Fool's Day. Makes it easy for you to remember."

"Oh, don't worry. I won't forget," he said. "I can't get you out of my mind. I need you here. With me."

I whispered my response. For all I knew, any of my family members were standing right around the corner, able to hear the longing of one lover for the other.

We'd been talking for several minutes when I asked, "Is someone waiting to use the phone?"

"How can you tell?"

The abrupt change in his tone of voice and the topic of conversation was my one and only clue. A soldier doesn't carry on sensual chit-chat where another soldier might overhear.

I gave my notice at work and negotiated a price from a guy at church who had been waiting to buy my car. We both felt like we got a great deal. God's goodness, I decided, was better than my good enough.

The deadline to drop my German course without receiving a failing grade was within days. When I told the instructor my reason for dropping, she offered to let me drop officially, and still attend class without taking the tests or turning in the assignments. The next few lessons added to my vocabulary, and helped alleviate some anxiety about navigating a foreign airport and train station, should Jack not be there when I arrived.

Mom, Dad, Rhonda, and Kevin got up very early on April 1, 1975, to take me to O'Hare International Airport. The weatherman had predicted a winter-like storm and got it right. A fresh snowfall made the roads treacherous. By the time we reached O'Hare, a record-breaking snow cover was crippling Chicago.

We checked my luggage and made it to the gate in time to hear that all flights were delayed until morning, and all major roads in the greater Chicago area were closed. The five of us began searching for a comfortable place to camp. Wind had blown more than a foot of snow into the deck, covering cars. No one was arriving or leaving from Chicago O'Hare.

Because of the huge number of non-passengers stranded in the terminal, I was welcomed aboard the plane and allowed to eat and sleep there. Snowplows worked all night, and planes were deiced the next morning. I wondered where Jack had spent the night. My flight departed before the roads were clear enough for my family to travel. People talked about that horrible storm every April Fools' Day for several years.

In Frankfurt, I thought I saw Jack on the other side of a glass partition and maneuvered my way to a short line, but the customs officials were thorough. Once I made it through customs, I saw the man who wasn't Jack. Two minutes seemed like an hour, and all the uncertainties of the past months crashed down on my tired body and anxious soul. *Was it over after all? Should I go to the Lufthansa desk and use my traveler's checks to buy a ticket home?*

Melodrama is ineffective without someone around who cares and will buy into it, so of course I would stay. Maybe I should go ahead and exchange some of my dollars for marks. Maybe he was looking for me to be wearing last year's winter coat? I spotted an out-of-the-way place to adjust my bags and organize my thoughts. When I looked up and began calculating the best way to proceed, I saw a familiar face. And he saw me.

In a lot of movies, lovers run toward each other. Not us. We walked slowly, partly because of fatigue, but also because we were savoring the moment. He felt good and he smelled good, just like he had eight months earlier when we said good-bye. White and yellow daisies surrounded the two red roses he was carrying.

I exchanged my heavy carry-on bag for the flowers, and in the process, one of the thorns punctured a finger.

I'd just completed my first ride in a plane, an international flight. Exciting enough, and now the train ride to Aschaffenburg was another first for me. But our eyes were on each other, and I wouldn't notice the scenery until weeks later, during my second train ride.

Once in a taxi, I began to notice the Germany I'd seen in my textbook. Jack was still in the mood for hand-holding and romantic gazes, but my eyes and pointer finger were busied by the narrow brick roads and tall buildings. After a couple weeks of hiding behind clouds, the sun had come out to welcome me. But it had not melted all the snow from the mountaintops on the horizon nor warmed the air from the taxi driver's open window.

"Can we go inside that castle? Have you been in that shop? I don't see any churches. Look! An old fashioned baby buggy! Is there a mall?"

I was in Germany. With Jack! This was going to be home for almost two years. It was fun and entertaining to be able to read and understand most of the signs.

The taxi pulled up to the guesthouse where we would be staying for the next two weeks. Jack paid for the trip, then told me, "Taxi drivers never admit to having change, especially if you are using

American dollars, so always carry marks and always have some small bills."

Three or four times in the train or taxi I remembered Jack's letters and wanted to question him. Why had he been so hot and cold in his letters? What was going on that was so terrible for me to know and understand? Had he really wanted an annulment? If so, why? I stifled the urge to start a conversation that might send me back to the states before we enjoyed our second honeymoon.

The owner of the guesthouse showed us to our room. Again, I stuck myself when I placed my flowers in a glass of water. The roses were slightly wilted by now, and I had two sore fingers, but the daisies had survived the day beautifully. The comfortable sitting area, the feather bed, and the plain, stand-alone sink attached to wall at the foot of the bed reminded me I was a long way from Illinois. We shared a bathroom with other guests. Fortunately, the winter sports season was over and summer vacations had not started, so most days, there was no waiting.

The food was amazing, but I quickly tired of drinking room-temperature cola. Iced drinks cost extra. What I would have given for some ice cold Kool-Aid. We got strange looks and chuckles from the other guests for turning down beer, especially since a small soft drink cost nearly twice the price of a big mug of beer. After a day or two, the teenaged daughter of the guesthouse owner approached us cautiously to let us know it was legal for us to drink alcohol.

"The U.S. is the only place where you have to be twenty-one. I still want to go there someday."

More times than not, we were the only guests in the dining room. Rather than sitting with her family on the other side of the room, or in the kitchen, the daughter would serve our food and then join us at our table. Her mother suggested we would rather eat alone, since it was our honeymoon, but we enjoyed her company and her numerous questions about life in the United States. She offered pointers on our language skills between bites of brats and kraut.

The mountain view from our guesthouse room turned missing some of the comforts of home into a longing to make this our home.

Jack patiently listened to my dreams and fantasies of staying there forever. And he let a few of his life's dreams and desires escape through the clean mountain air and into my heart for safekeeping. In that place, I knew I was loved.

"Jack. I'm so glad God finally answered my prayer."

"How do you know God answered your prayer?"

"I'm finally here with you."

"I think he's been answering your prayers all along. You only call them answers when you get your way."

I let that one pass. "Let's go for a hike?" I suggested with a touch of assumption. "Today would be a good day to see what's on the other side of the mountain."

"Are you asking, or are you telling me how to answer?" Jack grinned like he had when we were in high-school.

"That depends." I could play his game. "Are you going to give me an answer today, or are we going for that hike tomorrow?"

"Here's an answer for you. Grab a jacket. It's chilly out there."

The day came when the roses had to go. I had trimmed the stems, gently plucked the dry petals, and otherwise nursed them along, but they were finished. On that morning, Jack didn't seem to want to get out of bed, so I rejoined him.

We reflected on how wonderful yesterday had been and how good today would be. I thought of the months before, of sitting in bed alone, looking at the solitaire diamond on my ring finger and watching the morning light shine on my messed-up life and marriage. But no more mornings like that. My rings had never looked so good. I turned them to play with the light and noticed multiple scratches on my hands, sore and itchy.

"Jack. Don't ever feel you need to buy me expensive roses. Those thorns can really do some damage."

That comment opened the subject of spending money.

"But if a few bucks for flowers makes you happy, and I have the few bucks, I'll get the flowers."

How could I argue? We sat on the bed, leaning against the headboard, and began to outline plans for our future, decade by decade. We covered the essentials: where we would live when we returned to the States, how we would manage our money, what type of vehicles we would drive, and how we would discipline our children. It seemed we agreed on everything, even the style of furniture we preferred. Deciding who would do what household chores was so easy, we wondered if we shouldn't schedule all of our marital conferences to be held in bed, with only the sheets to come between his opinions and mine. Meeting adjourned. The business he wrote about in his letters wasn't on the agenda. An annulment was old business that neither of us reintroduced. We fell asleep on the same continent, under the same roof, and in the same bed.

Jack woke up while I was still snoozing and slipped out. He returned with a hand painted vase and a dozen fresh, red roses. Before I could finish saying the socially correct, *but you shouldn't have*, he held up a finger to interrupt my thought.

"When you got me, you got a bunch of thorns."

11

THE OTHER SIDE OF THE MOUNTAIN

The housing office at the army base had a list of recommended landlords and their properties. We spotted an apartment, priced within our budget. The rent was exactly one-fourth of Jack's monthly take-home pay; high school economics class wasn't a waste after all.

Jack's walk to work would be about a mile and a quarter. Between the price of insurance and fuel, having a car would have taken a huge bite out of his paycheck and left too little fun money at the end of the month. The apartment was within walking distance to downtown Aschaffenburg, and we went prepared to make a deposit.

It was fully furnished and clean. We signed on the dotted line. The landlord spoke in broken English until we were ready to walk out the door, when he articulated very clearly, "If the rent is not paid by the first of the month, I will call your commanding officer."

We made sure to pay by the twenty-fifth of the previous month, every month.

The benefit of location was offset by some disadvantages. The apartment was on the fifth floor of a building with no elevator. The stairwell smelled like the sweaty men and boys who frequented the karate school on the fourth floor, right below us. We grew accustomed to the quakes created by twenty to thirty synchronized yelling and high-kicking karate students.

Some of the windows were permanently sealed. We could not determine if that was a purposeful feature made to somehow benefit the landlord or if the window frames had been permanently knocked off their tracks during a particularly powerful karate session. The windows we were able to pry open, had no screens.

The landlord made only one surprise visit during our time there. We took the opportunity to ask about the window situation. He told us they had been jarred permanently closed during World War II. Aschaffenburg had been bombed heavily.

He seemed to have made amazing progress on his English during the two or three months since we'd moved in. "My grandfather was a wealthy man," he said. "A very smart business man. Responsible for most of the buildings in this area. Mother's family lived here. They felt the blasts and lived in the aftermath of Allied bombing and tanks blowing holes in everything our grandfather worked hard to accomplish. They hated Americans. Me, I like Americans. Because of the Americans, Aschaffenburg was rebuilt, and my family profited."

I wanted to, but didn't, respond with, *but not enough to fix the windows?*

He offered good reasons for leaving the windows sealed. Number one on his list was that I wouldn't need to wash them. As he piled on the excuses, it was easier to see through to his stingy ways than it was to see the building across the street.

Jack was interested in seeing a building our landlord told us about. It was around the corner from us. Damage from a tank remained visible as a memorial to both the Germans and the Americans who lost lives and loved ones during the war.

Würzburger Strasse was a busy thoroughfare with truck noises all hours of the day and night. Leaving the quiet guesthouse where we'd honeymooned meant exchanging a picturesque mountainous horizon for one of brick buildings. A large grassy courtyard in the middle of our square block of buildings was void of children, pets, or any activity. It was *verboten* to everyone except the groundskeeper.

The kitchen was five feet wide by seven feet long. It had a functioning window but very few cupboards. A two-burner stove and a dorm-sized refrigerator had to do. Somehow the landlord had managed to squeeze in a two-foot square table and two stool-like chairs. Summer or winter, if the oven was in use, the kitchen was unbearably hot.

The apartment was furnished with an eclectic collection of hand-me-downs. No two pieces matched, unless the orange, corner sectional could be counted as three pieces. There was no air-conditioning. Hot water was not stored in a big tank hidden away in a closet or basement like we had in the States; instead, small, individual heating units above the tub and the kitchen sink could be lit with a match to heat water, as needed. No hot water at the bathroom sink.

In the bedroom, two twin-sized feather mattresses were placed on a platform with a wooden frame. It was comfy. Our problem was with the large wooden board strategically and structurally dividing the bed into two halves. It might have been more functional in the early 1900's when large families had to separate the boys from the girls.

The plumbing vibrated and made noises in the middle of the night. The radiator heat worked well, except during some of the coldest winter months. It wasn't the radiator's fault.

During the nearly two years we lived there, we woke up at least four times to a freezing apartment on the first day of the month. If payment had not been credited to an account, the utility company would turn off a customer's service on the last midnight of the month. The landlord wasn't as committed to forwarding our payment to the utility company as he was about collecting from his renters. Too bad, if the last day of the month happened to be a Friday. The heat was not turned on until late Monday morning.

Despite all of that, we were comfortable. A large second bedroom could be used as a sitting room, and we ate most of our meals at the coffee table in the large living room, where the odd and well-worn furniture made us worry less about spilling. Large oriental rugs came close to covering the antique hardwood floors.

Jack had befriended a soldier from Tennessee whose wife had arrived a few months before me. The guys would be going to the field within a few days of moving to our new place, so Jack arranged a dinner out with Gene and his wife, Paula. The guys sat back and let us girls get to know one another, hoping we would be able to keep each other company, and out of trouble, while they were gone.

Paula was easy to get to know. I admired her for the way she had acclimated to our new environment so quickly. She was smart, enthusiastic, and fearless. Like me, she was a church going goodie two-shoes, almost newlywed.

Gene and Paula lived in a government housing complex twenty minutes away. It was furnished, but simple by American standards. Their small kitchen had a separate dining area, with a table and four chairs that could have been shipped from a factory in the States. A playground, with actual children could be viewed from their seventh-story living room.

Paula had a vacuum sweeper and no carpets. Their floors were newer tile, and she had only small area rugs. She shared her vacuum sweeper with me, only possible because their building had an elevator and they had a car. Those oriental rugs looked like new after Paula paid a visit.

We saw each other a few times while the guys were gone. We went to chapel together, and she showed me around the base so I could learn the ins and outs of shopping, banking, doing laundry, the library, and everything Jack had no interest in doing. Johannesburg Castle was nearby, and neither Jack nor Gene wanted to go, so Paula and I made a day of it. The castle reminded us of some of our childhood fairytale books and filled our heads with daydreams.

Within a few months of my arrival, Paula applied for a job at the commissary. They called her to work the next day. That severely interfered with our running around. We had a lot of Aschaffenburg yet to explore. Working on her feet was tiring, and she wasn't comfortable driving after dark. Our get-togethers were suddenly limited to three or four times a month.

Jack bought an old black-and-white television. An English-speaking station offered programs weeks or months after they were originally aired stateside. At least the military news and weather were current. Watching TV did ward off some of my loneliness, and the feeling of isolation from many of the persons and places that gave me comfort.

I read a few verses, or maybe a chapter, in my Bible every day. If a story or passage kept my interest, I might read more. I discovered romance novels. I could get immersed in a book and read all day. If Jack was in the field, I would lay around, reading and watching television most days, then clean like a madwoman the day before he came home. When he was in town, he jogged home for lunch, ate fast, and then jogged back to work. I could do a little work right before time to fix lunch, a little bit more before time to fix dinner, and still keep the house in order.

The romance novels were both addictive and unhealthy. Jack's best attempt at romance was no match for the unrealistic, hyper-masculine characters in the books. I tried to appear natural, while acting out some of the dramatic scenes, and Jack was entertained, but not in the way I expected. He could only laugh for so long. At twenty years old, I figured out that I needed to check out books from a different section of the library.

The freestanding sink in the hallway, right outside our apartment door, created a bit of a mystery, but until one day when our apartment was clean, there was nothing on TV, and I had nothing new to read, I didn't think about it much.

That day, my mind was looking for adventure. It wasn't just a sink—it was a *used* sink. The faucet dripped. Careful not to leave a fingerprint, I checked to make sure the handle was turned as far as it would go. A bar of soap lay on its lip, diminishing from use, but there were never any water spots in the sink or on the floor. I wondered who swept the hallway. Who changed the towel every day?

That evening I made Jack stand guard as I peeked into the small unlocked closet next to the sink. There was a toilet, and nothing else. It was old, but spotless like the sink.

Several more days passed before I realized a couple lived next door. They had a one-room apartment, smaller than our living room. A bed, just like ours, a small table, and a couple of chairs completed the major furnishings. The hallway facilities were for their use.

I assumed my language classes had failed me. Using a sort of sign language that would make the deaf community ill, I invited her into my apartment for a cup of tea. Jack drank hot tea instead of coffee, and I enjoyed a cup now and then. Tea, I thought, would be a safe international option. I was correct. She drank her first cup and asked for a second.

We toured our apartment while waiting for the second pot of water to boil. She nodded politely, and smiled as she pointed to objects. I gave the English word for the object, and then translated to German. It was all very scholastic. I played the role of teacher. She played the eager student. Before long, we laughed and came to the understanding that our best means of communication would be hand, face, and body language.

She invited me into her apartment for tea the next day. My new friend pointed out the obvious contrast between our living spaces. We had four rooms. They had one. We had two water heaters, they had none. No tub. No shower. We had closets. Their clothes hung on a couple hooks behind their door.

I complimented her on her delicate and fine china tea cups and saucers. If I owned a teacup or saucer, it was stored in my old bedroom in the states. Jack and I drank out of ugly green glass coffee cups. I think my attempt to communicate how much I enjoyed her company and appreciated drinking tea from her lovely china was successful.

We both dreaded cleaning our rugs. They were too big to carry down the stairs and shake. I used a stiff broom that had been left behind by former tenants. The dust would fly, and much of it landed right back on the rug. She had heard Paula's vacuum and hinted to borrow it. I tried to explain how the vacuum was not available and not mine to loan. I was never sure if she fully understood.

In about four months, she would be delivering a baby and was terrified about going into labor. She was giddy, in a reserved sort of way, as she held newborn sleepers over her baby bump for a newborn fashion show. She let me know she didn't care about the sex of the baby, but her husband wanted a boy. It took minimal sign language for her to communicate that bit of information.

She handed me a letter she had received, still in the envelope, and pointed to the return address. The letter was from her mother in Turkey. She was Turkish, not German. She and her husband were living below their means (a novel idea to me) in order to save money. They were living in Germany temporarily. Her husband, an educated man, could earn enough money in five years for them to return to Turkey and purchase a nice home near their family.

The amount of information a couple of women, speaking two different languages, could exchange in the amount of time it took to sip a couple cups of tea was nothing short of amazing. If absolute accuracy wasn't a factor, I would say it was no less than a miracle.

I told Jack about our neighbors and urged him to befriend the husband. Guys have a hard enough time communicating, even without a language barrier, but he made a point to nod and smile at the next opportunity. Neither of the guys was fluent in hand, face, or body language.

When I passed the husband in the hall or in the stairwell, he avoided eye contact. I supposed it was a cultural thing, and thought I should probably respond to him in kind, so my typical friendly greeting was restrained the next few times we met. Then, I came to the conclusion that he had as much duty to assimilate to my culture as I had to assimilate to his. After all, Germany wasn't home to either of us. I went back to my friendly greetings.

The day finally came when all four of us met in the hallway. It took over five minutes for us to establish that Jack spoke only English, except for a few German phrases; I spoke English and enough German to get me into trouble; my new friend's parents thought a second language was unnecessary for girls, and she only spoke only Turkish, except for a few English words she had learned over tea with me. Her husband could speak Turkish, enough German to struggle through at work, and a little English.

Our new friends knew Jack was American because they had seen him in uniform, but they thought I was German, because I wore German-style jeans and had used German greetings. Once our language barriers were understood, we had little to say, but "the husband" (as I called him) began to smile when we passed on the stairs.

I learned a few Turkish phrases over the time we were neighbors, and she learned a little English, even though most of our encounters were brief and in the hallway where she washed her dishes, laundered their clothes, and collected cold water for cooking or bathing.

We were in Germany long enough to see their adorable baby boy begin to toddle around. I loved bringing him little, inexpensive toys from the military exchange.

At one point, I was told (using our unofficial sign language) not to bring him so many gifts. He had come to expect my little surprises and begun to automatically grab at my bags. From then on, I would slip any irresistible purchase to his mother instead of giving it directly to him. He still smiled and reached for me with his chubby little arms and a cuter-than-humanly-possible smile. To that point, he was the most adorable baby I'd ever experienced.

I made another friend. Her name was Rose. She lived across the hall.

The second time Jack's company went to the field, Rose knocked on my door. It was 9 a.m. on a Saturday morning. Her manner of dress was less modest than mine, but in keeping with what most German girls were wearing.

After a brief introduction, she offered me a shirt as a gift. It was not something I would wear in public, so I tried to explain that she did not need to give me anything, and that I had nothing with which to reciprocate. She insisted, so I accepted. She knew I was home alone, and that Jack was in the field. How she knew was a mystery to me. Her invitation to go downtown shopping sounded like a fun idea, so I accepted.

I freshened up while she waited. She watched as I washed my face and put on lipstick and mascara. After all, the bathroom was right inside our apartment door. Evidently, it didn't seem like enough makeup to her. She offered to fetch her eye liner and shadow from across the hall. I declined her offer, not because I wasn't interested in adding some drama to my appearance, but because I'd been taught not to share makeup.

She followed me toward the bedroom as I went to change clothes. I had to close the door in her face or she would have watched me dress. Her comment that American women were too private didn't change a thing. I felt uncomfortable with her looking around the apartment unsupervised, but stripping down to bra and panties in front of her would have been worse.

In case of an emergency while we were out, I tucked a map of the area into my purse and checked to make sure I had small bills.

Once we got down the stairs and onto the sidewalk, she hooked her arm through mine. I flinched and pulled away. It was a frequent sight—two girls or women walking arm in arm. I knew it was simply a sign of friendship, but it was just one of the customs I never adopted—along with drinking beer for lunch.

"It's hard to be friends with Americans," she said.

"I'm sorry to hear that. I hope we can still be friends. Have you known many Americans?"

She told me about soldiers she had met, and about the couple who lived in the apartment before us. They hadn't made the U.S. look good.

"I'm not like that."

She announced she was an atheist before I felt comfortable asking or even hinting of religion. She thought all Americans were Catholic.

Rose would prove to be a challenging friend. We were not only from different continents, but different worlds. It took a while for me to realize the full extent of our differences, but I loved that she listened without judgment and spoke her mind without offending.

We window-shopped all morning. She showed me the stores where I could barter and where to find the best bargains. We grabbed lunch from a street vendor and sat on a park bench to eat. An older man, not quite as old as our landlord, stopped to speak with her. He acknowledged me with a look, but then continued to have what seemed to be a business conversation with Rose.

When he walked away, Rose quizzed me. I gave her a partial

interpretation, and was curious about what I had missed. She wouldn't fill in the blanks for me. It was great to practice my German with her. She would become a tough teacher who wouldn't accept excuses, but I think, in this instance, she was grateful I hadn't understood that particular conversation.

We spent the afternoon relaxing in her apartment, which was similar to ours, except she had art on the walls, and her furniture was not eclectic or hand-me-down.

Her father had sent her from their home in Czechoslovakia to a school in Germany when she was thirteen. She was single, in her mid-twenties, and her father had recently cut her allowance in half. She told me she had started working a few months before we arrived. In addition to her native language, she spoke fluent German, English, and French.

A photo of men wearing expensive suits was displayed in a silver frame on top of her elaborate and state-of-the-art stereo system. She acknowledged that the man, who looked like her, was her father, and the man who looked like Henry Kissinger, was indeed Henry Kissinger. Conversations about her work or her mother ended after a word or two.

She knocked on my door nearly every morning. I learned to drink warm Pepsi. She learned how to make cinnamon toast in an oven. I learned not to raise my pointer finger when I wanted one of something. Even with my thumb tucked, raising my pointer finger meant I wanted two of whatever I was requesting. My pointer and my middle finger meant I wanted three.

Rose learned the word "Jesus" was more than an American curse word. She laughed when I told her I was offended by her swearing. "That's not swearing! I don't swear."

"But it is. If every time I was angry or frustrated I yelled or grumbled your name, how would that make you feel? Besides, it's not very ladylike."

I don't know which was reason enough for her to change her habit, but she quit using the Lord's name in vain when I was around.

She thought the Bible was a book of fiction, a book of philosophy, and a means by which "the Church" controlled people. I would say, "Jesus is," and she would interrupt with, "Jesus was." We talked of creation, evolution, heaven, hell, and every VBS story in between. She knew many of the proverbs, but didn't believe they were in the Bible. She said they came from Confucius.

"If Confucius wrote these, he plagiarized King Solomon," I said.

She asked me what plagiarize meant, then pretended not to understand my English when I defined it. As fluent as Rose was, she knew when to use language as a barrier, or change the direction of a conversation. I promised to back up my statement by showing where the sayings were in my Bible.

She thought that surely I would be found mistaken, but in the meantime, I told her the story about the two women who claimed the same baby as their own, and how King Solomon's wisdom had reunited mother and child. She'd heard that story before.

"My grandmother told me that story. It's a Czechoslovakian...what is the word?"

"Folk tale?"

"Yes. A folk tale." Rose was grateful for the English word, and astonished that one of her ancestor's stories had made it around the world to someone like me.

"That's a Bible story."

My exuberance in announcing the error in her claim was too strong. I had turned our conversation into a juvenile *I know something you don't know* moment, and once that happened, the conversation died.

The base exchange was off-limits to civilians unless they were accompanied by someone with a military ID, so it was a big deal for her to tag along on my shopping trips. I offered to buy her a Bible. She refused. We stood in the isle as I thumbed through a modern translation, hoping she would change her mind. I showed her a couple of the proverbs we had talked about, and then I skipped over to the Songs of Solomon, hoping that would ignite some interest. It did, but she still wouldn't let me buy her the Bible.

Rose was in my daily prayers. Because of her, I learned to pray silently, instantly, in the middle of conversation and with my eyes wide open. I saw prayers answered. Most of them had something to do with what I should say, how I should say it, or should I speak at all. It was in those moments Rose asked questions, and words I'd never put together before came out as answers.

As we walked and shopped, she would request, "Tell me another story."

My Sunday school teacher would have been so proud.

Rose didn't believe Noah could fit all the animal couples on an ark or that God parted the Red Sea, but she loved the stories. She listened with childlike awe to the story of Jonah. I told the stories of Eve, Ruth, Esther, Job's wife, and the Marys of the New Testament. She handed me opportunity to tell one or two stories a day, but at the end of each day, that's all they were to her—stories.

Rose gave me reason to question, not what I believed, but why I believed it. In a sense, I used Rose. She didn't mind. She was a test, and I studied. My Bible became a tool, but I didn't really have the skill to use it with someone like her. For the first time, I was reading God's words from the perspective of someone who didn't have a life like mine.

In our entire time as neighbors, she avoided talking about the years between her thirteenth and eighteenth birthdays, but she asked lots of questions about me and my teen years. As far as I know, Rose never believed Jesus to be anyone more than a great teacher from ancient history. It made me sad. I cared for Rose. She would be a person I would never forget.

Jack came home from the field, late on a Friday, and Rose was knocking on our door at nine o'clock that Saturday morning. She whimpered when I told her of my plan to spend the weekend with my husband and didn't invite her to join us.

I dragged Jack to the door for a brief introduction. They shook hands. Rose flirted with him by telling him how handsome he was and touching his arms, making me uncomfortable. Jack told me later that he too was uncomfortable with Rose, but in the moment, it didn't seem that way. Just like she would have followed me into the bedroom while I dressed, she would have spent the entire day with us if we had let her into the living room. When Jack told her we needed to go, she begged him to let me go with her instead.

"Rita is my only girlfriend!"

His cherished comeback: "Rita is my only wife."

12

THE FIRST FIGHT

Rose and I went out and about nearly every day while Jack was in the field. I think I would have gone stir-crazy had it not been for her. She was used to shopping for groceries every other day or so, and I had to learn to do the same. Our refrigerator would hold only quart-sized milk jugs, and our freezer was only large enough to hold four ice cube trays and a couple quarts of ice cream.

We were always home before dark, except for the day we wandered a little farther away than usual.

On that day, we walked to a guesthouse about a half-mile beyond the army base. We hadn't been spending much money on our outings, and this was a day to splurge a little. I noticed that Rose was recognized by some of the guys as we walked by the entrance to the Army base, but I didn't think a lot of it. According to her, this guesthouse had the best wiener schnitzel around, and it was about supper time, when GIs were heading out for the evening.

Going to a restaurant with a bar was new to me. In the States, few family restaurants served alcohol, and taverns with more than one billiard table were called pool halls. According to both of my grandmothers, "a good girl would never be seen in a pool hall."

But this was a guesthouse, and Rose knew the owners. They greeted with smiles and waves, calling her by name. We were the only two customers in the place for a while. Rose got some billiard balls from the bartender and set up one of the tables.

We drank warm Pepsi and played billiards. Rose asked if I would like to make a wager before we started, and I declined, explaining my conviction against gambling in much more depth than was necessary. She listened patiently, all the while using a pool cue with the kind of skill I hadn't seen in the rec rooms of my few friends who were fortunate enough to have billiard tables.

Our food was hot and ready, so I cut my lecture about gambling short, and Rose laid down her pool cue. Had I known this would be the best wiener schnitzel of my life and that I would never return to this place, I would have savored every bite. Instead, I finished the entire meal without a word, barely breathing between bites. Rose did the same.

While we were swallowing the last of our supper, some guys wearing fatigues came in and ordered beers. They grabbed the cues and proceeded to finish our game. Rose gulped the rest of her Pepsi, then spoke up. "That's our table. Our game."

One of the soldiers cleared the table as though he hadn't heard. Rose stood, her temper with her. To my amazement, the fire of anger showing on her cheeks turned immediately to a flirtatious blush. I watched as she teased the soldier toward agreement.

My warning about the evils of gambling had no impact. American currency was slapped on the side of the billiard table. I sipped Pepsi while Rose stuffed one ten-dollar bill after another into her skin-tight, American-made blue jeans.

I sat by myself, nursing my third warm Pepsi, as Rose managed the room and the table. Soldiers lined up, waiting for a chance to lose their paychecks. She spoke softly to some, her face close to theirs, and made them smile. There were a total of five young men vying for her attention. I strained to hear what she was saying, but someone had turned on the jukebox. Rose clearly had something extra that appealed to the opposite sex. I wanted to know what it was, and if I had it.

As each young man slapped his money on the table, Rose stroked his arm and his ego just like she had stroked Jack's, then proceeded to demonstrate her talent and take their money. None of them complained. They encouraged her. Who could blame them? She was attractive and friendly, in a forceful sort of way.

When a pack of cigarettes was held out for her to take one, she pushed it away and stuck her face, teeth first, into the soldier's personal space. I wasn't close enough to hear, but knew she was telling him the same thing she told me when, earlier in the day, we saw a store clerk with horribly stained teeth. "See these teeth?" she asserted. With her eyes squinted and lips retracted, "I wouldn't have pretty teeth if I smoked!"

One of the guys stepped over to my table and invited me to a game with him, but I flashed my wedding rings and politely declined. He asked a few questions about how I liked it in Germany, and I asked him if he knew Jack. It occurred to me that he might know Jack as *John,* but I had no desire to continue the conversation. He gave me an uneasy feeling.

Rose was drinking beer now, and I could see this could turn into a long evening. I was bored, and without knowing why, increasingly uncomfortable. I wanted to get home before dark, so I got up to leave. Rose begged, and I consented to wait until she finished, "this one last game."

She had won a good sum of cash and offered me half. Of course, I didn't accept, but how can you not like such a generous soul? Our two-mile walk home started out at a leisurely pace. Except for the last thirty minutes or so at the guesthouse, it had been a fun day.

Lights on the street and in apartments were starting to come on, so we picked up the pace. When a young woman (or maybe she was an older girl) approached a man on the street and opened her sweater to reveal a provocative undergarment, I realized this was the first time I had been out after dark in my own neighborhood. I hadn't noticed we were living in a red-light district.

The man handed the girl cash, and they turned into the shadows together. I clutched my purse a little tighter. Feeling sick, and having a full stomach didn't prevent me from jogging ahead of Rose, up the five flights to our apartment.

A sigh of relief slowed my heart rate after I said good night to

Rose and rested against the inside of our locked door. I contemplated what it would take to move, and whether our names were still on the list for government housing.

I hadn't settled in for the evening when I heard Rose's door open and close. Surely, she wouldn't ask me to go out again. She didn't. I heard her go down the stairs. A few minutes later I heard her laughter and a man's voice.

I asked Rose, the next morning, about her date. She gave no detail, not even a first name, but she told me about several boyfriends from her present and her past. Ordinarily, there would have been some back-and-forth girl talk, storytelling. Not this time. Nothing about me was remotely interesting compared to Rose.

"I got these shoes last weekend from a boyfriend. He would have bought me the whole outfit, but I didn't see anything I wanted."

"He just bought you the shoes? Was it your birthday or something?"

"No. He likes me. Last month he bought me a TV."

"Wow!" My astonishment came partly from envy. "I've never had a boyfriend buy me things like that."

"You don't need a boyfriend. You have Jack."

She told me about the man who was currently helping to pay her rent, and another who was only good for a little spending money. After she mentioned the third or fourth "boyfriend" I knew we didn't have the same definition of the word, and Rose knew she had opened herself to judgment. I saw shame on her face, and prayed. I tried not to judge. It would be wrong. So I intentionally put grace and mercy on my face. Mom and Dad had shown me how that was done.

Jesus would have known what to say, but Rose was the next to speak. "I hope we can still be friends."

"Of course we can."

I hadn't much practice with a nonjudgmental, hate the sin, love the sinner kind of attitude. I worried that Rose saw my hesitation. That was the first time I remember praying to be like my parents.

Living in Germany, away from family and old friends, caused Jack and me to grow deeper as friends. The cost of a long-distance phone call promoted our independence as a couple and our dependence on each other as partners and confidants. It was a healthy newlywed lifestyle. Rare arguments never lasted more than a few minutes, and apologies were passionate.

Shortly after that memorable outing with Rose, Jack came home from his third time in the field. He had been outside, in either heat or rain, for fourteen days, and it was evident when he walked in the door. He had carried his field pack all the way home instead of taking a taxi. I assumed his mood reflected how tired he was. I was only partially correct.

The apartment was clean and tidy. Laundry was done, and supper was almost ready. He proceeded to the living room where he emptied his arms, and rather than acknowledge my cheerful greeting with a hug and a kiss, he opened his pack full of dirty equipment and pungent fatigues, still moist with sweat and mud. Then, he dumped it all onto the oriental rug.

Whoa! That got my attention. "Yeah, it's good to see you too. What kind of greeting was that?"

I was new at the welcome-your-husband-home-after-a-bad-day thing, so I expected him to cut me some slack. Not so. I offered to hold dinner and fill the tub for him.

"I'll do it myself."

I let him. The meatloaf was dry and the potatoes too salty, but he gobbled it down anyway. His mood didn't improve, so I pushed. "What's the matter?"

"I don't know. You tell me."

"Nothing was wrong until you unloaded all that filth on *my* rug?"

No response.

He went into the bedroom and closed the door. Dad would have given my Mom a good argument. I knew how to argue, but I had no clue how to deal with pouting silence. When Jack refused to answer through the bedroom door, I quit knocking and yelling.

I changed my strategy to making as much racket as possible while I cleaned up his mess. I wanted him to hear every moan and groan as I brushed the mud off every pair of pants and cleaned each piece of his gear. I calculated what my huge reward might be for this act of self-sacrifice.

As a young wife, I didn't understand that to sacrifice means to give with no expectations. I wanted Jack to be punished, so I pouted. With or without noise, pouting is pouting. I wanted Jack to pay. It would take a few more fights before I learned that if Jack paid for my sacrifices, they weren't sacrifices at all.

My own long bath was all the thanks I received for the sum of my efforts. I watched television until the fuzzy signal and annoying static notified me it was midnight. Then I sneaked into my side of the bed, ready to rest my head on the pillow, and grateful for that wooden partition. Jack was breathing easy and deep—eyes closed.

He waited until I was in a deep sleep to wake me and begin the discussion of what the matter was. Too tired to argue, I listened.

He wanted to know why I was "running around flirting with GIs."

What could I say to that? I didn't know what he was talking about.

Jack told me about a GI in his unit who had become notorious for creating excuses to stay behind, while the rest of the company went to the field. The guy would brag about spending time with someone else's wife or girlfriend instead of sweating and getting dirty out in the woods. This time he had bragged about spending time with me.

I was speechless when I heard a physical description matching one of the guys from the guesthouse where Rose and I had dinner.

Jack demanded an answer, "Did you hang out with him?"

I couldn't speak, but the tears were building, and the look on my face was all the answer Jack needed.

He sprang out of bed and threw on jeans and a T-shirt. His mumblings let me know he was leaving to put his fist in the face of a man (Jack had a name for him) who needed something to think about before messing with someone else's wife. I begged Jack not to go. He ignored my plea, grabbed his shoes and was putting them on with firefighter-like urgency.

"Wait until morning, after you cool down."

With his hand on the doorknob, I turned to logic.

"Spending the next few years in prison would be punishing the wrong man. His nose will stop bleeding before you've spent your first night in jail. Please Jack. Don't."

He hesitated, and I seized the opportunity to tell my side of the story. I told everything that happened that evening and then how, a few days later, the same guy had approached me in the commissary and offered to help me get my groceries home. Nothing about his offer was inappropriate, but I didn't accept. When I ran into him again on my walk home, I thought it more than coincidence.

But wasn't Jack's response an overreaction? Nothing had gone on between us.

"You remember my letter?" Jack asked. "How I didn't want you to come here?"

A sinking feeling gripped my stomach. I remembered. That letter had been torn to shreds in my attempt to forget.

"Same guy." Jack wanted me to know how close I'd come. "And there are more just like him. I don't want you talking to GIs!"

I mumbled loud enough to send Jack a message as I turned away, "I'm not a five-year-old."

He grabbed my shoulder. "You don't get it. You can't talk to GIs!"

I would have verbally escalated Jack's aggression, but it was late and I was tired. Grabbing my shoulder was Jack's way of showing he cared and indicating his level of commitment to my protection. At least that's what I believed.

I relaxed my shoulders, letting Jack know I was done with fighting. "Kiss and make up?"

Jack's hug was weak at first. Then, I think he hugged me tight so I couldn't see his tears.

The GI that had caused our fight was still bragging about his exploits the next Monday morning, but his storytelling ended unexpectedly. He was interrupted with a softly spoken, no-room-for-misinterpretation verbal message, followed by a blow to the storyteller's right rib cage. Jack had stored a weekend's worth of adrenaline in his angry left arm, and released it as a physical warning of what would happen if my name was mentioned again.

Jack was one of the ones called to assist the injured soldier to the clinic for x-rays, but each of the five or six men who had witnessed the altercation declined comment to the military police.

Our first big quarrel was over. I'd stepped onto the other side of Goliath's Mountain, and returned to Jack unscathed. We agreed I would remain friends with Rose as long as we stayed out of guesthouses and always made it home before dark. As for the guy who had caused our trouble, I saw his backside several more times, but never again saw his face.

There is a chapter in the Bible that speaks to being a good wife. I knew it was in the Proverbs somewhere, but I wasn't sure where. I scanned verses and read God's instruction to "turn at my rebuke; surely I will pour out my spirit on you" (Proverbs 1:23a). The second chapter reminded me to treasure God's commands, listen to his wisdom, and apply it to my heart, mind, and actions.

In the third chapter, I read about keeping "sound wisdom and discretion" if I didn't want to stumble. Not an easy task, if I wanted to keep Rose as a friend. Then I read the fifth verse: "Trust in the Lord with all your heart. And lean not on your own understanding." And the sixth: "In all your ways acknowledge him. And he shall direct your paths."

I kept reading, three or four chapters a day, until I reached the thirty-first chapter.

"Who can find a virtuous wife? For her worth is far above rubies. The heart of her husband safely trusts her; so he will have no lack of gain. She does him good and not evil all the days of her life" (Proverbs 31:10–12).

I wanted to be that kind of wife.

I read the entire chapter aloud to Jack. He got out of it that the husband of a Proverbs 31 wife would be well-fed, have his fatigues ironed sharp and stiff, come home to a clean house, and never have to worry about what the guys at work were saying about her.

"Do I come close?" I asked, hoping for some affirmation.

"You could make a better meatloaf."

Jack promised not to dump his dirty pack on the rug again. The husband of a Proverbs 31 wife would be "more considerate."

Before the week was over, he brought home one of those sweepers with a rotating brush. It was the next best thing to a vacuum cleaner. That, and a minor adjustment to my meatloaf recipe, helped return us to newlywed status.

13

HONEYMOON CONTINUED

We fought the old saying that, "when you have extra money there is no time, and when you have extra time there is no money." Surrounded by vacation hot spots that most people only dream about while living on an enlisted man's salary wasn't easy, but we managed. Trains were cheap, and buses were cheaper.

Frankfurt, West Germany was a hot spot based on my experience, and it satisfied our criteria for bragging that we had been to a big city. The burgers and fries at the McDonalds in Frankfurt didn't have the standardized taste we were accustomed to. We didn't go back. In contrast, ice cream at the Dairy Queen provided a perfect taste of home. We tried to stop in any time we went to the big city.

Gene and Paula joined us for a bus tour along the border between East and West Germany. Farmers on both sides drove tractors that would have been revered as valuable antiques in the States. Crops were grown on small plots of land that looked like family gardens compared to cornfields that met the horizons of Illinois. Everything on the east side of the wall appeared barren and gray or brown. The west side had color, with bright flowers growing in yards and printed on fabric curtains.

Much of the road wound alongside a mountain, and depending on which way the road curved, I could have been led to believe we were on either the west or the east side of a high barbed-wire fence separating us from an un-American ideology. We were, at times, close enough to factories and buildings on the east side to see faces looking through open windows. The soldiers on our bus could identify the caliber of weapons held by East German guards manning the frequent and strategically placed towers. Our tour guide instructed us not to wave. For the people on the east side to return a wave from someone on the west might invite consequences. My imagination robbed me of sleep that night. Sad thoughts of East Germans so cruelly separated from West Germans continued the next morning.

I asked Jack, "Can you imagine what it must be like to have a brother, sister, or cousin you are not allowed to see? Grandparents who might never have met their grandchildren. It's horrible."

"They have their stuff to deal with, and we have ours."

I cried for Jack. My attempts to apologize for the insensitive question met with a cold stare. Lesson learned: It doesn't take a world war to tear parents away from sons and daughters or to rob children and grandparents of the joys of relationship.

My favorite trip was to Munich during the Christmas season. Traveling through Southern Bavaria to get to Munich set an amazing stage. Private chalets, perfect enough for a postcard, and snow-covered mountains like we'd never seen, made the bus ride alone worthwhile. Then we stepped off the bus into the winter wonderland of the city, where snowflakes drifted onto our chilled cheeks and noses. Jack and I drifted away for a moment of our own, and missed being included in the group photograph, but we'd have a memory that wouldn't fade over time.

I'd never seen a city more beautifully adorned for the holidays. It wasn't only the lights, ribbons, and wreaths. It was the mood of the residents and merchants in the city. Unlike Frankfurt or Aschaffenburg, strangers greeted us with "Merry Christmas" when they learned we were American. The people in Munich smiled more, and the shopping was great.

I heard a live boys' choir for the first time. They were singing from the massive steps of a church that appeared to serve as much as a museum as it did a house of worship. The air was crisp, clear, and filled with Christmas spirit as their young voices traveled for several blocks. Nearby stores had no need to pipe in music. Padded pews and beautiful stained glass weren't necessary to enhance that worship experience for me.

I didn't want to go home. To my home above the karate school or to my home in Illinois. Munich was perfect.

Having more time than money was not so bad. Every household task, from making the bed to cleaning the bathtub, required more time and effort than it would have in the States. The little sweeper Jack bought for me was nice, but it took three or four passes over the same spot before the rug looked clean. Dirt seemed to truly come out of the woodwork in that apartment. Shaking out the small rugs required descending the five flights of stairs and climbing back up with rugs in tow. Other women shook their rugs from upper apartment windows, but Rose warned that the owner of the karate school would complain if dirt from the upper stories landed on his customers' vehicles, or his own Mercedes.

Except for those stairs, short trips to the local market were fun for me. Nearby market owners got to know us and were ever so patient with my language skills, or lack thereof. They also enjoyed speaking English with me. I tried new foods just to please them, and Jack stopped in on Fridays to buy a dozen thorny roses. Their daughter had married an American and moved to Chicago. Each time they received a new photo, they pulled it from behind the counter and took the opportunity to share an update.

"We're from Illinois." I answered on the first day we met.

"Chicago!"

I clarified, "No, three hours south of Chicago."

"Illinois. Chicago!"

Our merchant friends never did get it. It was difficult for them to understand we were from Illinois, but three hours from Chicago where their daughter lived, and where they planned to visit one day. They weren't the only ones. Depending on our mood or the amount of time we could spare, we might just let acquaintances hold on to the assumption that Jack and I were Chicagoans.

Shopping at the commissary meant an uphill hike to the base. I pulled a tall, two-wheeled wire basket. The first time I saw one of those baskets, it made me think of an old wino pulling the sum total of his belongings—not an image I wanted to project. But with the blisters on my hands barely healed from carrying bags home after my first trip, I bought one of those baskets for my second and subsequent trips. It cost about the price of two taxi rides and pulled my shopping bags and laundry for the duration of our time in Aschaffenburg. I blended into the sidewalk traffic.

September's Oktoberfest was one of those cultural tidbits I'd read about in German class, but it turned out to be a feast of activity and food that my textbook had not fully explained. Ordinary, hardworking, serious Germans put aside image for a few days and went crazy. The parades, polka music, and dancing must have lasted for a week. It reminded me of our Halloween, except adults were the ones trying to win the most creative or ridiculous costume contest. We felt a little out of place with our everyday clothes on.

The city of Aschaffenburg posted invitations to an Oktoberfest festival and specifically included the military personnel and their families. Jack and I went because the signs mentioned "American musicians." Our hearts were set on some good old rock-n-roll. I counted picnic tables, figuring there were at least five hundred people crowded into the beer tent where everyone gathered.

The autumn chill had arrived, but it was warm inside the tent. Waitresses carried trays of brats and liter-sized beer mugs. Beer sloshed on the heads and down the backs of two people at our table. I was one of them. We listened to the American musicians and wondered how far and wide the city had looked to find Americans who played authentic polka music.

The brats were good, but it was watching some of the GIs try to polka and gain the attention of the German girls that made the evening worthwhile. Jack refused to take me to the dance floor. I only asked once. Three drinks were available: beer, kinderbeer, and Perrier. I didn't like Perrier, and wouldn't drink beer, so my only option was kinder (as in kindergarten) beer. The first sip tasted nasty. "This smells like beer."

I took another drink. It wasn't what I expected, but I was thirsty.

The mug was empty before I learned that kinderbeer is half-cola and half-beer. It wasn't the German version of root beer, like I thought. The word *kinder* referred to a kind or size of a mug used to serve children, rather than the drink itself. We saw plenty small children drinking kinderbeer during our time in Germany. I had some difficulty accepting that cultural difference.

It was a nice evening out with some of the guys from his unit. Our landlord, local store owners, and a few of our neighbors noticed our presence. Each offered to buy us another round of brats, kraut, and beer. Jack, the less social of the two of us, wanted to stay, but I felt ill.

Two days later was my first official trip to the base medical clinic.

"I think I'm pregnant."

The medic who took my history was about my age. He created my medical chart, which consisted of one handwritten line, and collected a urine specimen. He asked me to sit in the waiting room, but no seat was available, so I stood in a corner. When my name was called from the busy reception window, I expected to be guided into the clinic area and a private room, but the same medic announced through the window, loud enough for the people around me to hear, "Your pregnancy test is negative."

He turned to walk away.

"Wait. I'm sure I'm pregnant."

He glanced back at me. "The test is negative."

The clinic was obviously busy, and I sensed my needs were not as urgent as some, but I wasn't wasting this trip. "What do I do now?"

"Can't help you. That's something you'll have to talk to your husband about."

Everyone around me laughed. I was more angry than insulted.

"But I know I'm pregnant!"

Another medic stepped toward the window.

"Come back in a few days. We'll retest. It may be too early to detect a hormone change."

I told Jack how I'd been treated. He laughed and told me to "get over it."

I got over it a few days later, when the pregnancy test was positive.

14

PRECIOUS MEMORIES

Dad's response, when I called home with the news we were pregnant, wasn't what I expected. I interpreted his concern as a lack of confidence in my preparedness for motherhood. Mom took the phone and tried to make up for his lack of enthusiasm.

I called again after a few days. Dad's apology came with everything needed except the word "sorry." Then, he overstated how Jack and I would make great parents.

"I don't want this baby to call me grandpa. My name is Howard."

That statement, more than anything else Dad said, explained his short-lived reluctance to share our joy.

This baby would be my parents' first grandchild. If it was a girl, she would never lack for pink ribbons, bows, and lace. John and Ginny already had grandchildren, but if this baby was a boy, he would be given the name of his father, grandfather, and great-grandfather. Jack and I talked about how exuberant grandparents might get annoying were it not for us living on a different continent.

Morning sickness and cold, damp weather weren't going to taint my excitement. Orange soda and saltine crackers helped me make it until lunch, when my craving for peanut butter on one slice of bread with thin dill pickles and a sprinkling of sugar took over. I called it peanut butter pizza, and I washed it down with a tall glass of whole milk. For the first time since my mother spoon fed me, vegetables and fruit became a staple in my diet. The pregnancy turned a previous aversion to broccoli and frozen peas into a craving.

Other than the expected nausea and twice the recommended weight gain, it was an uneventful and healthy pregnancy.

Jack bought me a sewing machine. I planned to make some simple maternity outfits for around the house and save the more expensive, store-bought, clothes for going out. After a few mistakes and some wasted fabric, I learned to follow a pattern. My favorite maternity dress was sewn in my living room. I wore it everywhere.

Friends I had made during my weekly trips to the laundromat brought their mending and patterns over when they learned of my machine. Our sewing group was nearly disrupted when I broke my last machine needle. We caught up on our cutting, pinning patterns together, and hand stitching while we waited an entire week for a replacement.

My Illinois family and friends gave me a baby shower. It was a regular shower, including a cake, punch, nuts, mints, party games, and presents. Mom and Ginny alternated opening gifts. The only thing missing was me, and someone assigned to turn on the brand new video camera aimed at capturing the event. They all had a good time, and I was thrilled to receive boxes of baby clothes and necessities with familiar department store labels.

My small group of American friends in Aschaffenburg gave me another shower. Paula had been busy working, so I was surprised when she suggested we help each other with some deep spring cleaning. She knew Jack would be in the field for another week and our apartment would be untidy for at least another six days. Not wanting to accept responsibility for a potentially embarrassing shock when she brought cake, punch, and guests into my apartment, she proved herself a genuine friend. It was a perfect surprise.

I loved being pregnant. I loved the anticipation, the planning, and the dreaming.

Bus transportation to Frankfurt for health care appointments was provided, courtesy of the U.S. Army. Jack arranged to go with me the first time. It was mostly soldiers on the bus, but I made friends with a couple of the other pregnant wives, and there were usually a few NCOs (non-commissioned officers) riding along, which kept the rowdiness under control.

The ride was smooth, and I felt safe with cars flying past us on the autobahn between Aschaffenburg and Frankfurt, but more than one woman went into labor because of the uneven cobblestone streets in the cities.

Visiting Frankfurt was an all-day ordeal, without a stop at the Dairy Queen. Seeing modern equipment at the 97th General Hospital was comforting. My pregnant friends back in the States were having sonograms and sharing funny pictures. Some of them were able to know the sex of their unborn baby. Not me. Military insurance provided sonograms only for what was deemed to be a significant problem.

The climb up the stairs to our apartment would have been impossible with all my laundry or grocery bags in hand. I had no choice but to leave bags at the foot of the stairs and carry them up a few at a time. Only once was something stolen during what I called my "one-woman five-flight relay." I think it must have been one of the karate school customers who couldn't resist a box of American cereal. I was looking forward to those Sugar Smacks, and since I was about eight months along, I felt the despicable act of thievery was akin to stealing food from my baby's umbilical cord. However hungry the thief was, I prayed for him to get a cavity.

Rose offered to walk with me to the base for my weekly shopping. She loved looking at American merchandise and flirting with GIs. As my attention turned more and more toward motherhood, she came around less often, but she intuitively knew when I needed something from the commissary, and she knocked on my door those days.

Jack was at work when I had the first contraction, and Rose wasn't home. There had been some random aches and pains, but nothing so severe. I was three weeks past my due date. This had to be the real thing.

The second contraction happened as I stepped into the bathtub. The sound of Jack's key turning the lock never sounded so good. He came through the door while I was still in the tub. Using the one-Mississippi, two Mississippi method, the contractions were seven minutes apart.

Jack took control with none of the scatterbrained stumbling around like we'd seen in movies. He took a quick bath, dressed hurriedly, and helped me put on my shoes. He grabbed my packed bag and the diaper bag. I carried my purse.

It was the dinner hour, and taxis should have been surrounding our block, but not that evening. We walked a couple of blocks before we spotted one of those Mercedes with a light on top. A young couple turned their taxi over to us before arriving at their destination, and the driver wouldn't take the money we had tucked away in my bag just for this occasion.

We climbed a tall set of stairs before walking into the clinic, and after a total of ten contractions. The clinic was staffed with a clerk and one medic, who immediately assessed my contractions as Braxton-Hicks.

"Go back home and come back when the contractions are seven minutes apart."

"But they are seven minutes apart."

Did this kid, younger than me, think I didn't know about Braxton-Hicks? Did he have any idea how many books I had read in preparation for this event?

"Aren't you the same medic who told me my pregnancy test was negative nine months ago?" I asked. We both knew he was.

Still in control, Jack suggested we walk to the commissary to get something to eat, "Just in case the contractions get worse."

I wasn't about to climb another stair, so I offered an alternative idea. "You can all go to the commissary. Have yourselves some greasy hamburgers and fries. I'm staying right here on this uncomfortable gurney."

The medic pulled a curtain as though it would block his voice while he told Jack it was okay to let me rest there for a while before we left.

"No hurry, unless someone else comes in," he said.

A soldier came into the clinic seeking attention, and I heard his every groan and complaint through the curtain. I don't recall the exact nature of his problem, but it was trivial from my perspective. No blood. No broken bones. I suspected he had a case of hypochondria, not severe enough to move my backside from that thinly padded metal cart.

I timed a few contractions at five-minute intervals, using the clock this time.

The medic sauntered in while a contraction was still in progress. He placed both hands on my belly, pretending to have confidence in what he was (or wasn't) doing.

"Maybe I should do an internal exam before you leave?"

He wasn't asking my permission. He was thinking out loud. With his first attempt, the young medic was unable to determine how far I was dilated. He made a phone call. Jack and I trusted that the person speaking instruction to him was actually a medical doctor, and not another medic with the nickname "Doc."

Two off duty medics had now arrived and were about to observe their first obstetric exam. The three of them were recipients of my philanthropy, although it wasn't offered as much as assumed. I remember thinking I deserved a plaque on the wall for providing them with such an educational opportunity.

With a second exam, according to this novice, I was dilated to five centimeters. The "Doc" ordered transport via ambulance to 97th General in Frankfurt, never mind the military car, which was their usual protocol.

It was a fast and wild ride through those narrow streets. Jack knew the driver and the ride-along medic who had been privileged to observe my exam. They had done guard duty together. The three of them held a casual conversation having nothing to do with me or my impending childbirth. The contractions continued every five minutes at about the same intensity. I interrupted their conversation to suggest they should be documenting things about me, but they had guard duty stories to tell.

I was glad to get off their cart and into a comfortable bed. The medics waved at Jack with a "See ya around," then wheeled their cart away.

Only a curtain separated the four beds in the room; all four occupied now that I had arrived. A sink intended for the four of us and our visitors was attached to the wall near the door. The community bathroom, with several stalls and a couple of showers, was at the far end of a long hallway.

The nursing assistant assigned to our room kept fresh ice chips at our bedsides, and every time one of us left to walk to the bathroom, she appeared from nowhere to straighten the bed of the absent patient. She was there when we returned to pamper us back into bed.

Each time, before leaving the room, she washed her hands, then used the moist paper towel to wipe the sink. She held the towel high before dropping it into the waste basket as though her example would cause us to do likewise, and her sink would remain spotless. I made sure to mimic her when I washed my hands, and so did the other mothers. *Maybe actions really do speak louder than words?*

Twelve hours after the first contraction, my cervix was at six centimeters, and I was hungry, fatigued, and asking for Demerol at the shortest possible intervals. They were giving it to me. The narcotic that had helped me relax and sleep a little between contractions was no longer offering the same level of relief. My three roommates had been to the delivery room, but my bassinette was still empty.

Contractions were now coming almost back to back, with increased intensity and a strong urge to push. I'd heard my roommates being instructed and knew that unsupervised pushing was against the rules. With the next two contractions, I pushed. I couldn't not push.

Our nursing assistant caught me: "Don't push!"

They were the only two English words she knew. I remember her well. Not her face or her hair color, but her attitude toward service and duty. Her smile and attention to the little details made me think she cared and was serious about her job.

She ran to retrieve the nurse, who called for the doctor right away.

"No more pushing and no more Demerol. Your cervix isn't cooperating with us," he said.

They rolled me to the radiology department for an x-ray. The nursing assistant came along, apparently for the sole purpose of sporadically calling out, "Don't push!" She did her job well.

The doctor stopped us in the hallway when we returned, slapped a piece of film on a lighted viewing box, and explained that the abnormal shape of "the pelvis" would not accommodate delivery through "the canal."

I'm not Panama, I thought, *and that's my "pelvis" and my "canal" you're talking about!*

I would need an urgent C-section. Jack, who never questioned authority, had lost enough sleep that his inhibitions were drowsy. He protested, "Isn't there something else you can do?"

"If we had known about this anomaly, we would have planned for and scheduled a C-section. Natural childbirth is out of the question, today and in the future."

One more contraction proved my ability to pant and not push. I was on my way to the operating suite before the next.

I was the only patient in the very large room. Curtains indicated that the operating suite could accommodate more than one surgery at a time. My panting with each contraction must have sounded like screaming. I knew they were annoyed because they told me so.

"Save your energy." "You're scaring that baby." "We don't give Demerol based on how loud you scream." Everyone in the room tried their own brand of humor. I gave everything I had to pant instead of scream. It wasn't working.

The operating suite was cold. They had strapped my body to a narrow table. I could see the doctor across the room scrubbing his hands and hairy forearms. With his back to me, he reminded me about the damage I would do to my baby if I pushed the head against my "noncompliant anatomy."

"What kind of mother would I be if I couldn't follow a doctor's order? What if I had already hurt my baby?"

Another contraction. It lasted longer than the previous ones. I prayed a silent prayer. *"I need help. I can't do this."*

It started as the most painful contraction yet. I focused on the clock's industrial-sized minute hand as it bounced audibly clockwise.

"That last contraction was different. The crescendo of pain felt different, painfully good—like progress." They heard me, but they weren't listening.

The doctor continued to scrub at what seemed to be a leisurely pace for such an "urgent" procedure. Someone was humming. I think it was him.

The surgical nurse watched the same clock as she continued to open instruments that, under any other circumstance, would have made for great conversation. She was working with a sense of urgency, as was the anesthesiologist, who held a mask about six inches from my face.

I caught a whiff of the funny-smelling drug meant to make me sleep, then interrupted his explanation of what he was preparing to do by rocking my head to stop the mask from making contact with my face. He must have seen my behavior as a stalling tactic or some form of hysteria. With one shot at convincing him I was sane and that something had changed, I spoke to him using the calmest voice I could manage.

"That last contraction *really* was different. Please. If someone will just take a look and tell me they don't see my baby's head, I'll cooperate and let you do what you need to do."

It would be less than thirty seconds until my next contraction. His eyes rolled, letting me know he was only pacifying me. I didn't care if he was condescending or what he thought of me. I knew what I was feeling.

He placed the mask on my chest where the escaping mist could moisten my face and probably wished I'd take a deep breath or two. As he walked toward the foot of my bed, I sensed he was still rolling his eyes. He loosened the restraint over my thighs. I assumed the position and threw back the sheet.

He confirmed what I already knew. "I can see the head."

I felt a strange euphoria during the next birthing pain. With a blink and a nod, I had permission from the anesthesiologist to push.

My baby was born into his ungloved hands.

The obstetrician, with mask, sterile gown, and gloved hands in the air, stepped over in time to observe.

When I saw the anesthesiologist's big smile, I dropped my head to the table. He moved the mask and placed a beautiful and wailing baby on my chest.

Then he took the corner of my sheet to swaddle his freshly delivered patient. For a moment—an awkward moment—I thought he was leaning down to kiss my baby.

The obstetrician invited him, "Go ahead. Cut the cord," So he did.

The anesthesiologist could have moved on to his next patient or the cafeteria, but he stayed behind and offered me a few whiffs of that funny smelling medicine. I was grateful for that mist while the obstetrician, at the other end of the operating table, did what obstetricians do after a delivery.

The nurse, holding her unused tray of instruments in one hand, leaned in from behind the doctors. "You forgot something. Something important. Maybe you should stick to anesthesia."

"It's a boy," the anesthesiologist said. "It's a boy. I get to be the one to announce. It's a boy!"

The mood in the room changed from professionally grumpy to happy they had come to work that day. No one complained about the screaming baby. John Robert IV was welcomed into this world on May 21, 1976.

15

PARENTHOOD

John Robert IV. A stuffy name, and not in keeping with our lower middle-class lifestyle, but the nicknames Robert, and Bobby were taken. Johnny seemed a generation too old. We tried them all on for size anyway.

"Robbie?"

I don't recall which one of us suggested it, but Robbie, as we stretched our imaginations, agreed to his new name with a newborn noise.

Ninety-seventh General Hospital had a rooming-in policy, which meant that newborns stayed in a bassinette next to the mother's bed. One of the four beds would empty, and it wouldn't be long until a laboring mom would fill it. There wasn't a lot of sleeping going on. And guarding our modesty wasn't easy with the fathers lounging in straight back chairs. Jack stayed by our side for the next couple of days. He left long enough to eat in the cafeteria or freshen up in the men's room.

The extra shirt I had packed for him was on its last hour. He was planning to bathe in the men's restroom again. I insisted he take the train home, get a good night's rest, and return the next morning with some clean clothes for me to wear home.

Before Jack left, I took the opportunity to shower and take a short walk around the maternity unit. When I returned and quietly opened the curtain to our quarter of the room, Jack was leaning over the bassinet ready to pick up his son. He had both hands around the baby's abdomen, then released him as though he knew he didn't know what he was doing. Then his left hand went under Robbie's head, and his right grabbed tiny baby feet. Just as I was about to step in, Jack maneuvered one hand under Robbie's head and the other under his diaper. He balanced our newborn son as though he were a well-done turkey on a platter.

Jack looked up and saw that I'd been watching him struggle. "He was getting ready to cry."

Robbie was sound asleep. The precious baby I had birthed over the course of about twenty hours, with only ice chips and too little Demerol, was being handled as though he were little more than a sack of potatoes. Jack clearly had some learning to do. I provided his first lesson, then, there, and loud enough for all the other parents in the room to hear.

"But the nurses handle him like that." Jack defended his method, but the nurses were confident and quick. Jack was hesitant and . . . well, he wasn't a nurse.

Robbie slept though the session, which Jack noted. His observation made me realize motherhood had not instantly make me the expert, authority, or head of household.

Jack walked away after gently stroking Robbie's back and bending down to get one more look at his namesake. One of the other mothers was trying to open a heavy window for some fresh air. Jack stopped to help, and commented on how pretty her baby girl was. There was no particular reason, but I didn't like the way she smiled and said "Thank you."

Three (maybe four) minutes later, Robbie was fully awake and hungry. My milk came in, and I started to cry. Mom and baby spent a frustrating afternoon trying to figure out what we were doing wrong.

I was in pain, tired, and emotionally on the edge of something, but I didn't know what. The hormone storm cloud surrounding me overshadowed everything. I had mistakenly thought reading and knowing about postpartum blues would prevent them.

The whole afternoon, I fretted and cried. Where was Jack when

I needed him most? He didn't kiss me good-bye or tell me he loved me. He didn't even say good-bye. Was I too young to be a mother? Would I have enough milk? Robbie was whisked off for circumcision, and I gave in to depression.

Every possible problem and a few impossible ones raced in my head, and then a nurse I hadn't seen before entered the room. She flung open the curtain between me and my roommate. Her eyes looked over the bassinette at my bedside and went to my belly, still round after childbirth.

"When are we doing your C-section?" she asked.

If her careless assumption didn't cause her some remorse, the indignation in the tone of my voice should have, when I told her, "My baby was born two days ago."

Hers, I thought, would be a very short nursing career. She couldn't complete her assessment and close the curtain quickly enough for either of us.

Another nurse returned my crying baby. "He could use a little soothing after his little procedure. It would be a good time to nurse."

She dropped a sheet of paper on my bedside table and told me to read it. I could read, and the instructions for post-circumcision care were adequately written, but I could have used a personal touch. The kind of care a mother, sister, or good friend would offer. I fantasized about buying a ticket back to the States until I heard one of my roommates talking about how long it would take to have her passport updated to include an infant—something I hadn't considered.

Jack returned the next morning, freshly shaven and smelling great. Mr. Shy and Introverted greeted each of the other mothers and proceeded directly to pick up his sleeping son. Clearly our plans to let a sleeping baby sleep would need to be revisited.

"She had a girl," he said. "Maybe we should give them the pink outfit since we don't need it?"

How thoughtful. Instead of telling him how hurt I'd been by his pathetic good-bye yesterday, his absent hello this morning, and his attention to the other mothers, an unusual urge to pout came over me.

"Sure."

The feedings still weren't going well. They weighed Robbie before and after the next few feedings, and I think it was me he was talking about when the pediatrician told the nurse to give the nervous mom some extra samples of formula to take home.

Gene and Paula were in the lobby waiting to drive us, but they would need to wait. I was dreading the long drive, and hoping I wouldn't need to change a diaper or nurse in the car, but that's not what was slowing my progress toward the exit. It wasn't for the dread of the eighty stairs when we got there either. It was pulling on my pre-pregnancy jeans that was causing me anguish. The bell bottoms were fine, but the hip-hugging denim wasn't giving.

My pelvis and every other bone in my pelvic region had been compliant enough to expand, but not enough to contract; I had the pain and wider hips to prove it. The two sides of the snap and zipper were not going to meet. One of the nurses knew what to do. "Medical-grade silk tape!"

I had my figure back for the ride home, and I can recommend the stuff be used as a tummy tucker, but for no more than a couple hours, or only as long as one can hold their bladder.

The blues left me just about as quickly as they came, even though Robbie and I couldn't agree on a schedule. I tried. I read more books. They assumed the ideal. My days and nights were spent nursing, changing diapers, and rocking without the aid of a rocking chair. The cycle repeated, regardless of how long it had been since Robbie's last meal, diaper change, or nap time.

At night, Robbie napped for twenty to thirty minutes at a time in a comfy little portable cradle. During the day, he made up for lost sleep in my left arm while I did housework, ate, read, or watched TV.

We bought an old-fashioned baby carriage. It was big enough for newborn triplets or a spoiled five-year-old. Buggies like ours were used for both kinds of babies. When my arms needed a rest, I would take Robbie out for a long ride. He had some great naps in that baby buggy.

Jack was greeted on many afternoons by my outstretched arms, not asking for a hug, but asking him to take his son. Robbie was soothed by the smell and feel of sweat, whiskers, and a heavily starched military uniform.

My parents, Rhonda, and Kevin visited us in Aschaffenburg. They came to see Robbie, but Dad rented a car so we could also do a little sightseeing. He loved the autobahn but claimed to be disappointed with the Mercedes. It lacked some of the bells and whistles that were standard in most American cars.

I don't remember who wanted to go to Paris, but we drove into France. We aren't a beer or wine drinking family, and the bottled water and soft drinks weren't just warm, they were a sitting-out-in-the-July-sun sort of hot. The Mercedes didn't have air-conditioning, and the French people we encountered were less than enthusiastic about American tourists. We turned around before we made it to Paris. The people of Luxembourg and Belgium were friendly and grateful for American tourists and their credit cards.

Jack and I missed home after their visit. We missed our church family, too. Worship services at the chapel on base were not the same, and it didn't take much of an excuse for us to miss a Sunday. The end of our time in Germany was drawing close. The mini-vacations and sightseeing trips were limited now that we were a family of three, and one of us was too young to appreciate the scenery. Public transportation, with a baby in tow, made me miss my car. Things we had considered quirky before, were now inconveniences. We'd miss our new friends and the comfy feather mattresses, but not that wooden partition.

Jack and I were content, but ready to try something other than army life. The five flights of stairs had served their purpose, I was back to wearing my hip-hugging jeans. It was time to go home.

16

HOMECOMING

Munich had been Christmas card perfect, and the Chicago skyscrapers along Lake Michigan were something to see, but after being away from home for over twenty months, it was a silly Ferris wheel that made me cry. Strung with red and green lights, it takes on the appearance of a Christmas wreath to welcome travelers to Peoria, Illinois from the interstate or from the air.

Jack would be flying home a few days before Christmas. I hoped he would have a seat on my side of the noisy little prop plane that shuttles passengers from Chicago to Peoria every evening, or that his pilot would do a circle before landing, so Jack would experience the same welcome. He had stayed behind in Aschaffenburg to make sure our belongings made it onto the truck and to complete his commitment to the army.

Robbie and I had already left Germany when they offered Jack another promotion and an easier job in the States. He didn't consult me. There was no need. Jack was done with the army. Since the day he'd hurt his ankle, he had looked forward to when he could take off his combat boots for good.

Robbie was immediately spoiled by both sets of grandparents, aunts, uncles, and church ladies. It didn't matter that he had lost nearly all of the hair on one side of his head and still had a fair amount of red hair on the other side. Mom teased John that their grandson had inherited red hair from her and baldness from the paternal side of the family.

Within a few weeks, Robbie had a full head of blond hair, putting an end to Mom's claim of genetic superiority.

He started to take longer naps during the day, and in his crib. Maybe it was all the attention. Maybe he just needed more space, or maybe my left bicep had gotten too firm, and he preferred a softer place to rest his head.

Jack made it home for Christmas. We were jobless and uncertain, but happy. We found an apartment through the classifieds. It was cheap and fully furnished. Again, there were stairs. It was on the second story of a fifty-year-old house, and the stairs were rickety, with rotting wood. There were hardwood floors, but no big oriental rugs. The wood was splintering. We couldn't go barefoot in our own apartment, and it was not a safe place for a baby to crawl about.

If the dangerous stairs and large splinters in the floor weren't awful enough, smoke from an illegal substance wafted up every evening from the apartment below us. After thirty days, we gave the landlord notice that we were moving.

Our new apartment was smaller, but on the ground level. We could park right outside the door. It had clean carpet and tile floors, newer appliances and friendly neighbors. Breaking into our savings account for some new furniture was a pleasure.

I took pictures of Robbie and our new apartment. Lots of pictures. I tucked a couple into envelopes with letters to Paula and Rose. My Turkish friend only got pictures with our new address written in bold print and a one-sentence request, written in German, for them to reply with pictures.

Paula answered within a couple weeks, telling me Gene had re-enlisted. My other two Aschaffenburg friends never did reply. I knew I had made a lifelong friend in Paula, and I wondered if my Turkish friends owned a camera. And Rose . . . she was in my prayers for a long while.

Searching for a job became Jack's full-time job. The ladies at the unemployment office either tired of seeing his face every day or else succumbed to his polite mannerisms and handsome smile. They hired him to work in their office. He was overqualified as a file clerk, but without a college education he was not eligible for management. The perk was being in the right place to see the best jobs as they became available.

Within a short time, he landed a job as a laboratory technician at a nearby chemical plant. The work wasn't exciting or challenging, but the pay allowed him to take good care of our little family, buy a new car, and settle us comfortably. Within a few months we were into a routine. Our small apartment could be thoroughly cleaned within a few hours. Robbie was finally sleeping through the night and took long afternoon naps. I discovered TV all over again. Boredom set in.

I dropped by JC Penney to check in on Lucy and Edith and ended up filling out an application for employment. I was hired on the spot even though no opening had been posted. Jack agreed it would be good for me to work a couple evening shifts and a Saturday, or two, a month. We thought the extra money would be good, and I could easily spare sixteen hours a week. It would be fun to reconnect with old friends.

After the first week, Jack had to work overtime and would not be home by the time I needed to leave for work. Desperate, I begged a friend to babysit. After the first month, I was given a raise and scheduled for over thirty hours. Robbie didn't seem to mind being shuffled between Jack, Grandma, and the babysitter. The money was nice.

One night at work I received a call to meet my parents in the emergency room. Robbie had learned how to make his walker glide across a plush carpet. He had sailed down a flight of stairs before anyone could catch him.

No serious injuries. Just a few bruises. Accidents like that happen all the time. Still, I felt guilty. Shortly after, I gave notice to the store manager and decided my time would be better invested in volunteer work at church.

We didn't miss the money.

The third member of our family created a whole new set of safety standards for us. We waited for the icy winter weather to pass before we took our first road trip to introduce Robbie to family. We spent a few days in Kentucky with my side of the family. It would be the only time he saw his maternal great-grandmother, Sarah.

Then we headed to Wisconsin, where his paternal great-grandparents were thrilled to see us. Jack's grandpa walked around with Robbie on his hip for a couple hours, telling the ten-month-old about paintings on their walls, when and how they had acquired antique furnishings, and stories about various mementos on shelves and in glass cabinets. One would think John Robert IV would inherit his great-grandfather's entire world. That was the last time we saw Jack's grandpa.

Margaret was living semi-independently, requiring minimal supervision to manage her finances and medication. She was about an hour away from Jack's grandparents. We mailed a note to let her know we would be in town, and the approximate time we would arrive, but didn't allow her time to un-invite us. Neither did we share our plan for the visit with anyone else. To mention her name in front of John, Ginny, or Margaret's former in-laws would have been awkward, and probably ruined our trip, as well as some relationships. Up until the moment we rang her doorbell, Jack held an internal debate as to the wisdom of this reunion.

She was dressed and expecting us. We visited for a while, mostly small talk and sharing family photos. She declined our offer to take her out for a meal. Other than a full ashtray on every horizontal surface, her apartment was spotlessly clean. Jack was relieved that she was safe and had a few friends. She had a boyfriend and called him to come meet us. It was as if she needed to prove the existence of her children and her past.

It was too hot outside to open her apartment windows, and her smoking made it hard for us to breathe. We stayed only an hour or so. Hugging Margaret hello and good-bye in the same afternoon was bittersweet. I turned my head, pretending to be distracted while Jack and his mother embraced. I didn't know if one of them would cry, but my own tears were about to pour. Before we walked away, I invited her to visit us in Illinois.

"I'd like that," she said.

We all knew a second reunion would be nearly impossible to keep secret.

Whether our visit had been a treat or had opened old wounds for his mother consumed Jack's thoughts for several days. When a letter we'd sent with a photo of Robbie arrived with a hand-printed "Return to Sender," of course I wondered why. Had Margaret moved? Had there been an error on the part of her letter carrier? Had she refused the letter? If she had, did she realize a photo of her precious grandchild was enclosed?

Our phone calls were never answered. Neither were our questions. I was frustrated and thought we should take another trip to Wisconsin to check things out. Jack said, "Let the past stay in the past."

Jack resisted all attempts to have a conversation about his mother or pursue an adult relationship with her. He never gave a firm "No" to my hints, but I felt my suggestions could easily turn to nagging. I could push and nag to get my way in almost anything, or I could do the right thing and leave Jack's past alone.

Eventually, I stopped wondering what was going on in Wisconsin and assumed we would make it back when Jack was ready.

I stayed busy enough watching after a growing and busy little boy.

It's a wonder Robbie didn't break his back or at least a limb when he climbed out of his crib. We never caught him, but we often discovered him playing on the floor early in the morning. He wasn't the first toddler to use the drawers of a dresser like stairs to get to some priceless dust catcher or toy. Someone should have warned us that nothing in a toddler's sight is out of their reach for long.

I have a photograph of Robbie standing naked on a bouncing rocking horse. He was resting his chin on the window ledge and watching the comings and goings in the alley behind our apartment – specifically the garbage truck. I supposed he had heard the noise of garbage pick-up day and, naked or not, he wasn't going to miss the action. The next week, he used a stool to unlock and open the back door. Based on the intensity of his temper tantrum when I grabbed his arm to pull him back inside, I think he was planning to run away with the garbage man.

I loved being a mommy. I loved my life.

17

FOUR IS NICE

Our initial plan was to have a family of eight. About a month before Robbie's second birthday, the subject of baby number two came up. We (more me than Jack) had decided life would be easier with only one in diapers at a time.

Along with the usual cars, trucks, and balls, we gift-wrapped some big boy underwear for Robbie's second birthday party. Based on what we'd heard from family and friends, the potty-training process would take at least a couple of months.

During his birthday party, he put on his new Superman briefs, then left his new cars, trucks, and some unwrapped birthday presents in the living room to trot off and do what needed to be done. One of those unwrapped presents was a wood-framed potty-chair.

We followed him from a distance. Lid up. Seat up. He was standing poised and proper. He knew what to do. He was just too short to get it cleanly accomplished.

Jack was a proud daddy, and I sterilized the bathroom. We added a stepstool to his stack of presents that same day.

"You're such a big boy!" I gave Robbie an extra tight and long hug when we tucked him in that night. The potty-chair stayed in the box.

That was a really good day. One of Jack's quieter dreams woke me early the next morning. This time it woke him too.

"*Be a big boy.*" That's what Jack's dad told him when they took his mother away. It meant he should conquer his tears rather than wiping them with his sleeves. He confessed that many times, as a child, he had woken up crying because of that same dream.

"I only dream that dream once or twice a year. And it doesn't make me cry."

I wiped my own tears with the corner of the sheet. "Look at how far you've come. You're an amazing father. Right now, your son is probably dreaming of cars, and trucks, and balls, and big-boy underwear."

The next evening I called Bernie to tell her about Robbie's lightning-quick potty-training, but after dialing, I handed the phone to Jack. The only person he could talk to on the phone, for anything other than a business transaction, was Bernie. We saw her on one or two holidays every year, but the only time he could really talk with his big sister, without the entire family listening in, was over the phone. When Bernie spoke, Jack listened. No matter the context, I sensed his admiration when he spoke her name.

Bernie had been like an attentive mother hen when her brothers needed her. They joked about her being a bossy teenager, but they knew that if she hadn't taken charge, no one would have. The boys trusted Bernie's direction even into adulthood. She was their constant and their security. Jack saw her as the "glue" that held their family together.

Listening to his end of their phone conversation, I could tell Bernie was suggesting we provide her with another nephew or niece.

That night we prayed to be blessed with a second child. Paula Jean was born on her due date, January 22, 1979. You can do the math, or I can tell you I was already pregnant when we prayed that prayer. God is so much better than good.

Uneventful is the term used to describe that pregnancy. Stopping just short of critiquing the army doctor's judgment, my obstetrician let me know he was unconcerned with the shape of my pelvis. We planned for a natural delivery.

The pains started right before the alarm clock would have buzzed, so instead of going to work that day, Jack took me to the hospital. As the contractions steadily intensified, there was a sense of satisfaction that my labor would soon be rewarded with the sweet smell of a newborn baby.

My labor nurse spoke excellent English, and Jack took pleasure in disclosing my history as a screamer. The two of them talked about how well I was doing compared to the teenage girl down the hall, whose profanities we heard as the elevator doors parted.

In contrast to the maternity unit in Germany, he was able to follow me into the delivery room.

"Only a few more pushes, and we'll find out if you have a football player or a ballerina." I wondered how often the doctor used that line. A few more pushes, and nothing changed. I gave a good effort, but Paula stayed put. To this day, she's a stubborn little thing.

The conversation between me and the obstetrician went something like this:

"Can I have some Demerol?"

"No. It will make your baby sleepy, and we need a wide-awake baby."

Fifteen minutes later, "I think I need a C-section."

"Oh, so you're the doctor now?"

"No. I was just noticing the baby's heartbeat is getting a lot slower."

One, or maybe two contractions later, I felt some cool fluid in my vein and an almost instant woozy feeling. Jack saw the pair of forceps used to pull our baby from my womb. Whatever had been sent through my veins made my brain feel numb, but the rest of my body felt the pain. No one hushed my scream.

"It's a girl!"

The doctor's announcement lessened Jack's grip on me. He'd been holding tight since the sight of the forceps. I'd have his black and blue handprint on my upper arm for several days.

"I'll never let you go through that again." Jack's words stood unopposed.

Sore and tired, I cared only about seeing my baby girl.

I had just one roommate this time, and Jack went home in the evenings to spend time with Robbie and to sleep. On the morning we were discharged, he brought me a dozen pink roses and handed me a box wrapped in baby shower paper.

It was a pink sweater, Size 3. Not 3 Months, but 3 Toddler—the smallest pink sweater in the department store. The nurse helped me wrap it around Paula, with the sleeves making an adorable scarf to cover her head and ears before her first exposure to a cold Illinois January.

Paula was a pretty baby. Other than the huge bruise on her head, she was perfect, and the bruise was gone within a couple of weeks. She too, was showered with attention and affection from grandparents, aunts, uncles, and church ladies. By spring, her pink and purple owned controlling interest in the closet shared with her big brother, and her bassinet became a twice-a-week toe-stubbing fixture at the foot of our bed. We started looking for roomier living quarters.

The third house we looked at was a modest three-bedroom with a detached garage. The neighborhood, very close to a primary school, was made up of young families and retirees. We were welcomed on moving day by neighbors from both sides of the street. The kids each had their own room, we had a beautiful brick fireplace, and I loved the bright yellow kitchen with my large pantry.

Jack bought a lawn mower. I added a few flowers and planted a small vegetable garden.

Once we settled in, I suggested we take another road trip to show off our new baby girl. Jack had used his vacation time for the move, but we planned to do a couple of weekend trips. Late in July we were able to make the trip south for my family reunion. Jack drove. It had been a perfect weekend, until the six-and-a-half-hour drive home when I asked when we would be going to Wisconsin to see his grandparents. And what about trying to reconnect with his mother?

I hadn't forgotten Jack's decision against returning to Wisconsin, but I thought he had changed his mind. We'd talked about it again—well, I had talked, excitedly, and I'd understood his silence as agreement.

"We aren't going back to Wisconsin."

"But I thought . . ."

"That's right. You *thought.* I never agreed to go."

Within fifty miles of home, we were slowed by a long stretch of road construction. Jack started yelling and hitting the steering wheel as if his behavior would clear the road. I was smart enough to understand his fatigue and frustration, but not wise enough to guard my tongue.

"Getting mad isn't gonna get us there any faster."

His right hand flung toward my face. It was as though a tightly wound spring had released his forearm. My own hands were not fast enough to shield me. His knuckles stopped two or three inches from my nose. I wasn't sure whether he'd calculated exactly where a threat would meet injury, intending to scare me, or if some part of his brain corrected his original intent.

He didn't look my way, and I made a point to stare out the window, grateful he wasn't able to drive the speed limit. He yanked the car to the shoulder of the road, banged his hands on the steering wheel one more time, and then got out of the car.

"You can drive the rest of the way."

Other than a few noises from the kids in the back seat, the rest of the trip home was silent. No rock-n-roll on the radio. All through the following week, things were quiet and tense. I was slow to speak, other than the occasional sarcasm veiled in comments to our children about their father.

I was the one with the ill-controlled temper. Life's ordinary aggravations didn't seem to change Jack's good nature. Sometimes he would use the back of his hand to stroke my cheek or shoulder, reminding me that my anger was being wasted on a temporary and fixable little thing. He'd used his hands in a way that drew me closer to him. Never had I seen the back of his hand in anger. I supposed I was less of a bride, to be cherished and pampered, and more of a wife. The honeymoon was over.

After a week, I set a tuna noodle casserole on the table and a chocolate cake on the counter, ready to resume marital bliss—or at least see Jack smile. Men still claim it's impossible, but Jack read my mind. Or maybe he was also ready for reconciliation.

"We can't go to Wisconsin," he told me. He was calm. "My grandmother knows we went to see Mom, and she told Dad. How Grandma found out is anybody's guess, but Ginny says if we go again and Grandma finds out, she will change her will."

His family drama had put us in an unfair, if not ridiculous, position. Bernie, Bill and Joe felt the same conflict. Jack was not even sure if we had his mother's current address and phone number. I resolved to keep the situation in my private prayers. Making suggestions, or asking about issues concerning his family matters, served only to point a finger of comparison between his and mine. Jack's grandfather passed away that autumn without ever meeting Paula.

Paula's birth had been traumatic, but she and I recovered fully within weeks. Jack, on the other hand, was still talking about the forceps, the sights, and the sounds of the delivery room well past spring—at the dinner table, in the car, anytime he saw a newborn, and in our bed.

I protested his worries. "It's not like you're the one who birthed her!"

"I hate the thought of you going through that again."

"No two births are alike. It wouldn't be like that the next time." I thought I'd had the last word and won my case, but Jack was still thinking.

"It could be worse. I don't want to lose you."

"Don't be so dramatic, Jack. Nothing's gonna happen to me."

"I wouldn't be able to live without you."

"Don't talk like that. Give me a kiss and get some sleep."

Nevertheless, after a few long nights with a fussy infant and a toddler with an ear infection, I began to rethink our plans for a family of eight. Four was nice. I was happy with our little family, our little house, and our comfortable life. My dream of becoming a nurse was doable with two children. Not so much with six. The only thing left to decide was which one of us would have the surgery. Jack didn't hesitate to volunteer, but he didn't like talking on the phone, so I called the surgeon's office.

"Snip, snip," the surgeon told us. "Nothing to it."

Jack scheduled himself for a long weekend off work. His coworkers knew why. After the early Friday morning procedure, we looked forward to a quiet three-day weekend. Then Jack decided to get a head start on his weekend chores.

"Mowing? Really? The lawn can wait!"

He ignored me.

"Let me do the mowing," I begged. "The anesthesia hasn't completely worn off."

With his back to me, he waved at my comments, then yanked on the lawn mower cord.

An hour later, our yard looked like a lawn again, and Jack was in the shower. An hour after that, he was reclining on the sofa in agony. I called the surgeon's office for advice. The nurse instructed, "Tylenol and ice. That's all." I think that was the day Jack learned the importance of following post medical procedure instructions. The words "I told you so" crossed my mind, but not my lips.

A month or so later when a friend asked him what it was like, Jack grinned. "Snip, snip. Nothing to it."

We had no regrets. Robbie and Paula were meeting milestones and making us proud. We could afford to give them pretty much whatever we wanted them to have. They were a little spoiled, but not too much. They kept us busy, but we were not overwhelmed.

We wanted our children to have all the good from our own childhoods with none of the bad. We played the same games, sang the same songs, and read many of the same stories that my mom had read to me. I tried, but I didn't have my mother's flair. Both Robbie and Paula challenged me to try harder.

Jack worked a lot of very long days. His time with the kids was necessarily sporadic. Paula sat on his lap while he watched television and occasionally assigned him roles in her game of "house." He was a lousy actor unless his role could be played from his corner of the sofa.

Paula wanted to play with the boys. I recall her standing as a three-year-old, leaving tears smeared on the front window because she wasn't allowed to go play ball with Jack, Robbie, and the neighborhood boys. The stool Robbie had used for mischief was in her bedroom now—where it stayed. Paula wasn't a climber.

Summers in the neighborhood brought everyone outside. Kids played in grass, dirt, driveways, and sometimes the street. Parents talked over fences, on front porches, in driveways, and yes—in the street. Retirees mostly sat on their porches, watching for children who might step into their yard or throw a ball in their direction.

We taught Robbie and Paula to respect our retired neighbors, and our neighbors were lenient with them. After all, their own grandchildren were annoying a retired couple in another neighborhood.

Jack enjoyed running the track at the school. Robbie would take his bike and ride along. A weight bench, with an assortment of weights for Jack and barbells for Robbie, made our garage good for more than parking a car and storing tools, bikes, toys, and junk.

The street sign said Bellaire Ave. Everyone called it Bellaire Street. It was home.

I remember the time I convinced Robbie and his friend of my supernatural powers. I hadn't been present to witness, but I knew they had been walking on the picnic table, a forbidden behavior. I disciplined him in spite of their dramatic denials.

"How do you know we were on the table? You're mean!"

Robbie's friend was sent home with instruction to tell his mother what he had done, and a warning that I would be talking to her in a day or so.

Ten years passed before I told Robbie and his friend about the single-pane windows and thin walls that made many of their conversations less than private, or the distinctive muddy footprints on the picnic table. Ten years later, Robbie's friend still hadn't told his mother what they had done, and neither had I.

Then there was the time Robbie, along with the same old-enough-to-know-better friend, devised an experiment with a hypothesis involving how many crab apples would need to land on the neighbor's pool cover before it would collapse.

I still think their unwritten research protocol had scientific value, but they stopped short of calculating the damage. The boys tried to make amends. Our neighbor refused their offer to jump into the pool and clean up—an offer that probably should have been accepted. It was hot and well past Memorial Day. Their pool wasn't opened until the weekend before Independence Day. Robbie and his friend (both seven years old) spent their Fourth of July observing bikini-clad teenaged girls pull buckets of apple cores and debris from their pool.

Robbie held a kind of power over me when it came to discipline. Typically, he was apologetic and remorseful. I leaned toward quick and mild punishment followed by grace. Jack wasn't so soft. With him, the punishment should match the crime, plus a little something to remember during the next temptation.

For Robbie's act of vandalism, he was denied a trip to Kentucky with Grandpa Howard and Grandma Ellene, a punishment that hurt my mother as much as my son. They both got over it, and Jack's choice of punishment proved effective. Grandma Ellene learned to warn her grandchildren against acts of destruction, and offer frequent reminders when she had a trip with grandkids on the next month's calendar.

There were moments when I knew I was raising a genius with a considerate side. There were hours when I worried he wouldn't live to see another birthday. About three feet separated our garage from the neighbor's, and the neighbor lady waited several days to report Robbie's ability to jump from one roof to the other without injury. He was also busted for using a small tree branch to swing from the roof of our garage to the ground. I don't know how he got to the roof.

As far as I recall, Paula didn't break any windows, take apart any radios, play with matches in her bedroom, or use the back of the garage for BB gun target practice. Her big brother took care of all those things. I interrupted her one Saturday as she was digging a tunnel from our backyard to China (Peking, to be exact). A long soak in the tub dissolved the dirt under her fingernails, and a good scrubbing ridded her knees of the grass stains. She looked adorable the next morning—all dressed up in her Easter outfit, complete with new shoes and hat.

Robbie seldom repeated the same crime twice. Paula, true to her nature, tried several more times to revive her tunnel-to-China project. The multiple sinkholes in our back yard made it a dangerous place to mow or walk around. I'm not sure if she was too little to dream up more outrageous schemes or if experiencing some of the mischief on Bellaire Street caused Jack and I to hover a lot closer over Paula. In any case, four was enough. Four was nice.

18

FAMILY MATTERS

Jack's dad became seriously ill in November of 1981. He had been ignoring significant symptoms for months before pain sent him to the emergency room. Colon cancer was discovered during a surgery to remove a bad gallbladder.

"But we got it all," the surgeon assured us.

Everyone, except John, was happy with the news. He woke up from anesthesia as expected, but then he heard the word *colostomy*. And the other one. *Cancer*. We heard "full recovery," but John, barely fifty-six years old, heard those two C words and insisted he didn't want to live under those circumstances.

He didn't recover.

Paula was just old enough to know the adults in her world were upset. At the funeral visitation, she insisted on seeing what everyone else was seeing. I looked to Jack for guidance. He lifted her, and the two of them had a father-daughter chat in front of John's casket. With her curiosity satisfied, she went about showing her new shoes to family and friends.

Robbie was old enough to understand and ask questions. Jack was stoic during the funeral and after. I expected he might cry or show emotion once we were alone at home. But no. He answered Robbie's questions matter-of-factly.

"Grandpa went to heaven." A good answer, but it led to another question.

"When did he go there?"

"The minute his heart stopped beating." Another simple answer.

"What is cancer?"

"It's a bad disease." Great answer, but Robbie needed more.

"Do boys get cancer?"

"Not usually." Jack was doing well, but Robbie's questions seemed endless and gave us plenty to think about. The answers had to be appropriate for a preschooler. Paula was listening.

"What happens to our bodies when we die?" "How much does a casket cost?" "Will the hospital give Grandma her money back since Grandpa died?"

Robbie asked those questions using the same non-emotional, information-gathering tone of voice he used to ask the man in the dairy department of the grocery store, "How much college did you need to get this job?" and our pastor, "How much do you get paid to come to church?"

Jack was sure his dad had willed himself to die. Some close family members openly voiced the same sentiment. Others made comments like, "Maybe this was a blessing in disguise." I was glad Robbie didn't hear that one. He would have had a follow-up question. Jack wasn't standing with me, and I wouldn't have had an answer.

Robbie managed to save what I believe was the hardest question for me.

"Since Grandpa's in heaven, does he know that Dad is mad at him?"

Jack's grief emerged quietly and privately. If there were tears, no one saw them. He began to read his Bible more often. He also became fascinated with books that claimed concern for his spiritual well-being, but treated God as a tool or a crutch to be used instead of the relational, personal God we knew. I was bothered by the red-flag statements on the book covers and the passion with which Jack defended their teachings. Jack seldom read for entertainment. He studied.

"Why do you read those books?" I insisted. "They're nothing but lies."

I was tired after a busy day, and fatigue often attacks my ability to filter either the speech coming in, or the speech I let out. Jack did not excuse my weariness.

"What do you mean, *those books*? Have you read even one of them?"

"No. I don't need to. Why would I read their lies? You're wasting our money and your time."

Jack knew all my arguments and countered them as though he had authored the books. When he couldn't find the right words, he became agitated and defensive. I should have had a better way to say "Because the Bible said so," but I didn't. The last thing I wanted was for an argument to cause him to draw a line in some imaginary sand, so I eventually left him alone to study while I worked at being nonchalant, and I prayed.

The attractive, feel-good messages in the books told him life should be wonderful, he deserved to feel satisfied, and if he followed a formula, life would be easy. He read them from cover to cover, underlining passages.

And then one day, he brought home a book, written by a man I'd never heard of.

He would read a passage and call me to come and listen to what he had underlined on the page.

"This guy Oswald Chambers says . . ."

I was in the room, but my mind was on other things. Jack had yet to notice my inattention.

"Oswald Chambers says . . ."

Jack was more enthused about this Oswald Chambers book than any of the others. "Listen to this, Rita . . ."

I pretended to listen while I made a mental shopping list or planned the next day's dinner.

"You should read this, Rita."

"Leave it on the table, and I'll read some later."

But I didn't. I assumed Oswald Chambers was just like the authors of the other books. Jack finished reading *My Utmost for His Highest* and left it on the nightstand for me.

It was about an hour before the alarm would go off, and I watched as he fought with his pillow. He opened his eyes, startled, or maybe embarrassed that I was watching.

"You were dreaming. Was it a nightmare?"

"I wasn't dreaming."

"Odd. Your eyes were closed. You were hitting your pillow and mumbling like you were mad at someone. I call that a dream. And you've done that several nights in a row."

Memories from his childhood were so seldom shared, that I sat up in bed to give him proper attention. I heard the story of how his class in Kentucky hadn't yet mastered the multiplication tables when his family moved to Illinois, but his new teacher had completed those lessons and had no time for individual tutoring. John made flash cards and Ginny stayed up late flipping cards until Jack had memorized them all.

It seemed like an ordinary, if not pleasant, memory. Jack had accomplished in one week what took months for his classmates. I'd heard the story before. John told it (more than once) as a way to impress me with Jack's intelligence.

But now, Jack added some details I hadn't heard. "Did I ever tell you that Ginny smacked my hand for every wrong answer? Or that I was threatened with a repeat of the third grade unless I passed the test, but when I passed the test, I was sent back to the third grade anyway?"

Jack was clearly depressed. His work at the factory was not compromised, but he had no energy at the end of the day for meaningful communication or even casual conversation. So, on those rare occasions, usually late in the evening or the middle of the night, when he would open his huge vault of secrets and tell me a story from his past, I was a great listener.

There were some unwritten rules. I would not repeat the stories, I would not ask why or what-if, and I would not suggest how things should have been. Jack wanted no sympathy. Without knowing it, he was helping me learn the concept of empathy. I followed his rules. I wanted to help, to offer something, but all I had was words and they would never be enough.

He usually slammed the vault shut as surprisingly as he had opened it. If he was in a good mood I might hear, "Dwelling on my past doesn't help." Otherwise, his non-verbal cues allowed no room for discussion or inquiry. I prayed, asking for help during those silences. It was hard, letting him have the last depressing word.

I learned to be content with whatever details he shared. Right, wrong, healthy or not, my need to know about Jack had always been less important than my need to be loved by him.

During the days and weeks between bouts of depression, Jack was his old self. It's hindsight that allows me to name *depression* as the barrier between us. At the time, I labeled him *moody*. He was still introverted. He knew how and when to drop a memorable punch line, yet he only tolerated attention and he abhorred crowds.

Jack was a spectator when, most of the time, he could have been a star player. Me? Winner or loser, I was having fun as long as I was in the game. As an extrovert, finding a game and getting involved was my solution to almost any problem. Not so for Jack. Our differences kept us interesting as lovers and friends, but made problem solving tedious and often tempestuous.

His weight bench and other muscle building contraptions got more attention most days than me and the kids. His two, sometimes three times a day workouts were great for relieving stress—for all of us. I didn't feel responsible to cheer him up when he was out of sight, in the garage. When he was working out, he felt good. Physical exercise clearly helped, but it wasn't the cure. Was he depressed because he missed a few workouts, or was his lack of energy and desire to exercise because of the depression?

We didn't understand clinical depression. Depressed was what you got when your dad died, or when you couldn't afford a fancy car, or when you got a divorce. Wasn't it? But Jack's dad had been gone for months, and he hadn't been depressed enough to cry. He laughed at television shows and conspired with Robbie to aggravate and tease Paula and me. I saw no reason for him to be depressed.

Ginny announced her plan to move to Cincinnati within days of the funeral. Technically, she mentioned it to friends *at* the funeral, but she didn't inform us until we ask for confirmation of what we hoped was merely rumor. She wanted to be near her children. Debbie was divorced by then and would be moving along with her.

We knew Ginny would need to sell or give away John's belongings in order to downsize into a condo. I encouraged Jack to ask for mementos before they were all gone, but he refused. He hushed my words and told me, "Let it go." Jack blamed Ginny for some of the family's circumstances, but he kept the peace and never verbalized his feelings to her. He wouldn't ask for a copy of John's last will and testament, and none was offered.

One morning Paula and I were in Ginny's neighborhood, and we dropped by for a visit. She had most of her household belongings packed and was prepared to leave in a few hours. I could only assume she had no plans for saying good-bye. A misshaped iron griddle sat alone on her kitchen counter, near the trash. Ginny offered it, so I rescued it from the trash to give it a new home.

Robbie was in school and Jack was at work, so Paula and I were the only ones to get an official good-bye. I thought Jack would be angry. He only chided me for expecting more.

About a year before he died, John had given Jack an antique snuffbox with the family crest etched in the metal. It had emigrated with a distant relative from Scotland to the United States. According to Jack, his dad and grandparents had predicted this was how John's estate would be distributed. Other than the snuffbox and the old griddle, John's children received none of the family heirlooms or anything of value.

That old griddle was okay for making grilled cheese. I could do four sandwiches at a time. Jack remembered Margaret, before she became ill, using it to fry hamburgers. Any food I prepared on that griddle tasted great where Jack was concerned.

Jack's grandmother passed away less than a year later. Over the next few months, grief blended with Jack's depression, making the two indistinguishable. He went to work, came home every evening to eat, and then locked himself in our bedroom to sleep, read, or draw. I was impressed with his artwork and wanted to frame some of the pieces, especially some of the portraits. He wouldn't allow it. They ended up in the trash, torn to shreds.

The deaths of his father and grandmother changed me as much as Jack. I learned to make excuses for his refusal to leave our home and socialize with family and friends. It was easy. He worked long hours. I didn't see a man who was becoming a recluse. I saw a man who loved his family and worked hard to provide even when times were tough.

I was unhappy and impatient, but what kind of person would I be to complain about not having any fun while my husband mourned?

Months went by, and my unhappiness began to turn to anger. Passive-aggressive comments slipped into my explanations of Jack's absences. It was easy for either of us to start an argument. I pushed to move toward apologies, and Jack withdrew. On random days, he would behave as though we were the happiest couple on earth, but many of those days were cut short by an about-face and a return to depression for him and anger for me.

Soft-spoken and well-timed conversations comforted me, but didn't lead to answers. Jack continued to insist there was no problem. When I told him how I was feeling, he said he understood, but nothing changed. After we talked, one of two possible scenarios would play out: Either Jack would start an argument, and end up hiding out in our bedroom while I managed the household, or we would enjoy physical intimacy.

When he went to the bedroom alone, I blamed myself for failing him as a friend and a wife. When we went into the bedroom together, I allowed myself the false assumption that everything would be all right.

I knew this season would end. My way of coping was to stay busy with Robbie and Paula, along with taking night classes at the local junior college. I wanted to move toward my dream of nursing. It would provide a part-time income, and we had hopes of building a subterranean home on the side of a large hill overlooking the river.

I picked up Jack's book from my nightstand. I liked what this Mr. Chambers had to say. He named obedience to God in the ordinary and the simple things as a way to take the initiative against depression and despair. He talked about how everyone experiences despair, but it only defeats us when we allow it to stop us from moving forward. I didn't have time (or take time) to read the entire book. It was rather deep philosophically—not a quick read.

It would be years before I realized who Oswald Chambers was, but I decided to follow his advice in this one thing. I would not let past failures defeat me, and I would keep doing the ordinary, everyday things required of me.

We planned a Saturday at the park with the kids. Jack chose the menu and the park. I packed a bag. He loaded the trunk with outdoor games. During our final trip to the car, he decided to stay home. No particular reason. Robbie, Paula, and I spent the afternoon enjoying a day full of sun and play. We were so accustomed to changes in plans that, most of the time, we were able to adapt with little concern or effort.

We were invited to join a group of friends for a long weekend of canoeing and camping. Jack reserved a canoe, bought a tent, and picked up some camping supplies. My parents agreed to keep the kids. I was busy outlining things on our to-do list when Jack changed his mind—two days before we were to leave.

"We aren't going. Take back all the camping gear. We won't be needing it."

I called the friend who was coordinating the trip. "I'm sorry, but we won't be able to go canoeing."

"Oh no. What happened?"

"Nothing. Jack hasn't been feeling well. Probably just the flu."

At 9 p.m. the night before our friends would be leaving, Jack asked, "Do we need to take our grill?"

"Take our grill where?"

"Canoeing."

"I thought we weren't going?"

"We can go. If you want to."

"Okay. No, we don't need a grill."

It hadn't rained much that spring and summer, so the Current River was low. We carried our canoe over dry places in order to enjoy what white water we encountered, but canoeing was a first for us, and we found it worth the work. We prepared our meals on grills and camping stoves. In the evenings we sat around a campfire laughing, pushing our troubles back to Tuesday, and talking about woodsy creatures and rumors of rattle snakes in that area of Missouri.

We slept on air mattresses in the back of pick-up trucks and in tents. Early in the morning, Jack tested the power of suggestion and his ability to hiss and click like a rattle snake. He was thoroughly amused by my reaction. I raced off, looking for the outhouse, while he stayed smug and dry under the covers. It had rained overnight, and I was barefoot.

How many times that day did I pull my ponytail to my nostrils for a whiff and a reminder of the night before? I don't recall. But I always will love a campfire.

I loved to stroll through any mall. Jack came along one Friday night, probably intending to thwart my plans for his paycheck. I pushed Paula in her umbrella stroller. Jack and Robbie followed me into a piano store. We had a little money in our new house fund, but not enough to buy a piano. I ran my fingers over the smooth ivory, but it wasn't practical. An occasional plunking session at Mom and Dad's or a rare song for the children's class at church didn't warrant such a purchase. My keyboard skills had not advanced past my early years of piano lessons.

"Do you like this one?" Jack asked.

"It would look nice in our living room. Maybe someday, when we're in our new house and the kids are ready for lessons."

A zealous salesman had left his seat from behind the counter and was within striking distance when I turned and stepped back out into the main mall. Paula and I were a store away when I turned to see that Robbie and Jack hadn't made their getaway. Jack was shaking hands with the salesman.

Later that evening, Jack excused himself from the dinner table. He was gone for about forty-five minutes. A few days later, he was rearranging furniture to make room for my new piano. I never questioned his spontaneous decision or where the money was coming from. The smile on his face and the energy he put into making me happy clouded my judgment. A gal would have to be crazy not to love a guy like that.

We took a couple of college courses together. I needed chemistry, and he needed English composition. I saw Jack's unattractive competitive side, and he saw mine, but he helped me earn a better grade in chemistry, and I helped him write his English papers. Overtime at work made it difficult, and sometimes impossible for Jack to attend class. Rather than fail, he dropped the courses. We decided I should continue, so I did—one class at a time. He never re-enrolled.

Then an accident at work ruptured a couple of discs in his lower back. The pain was tremendous. There were days he could go to work, but with the aid of painkillers. Other days, he wasn't able to get out of bed. I expected he would become depressed with the pain and the smaller paycheck, but he had a fresh desire to study Scripture, and we decided I would practice nursing (without the formal education) and give him lots of TLC until he recovered.

When therapy didn't help, and taking strong pain medication was only an option if he wanted to be disabled the rest of his life, he agreed to see a surgeon. The procedure went well. This time, he came home and rested. He took his pills on time and did the exercises as prescribed.

The pain was definitely less severe, but his back was not the same. He'd been released by the surgeon, but still had occasionally disabling pain. He decided he was done with doctors, and invested in some gravity boots to begin his own, self-directed therapy. He tolerated the pain and seldom complained.

I completed all the prerequisite courses for nursing and was accepted into an associate degree program. We weren't sure what our lives would look like in five, ten, or twenty years, but we counted on being happy and fantasized the rest. Having our imaginations play together was a cheap form of entertainment that made us smile.

Jack's depression had become less of a struggle for me. We didn't know how to label his melancholy moods, lack of interest, and lack of energy, but it became something we lived with. It had eased its way into our lives, not like a goliath with a heavy, bounding foot, leaving a time stamp, but more like a worm that's been there, and only comes out after a hard rain. Then once the ground is dry, where is the worm? Still there. Waiting for another rain.

That year, I attended a women's conference and picked up a book called *The Total Woman*. It became a favorite among me and some of my friends. We read it from cover to cover, discussed it as a group, and agreed it held a lot of truth and some godly advice. The author offered more than lofty ideals. She included practical tips, including a suggestion to meet our husbands at the door draped in nothing but kitchen plastic wrap.

I was certain she didn't have me in mind when she put that in print, but I thought I should at least consider the potential value of a few feet of plastic.

"Jack. What would you do if one day I met you at the door wearing nothing but plastic wrap?"

"You have to ask?"

That's all it took. A simple question. That one book, *The Total Woman*, was worth far more than all the romance novels I'd read in the mid-seventies. No need for the plastic wrap. We didn't have a solution or a cure for our problems, but we agreed that physical intimacy was the one part of our relationship that needed no adjustment.

Jack often said, "Let's never stop loving each other."

I needed affirmation. "Am I good enough for you?"

"You're still my favorite sport, Sport."

It was following a late night of intimacy that Jack was ready to tell me about another recurring dream. One of his earliest memories had been stealing his sleep for weeks.

Jack was four or five years old. John was well established in a lucrative career requiring long periods of travel, and Margaret was left for days at a time to care for the kids and manage the household alone. John would take from his paycheck, only what he needed for his travels, and leave the rest with Margaret.

He would come home weary, counting on time to rest and prepare for another week or two of travel. The lifestyle had been comfortable during the first few years of their marriage. But things weren't comfortable now.

John didn't see the crisis ahead. He reacted to the piles of dirty dishes and laundry, the house in horrible disarray, and the unopened bills with anger. Then he did what most other proud and capable men would do: he washed the dishes, did the laundry, cleaned the house, paid the bills, and was grateful for Monday mornings when he could leave some cash on the dining room table and drive away from it all.

Whenever Jack found an opportunity, he would pick up coins from the kitchen counter, the dining room table, or John's dresser. He would only take what he thought would not be missed—nothing larger than a one dollar bill—and would stash it in the hollow tube of a brass bed. Joe witnessed this small-time thievery.

Within a few days after his dad would leave, a stove was required to make anything in the house edible, but the stove was off-limits to the young boys, and Bernie was in school. Jack took the stash of cash two or three times a week to shop for food at the gas station down the street.

His hand was too big to fit into the opening, so he would have Joe reach in to retrieve the money, and for the favor of keeping a secret, promised to return with candy to share. This went on for possibly months, until one day when Margaret overheard Jack coaching Joe to grip the money between his fingers instead of grabbing a fist-full. Joe's hand was stuck in the brass tubing. Jack not only got a spanking, but lost his cash and his best hiding place.

In Jack's dream, Joe was crying, his hand still stuck in that brass bedframe.

It was his dream, but I was the one crying. "I'm sorry, Jack."

"Sorry for what? It's only a dream."

"But it really happened."

"And now. It's only a dream."

As long as Jack was holding me and sharing his life with me, Goliath was a dead giant, buried in the pages of the Old Testament.

19

PAULA'S PRAYER

October 31, 1983. Paula was four years old.

I rushed to drop Robbie off at school in order to drive across town, buy her a Halloween costume, and be back in time to watch the school's mid-morning Halloween parade. Students and teachers would be marching around the perimeter of the school, displaying their Halloween costumes, while parents, grandparents, and younger siblings waved and made noise. Robbie would be watching for us. We couldn't be late.

The first thing we saw when we walked through the door of the department store was a stocker, loading Christmas decorations on a shelf. Seeing all the red and green banners, candy canes, and tinsel triggered something in Paula.

"I want a real baby for Christmas," she announced.

I agreed to go back and look for a real baby as soon as we had everything we needed for her costume. And so we did. Once in the doll section, we looked up and down, on every shelf, looking for the elusive *real baby*.

Paula, hand on her hip, kept telling me "we won't find her here," but we had no time to go to another store, and it was still weeks before Christmas. As I buckled her into the car, she clarified: "Mommy, you don't understand! I want a REAL baby, the kind that comes out of your tummy, not a box!"

I laughed. "You can't have a real baby, but you always get two or three dolls for Christmas."

"Why?" She asked, not using a whining voice, but her seriously inquisitive voice.

I had to come up with an answer in the time it took to walk around the car and buckle myself into the driver's seat. Kids are easily distracted, I thought. Maybe she will forget. I pulled a piece of gum from my purse.

"Why?"

"Me and Daddy decided, right after you were born, that we were happy with our family just the way it is. We're not going to have any more babies. We can't have any more babies unless God does some kind of a miracle. Paula, I'm sorry, but you can't have a real baby for Christmas."

There was nothing extraordinary about either the parade or the rest of the day, until Jack's car pulled into the driveway. It was a rusty, Ford Pinto, with an engine that leaked oil and a muffler in dire need of replacement. At a certain time, every week-day afternoon, Paula's ears were tuned for the sound of that muffler, and she would race to the kitchen, intent on greeting her daddy before I did.

She had a fascination with what sort of leftovers were in his lunch box, so I started packing extra treats. Jack made the most of this contrived interaction by placing his lunch box within her reach five days a week. Under the guise of helping him unpack, Paula would notice a treat and wait for permission like an obedient puppy.

When she started "supervising" the packing of his lunch, Jack and I considered putting an end to the game, but we enjoyed it as much as Paula.

That Halloween afternoon, she didn't come running to the kitchen. Like most experienced parents, we knew to check for trouble. The two of us went back to her bedroom, but stopped at the doorway. Paula was kneeling at her bedside, eyes closed, with her little hands in the praying position, as seen on the cover of a bedtime storybook.

We prayed with our kids before meals, when someone was sick, and even on the run when there was a problem. I was known to say

"Lord, please help me" or an impromptu "Thank you Lord", when the situation called for it, and of course we went to church three or more times every week. But we never, not even one time, had the kids kneel at their bedside using that posture.

What we heard went something like this:

"Dear Lord, please give me a real baby for Christmas. I promise to be a good big sister and help Mommy take care of the baby. I want a girl baby, but I will love a boy baby, too. Dear Jesus, PLEASE give me a REAL baby for Christmas. Dear Lord, Mommy says the only way I can have a real baby is if you think I need one. Please Lord, I NEED a real baby for Christmas. I promise to help Mommy feed the baby, change diapers, and fold clothes. I can share my room. If the baby cries, I will hold it. I will rock it until it goes to sleep. I will dress it in very cute clothes. I promise. In Jesus' name. Amen."

We were still in the doorway when Paula stood, burst between us, and headed to the kitchen.

She raced through the hallway to see what sort of treat she'd find, her burden lifted. I wished it were so easy for me to unburden my heart at the feet of Jesus and then go about my day. She was smiling and walking with confidence that something good was coming for Christmas.

The afternoon and evening went on with trick-or-treating and all things Halloween. Before crawling out of bed the next morning, Jack and I took time for a sigh and a minute to ponder Paula's Christmas wish. We wondered how we could preserve her innocent kind of faith after the morning of December 25th.

"We could adopt," Jack suggested.

"Really, Jack? Adopt a baby by Christmas?"

I would have been open to a discussion, but mornings are hectic. *He didn't mean it. Rita, don't go making a big deal over a simple comment. Jack was only teasing.* Besides the issue of Jack's surgery, there was the problem of time. I was midway through the first semester of the nursing program at a nearby junior college, doing most of my study after 9 p.m. I didn't have time for a baby. Between nursing school, church responsibilities, and taking care of the house,

I didn't feel I had enough time to take care of the two children I already had.

Many evenings, Robbie and Paula were put to sleep by listening to the signs and symptoms of infection, proper technique for inserting a Foley catheter, or (Robbie's favorite) the anatomy and physiology of the colon.

A friend from across the street woke us one Sunday morning by knocking (or should I say pounding) on our door. Robbie, fascinated by one of my expensive textbooks, had become the neighborhood tutor. His lessons included colorful drawings and were free of charge. His subject? Human reproduction.

The mother at our door didn't appreciate Robbie's gift for teaching. His biology lesson had forced a talk about the "birds and bees" over their supper table, and our neighbor "couldn't sleep a wink all night long!"

Robbie offered to let her see the book. Of course she declined. My hands were clamped tight on his shoulders. He seemed unaware of the reason for her drama. Not sure what a wise mother would do with him or to him, I offered some final words of apology to my friend. Then I closed the door and kissed the top of Robbie's head.

"If you have any questions about what you saw or read in that book, you should probably ask Daddy."

Jack had been in the hallway during the entire encounter, and he stepped into view only after he was sure our friend was out of our yard and not turning back. He did have a brief conversation with Robbie about that chapter in my textbook. I remember being dissatisfied with Jack's lesson, but not knowing how to improve on it. Their conversation ended with Robbie asking, "Do you like to do sex?"

"As a matter of fact, I do. It's about my favorite thing."

"Does Mommy like to do sex?"

"I'm pretty sure she does, but you should ask her."

Jack followed Robbie from the living room into the kitchen, where I had been listening. He was grinning, quite pleased with himself and his ornery setup, but I worked at nonchalant, "Yes, I like to do it."

After we got into the car and headed for church that morning,

Robbie accused us of lying to him. "Mark's mom and dad have done it three times. Jason's mom and dad have done it four times, and you guys have only done it twice!"

Between the two of us, we gave a rudimentary explanation as to why we only had two children instead of three, four, or more. I prayed for Robbie's Sunday school teachers as we pulled into the church parking lot. Jack couldn't wait to see their faces when the class was over.

That year, I looked early and often for a doll that looked as alive as possible. The rest of my Christmas shopping would have to wait until my winter break from classes. While some of my classmates were reading ahead for courses that would begin mid-January, I wanted to minimize the stress of the holidays by concentrating on Christmas and family. I did just that.

We had a wonderful Christmas with all the trimmings. The decorations, the food, the gifts, the Christmas musicals, and the children's programs all seemed extra special in 1983.

Christmas morning, the kids dragged us out of bed and steered us toward the tree where presents, wrapped late the night before, were waiting. We had already celebrated with Jack's family, so Robbie and Paula had a hefty stack of new toys already, but their enthusiasm was not dampened. They unwrapped and tested a variety of new toys until it was time to leave for my parents' house, where there would be another stack of surprises waiting under Grandma and Grandpa's tree.

Robbie and Paula were the only two grandchildren on my side of the family at that time, which meant they were spoiled to the level of almost rotten. We spent many Sunday afternoons in my parents' home, and the kids knew every nook and cranny of "Grandma's house."

After Christmas dinner, it was time to clear the table and make room for a board game. Mom usually tried to choose a game everyone could play—adults and children alike. This year, all the seats were taken when the game was spread out and the teams were chosen. No room for Jack and me. Our kids had taken our place.

The game had gone into round two when Jack stood to announce that he wasn't feeling well and needed to go home.

I searched his face for the hint of a bad mood, but he seemed all right. "What's wrong?"

"Maybe I ate too much. You can come back, but I need to go. Will you drive me?"

Mom insisted the kids would be fine without us, and we should not worry. In the car, I learned that Jack was feeling fine. All he wanted was some alone time with me. Although he sometimes had difficulty expressing it, he proved he was a romantic at heart that Christmas Day.

There was one more present hidden in his closet. A sapphire ring. That small gift, and an hour or so alone with Jack, made my Christmas complete—or so I thought. I wouldn't know until the middle of January about the best gift.

The second week in January I found myself feeling tired, nauseous, and generally ill. As time for classes to begin came closer, and my symptoms were not improving, I made an appointment to see the doctor. With one semester of nursing school under my belt, I had already diagnosed my problem as a virus, but needed a doctor's signature for the medication I knew I needed. My doctor had his own agenda, based on his years in medical school, residency, and over twenty years of practicing medicine. He told me I was pregnant.

When I told him about my husband having had a vasectomy four years earlier, he was slightly less confident in his initial diagnosis. He turned me over to his nurse for a blood and urine specimen. I felt too miserable to do anything other than comply. While the blood test results would not be available until the next morning, the urine test was done while I waited. It was positive.

My request for medication to relieve nausea was being denied because of a false positive pregnancy test. I explained how, with my first pregnancy, a urine test had been negative when I was pregnant, so why would I believe a positive pregnancy test now? There was no possible way it could be accurate.

While he seemed to appreciate my logic, the doctor let me know he was the doctor. I consented to a full exam, hoping he would find some other explanation for my symptoms and give me a prescription to make me feel better.

"You're *pregnant*."

With a sheet blocking his eyes from mine, he asked if I had been with anyone other than my husband. Looking toward the nurse, I emphatically, perhaps too emphatically, declared monogamy as my belief and my lifestyle. She looked down toward the doctor with her lips raised and pursed tightly. I knew her expression well. Why I cared what these two thought of me, I don't know. But I did.

My doctor had a reputation for being thorough and smart. I supposed he was both. He was also known to have a curt bedside manner. That, I was witness to. After finishing his examination, he plopped his metal instrument on a metal tray, rose to his feet, and looked at me, eye to eye.

"You're sure?" he asked, sounding like my high-school principal. "You haven't been with anyone other than your husband, even once?"

I wouldn't have been able to lie to him even if I'd had something to hide.

"I'm sure."

With no transition, and not in the head-to-toe assessment style I had learned in school, the doctor redirected his exam toward my thyroid. A lump had been identified during a routine exam four or five months earlier, but I had been too busy to follow up with his suggestion of a thyroid scan.

Like my high-school principal, he didn't have time for long speeches, so he delivered a few scolding words with some intense facial drama and expected I would receive his message. "You should have had a scan with radioactive contrast, but now that you are pregnant, we'll have to settle for a non-contrast scan. I need to know what we're dealing with here."

We agreed I would return the next day to repeat the urine pregnancy test and to hear the blood test results.

I cried all the way home and well into the evening. If I wasn't pregnant, and *I couldn't be*, then what kind of awful or life-threatening diagnosis was I facing?

Jack was just as concerned. He went with me the next day, confident his presence would force the doctor to a correct diagnosis, and prepared to take me to the emergency room for a second opinion. We sat on the exam table, holding hands and whispering small talk, while the nurse took my blood pressure, my pulse, counted my respirations, and checked my temperature just as she had the day before. The nurse was thorough, professional, and as expedient as the doctor.

I got the impression she would rather be helping "sick" people than preparing me to see the doctor. She reminded me of how I had complained of "severe nausea" the day before. She made a good point. The nausea that had caused me to make the appointment, and had been keeping me in bed, was all better.

The doctor came in and resumed the conversation from the day before, without as much as a simple hello. "Rita, we have two positive urine tests, a positive blood test, and my examination to confirm you are pregnant. I can't give you any medication for nausea or make you feel better. I would expect, as with most pregnancies, your nausea and fatigue will subside in a few weeks if not sooner. In the meantime, you need to be taking prenatal vitamins. I'll give you a script. My nurse can give you some tips for minimizing the nausea and keeping those prenatal vitamins down. I'll have her schedule a sonogram. You'll be able to see the fetus. It will also help to confirm a due date."

He offered his hand to Jack for a brief introduction before turning to a large calendar and counting days.

"What were you doing on December 25? Did the two of you have a merry Christmas?"

Jack's eyes met mine as though the doctor had dangled a magnet between us. We said the words in unison, "Paula's prayer."

I still remember the puzzled look on the doctor's face. He knew we had a story, but my appointment had been squeezed into his already overbooked day, and another patient was waiting.

"I'll see if we can get a sonogram and the thyroid scan scheduled on the same day, and we'll get you scheduled with the endocrinologist right away. Your thyroid levels are out of whack, worse than before. Who is your ob-gyn?"

He instructed Jack, "You'll want to call your urologist or surgeon, or whoever did your vasectomy."

We walked out of the office with too many pieces of paper and twice as many unanswered questions. With so many uncertainties, we decided to keep our circumstance private until we had some definite answers.

My next medical appointment was with an endocrinologist, who was to advise and treat my hyperactive thyroid.

"You will have to take some medication to keep your heart rate controlled," he said. "You'll damage your heart if you don't. You could have a heart attack, die during labor, so you would have to have a C-section. If we don't slow down your thyroid, you could die before you go into labor. The fetus, if it makes it to term, will have a large goiter and developmental deficits, profound and irreversible mental deficits."

He said more, but Jack and I were still hearing that our little miracle would come with a heavy price. We agreed to see the out-of-state physician he recommended, thinking a "highly skilled specialist" in a big city would give our baby every advantage. A call to the clinic for driving directions revealed that my "elective abortion" was scheduled for the next day. I had *elected* to no such procedure! We canceled the appointment.

I had yet to be examined and evaluated by my own obstetrician. His schedule wouldn't have an opening for another week. We waited, and I took the prescribed medication. It didn't keep my heart from racing like it was supposed to.

As soon as we entered the exam room, my obstetrician told us that my primary doctor had called to discuss my case, and that he had heard from the endocrinologist as well. Then, he started his own examination.

"Your heart rate is over a hundred, your blood pressure is high, but other than your thyroid, your labs look good. How are you feeling?"

Jack answered, "The nausea is about gone, but she's tired, and weak."

"To tell the truth, I didn't expect you to come in today."

We were confused by his comment. He went on to explain how, over the past couple of years, some of his patients had gone to the same "clinic" I'd been referred to. "If they returned to my office," he said. "It was for the management of their complications."

"You changed your minds?" he asked.

"No. We never wanted to do that," I answered. "We thought he was recommended to help our baby."

Jack came to his feet and reiterated, "This was not a simple misunderstanding. We were upset. Who wouldn't be? That jerk mentioned 'terminating the pregnancy,' but we didn't think that was his plan. We didn't, for one minute, consider it."

The doctor nodded. "Glad we got that straightened out." He motioned for Jack to return to his seat and offered a hand as I stepped down from the exam table. He discussed the same fetal outcomes but added terms like "manage" and "mitigate." He paused and took questions as he laid out a plan.

"Let's get this thyroid under control with the lowest dose possible. You'll need weekly blood tests, and I want you to see my nurse every week. At least for a while. Call me if you have any of those problems we talked about."

As we stood at the front desk, waiting to make my next appointment, I felt my heart rate slow and my diaphragm relax. The doctor appeared from behind us and added some instruction for the lady behind the desk.

"Give them my home number," he said.

The next Sunday, during a family dinner, we announced our pregnancy to my parents. We told them about Paula's prayer, competing with each other for a turn to share what we remembered of the previous Halloween. Jack bragged about how we had conceived in spite of his surgery four years earlier. He was the first to call this our "miracle baby."

"There's a verse about this sort of answer to prayer isn't there?" Jack asked.

Mom knew the verse Jack was thinking of. "It's James 5:16. The effective, fervent prayer of a righteous man availeth much."

Then she paraphrased, "The effective, fervent prayer of a righteous *little girl* availeth much."

At his place of work, there was a different dynamic. The guys teased and called him naïve to think the baby could be his. The comments and jokes, no matter their intention, began to agitate him, and then someone stuck a note and an offensive cartoon in his locker. That was the day he came home accusing me of being unfaithful, repeating some of the things his coworkers had said about me in the locker room.

We yelled and argued for about an hour. He was accusatory and threatening, and I was aggressively defensive. I offered to get paternity testing. He was still angry. I pointed out that my life was too hectic to include time for any other man. Still angry. I pulled out argument and debate techniques that had worked in the past. They were ineffective this time. We said some things that needed to be said, but nothing that Robbie and Paula needed to hear.

I wish I could say they were outside playing, and not able to hear any of our angry words, but it was winter. Neither of us won the argument. Jack probably conceded to the pregnancy hormones and the tears. "You do know that not everyone sees this as a miracle," he said.

We held each other and apologized. In the end, it was Paula's prayer that gave him peace about our situation. Without that prayer, I wondered if Jack would have trusted that he really was my first and only love.

20

GOLIATH IN OUR HOME

March 1984.

"Jack. Dinner's ready."

No response. I knocked a little louder.

"Dinner's ready! Ginny's tuna noodle casserole."

It was one of the recipes he had insisted on getting from Ginny when we married, and I made it at least once a month.

Robbie and Paula took their places at the kitchen table.

"Dad's going to eat later," I told them.

Later was 10 p.m. The kids were bathed and in bed, asleep. The dirty dishes were in the sink, waiting for Jack's plate, fork, and glass to join them.

I knew where it could lead, but I still pressed. "What did I do to make you so mad?"

"Nothing."

"Then why are you so mad?"

"I'm not mad."

"You're acting like you're mad."

He plopped a large serving of the casserole on his plate, took one bite, and then threw it, plate, fork and all, in the trash.

"I would have heated that up for you."

We both knew I was not bothered by his cold dinner.

"I'm not hungry." And with that, he walked out of the kitchen.

Twenty minutes later I was still interrogating. *If he would simply tell me what was wrong, I might be able to fix it.* My probing accomplished the expected. Nothing.

Sleep came sometime after midnight. Possible scenarios and a few impossible ones wrestled in my thoughts. I pulled out the imaginary checklist I'd been working on:

- He left home, just in time for work every morning.
- He came home, on time, smelling like a chemical factory, every afternoon.
- If he worked overtime, he called home during a break, and there were factory noises in the background.
- I had the checkbook. His money was accounted for.
- No secret, or hang-up phone calls.

If one of us looked guilty, it was me with my baby bump. Jack was smart though. He would know how to cheat and not get caught.

In the middle of one of those nights, I snooped through his wallet. Nothing tucked away, except a receipt for one burger, one order of fries, and one drink. A picture of our smiling family was displayed prominently in the clear sleeve across from his driver's license. He didn't look like an adulterer.

The next morning, he laid money on my nightstand. "Were you looking for some cash?"

He wasn't just smart, he was a light sleeper. I wished I had checked his car. Any evidence there would be gone before he came home from work.

The busy daylight hours wouldn't allow me to dwell on my troubles, with one exception. About an hour before Jack was expected home from work, I would begin to prepare for what I hoped would be his new attitude, a good dinner, and a pleasant evening. In that hour, it was hard not to let worry reign.

I remember the details of an afternoon when supper was in the oven and the table was set. Homemade cookies had been pulled from the oven just in time to cover the scent of pine cleaner. The kids were complaining, but picking up the last of their toys.

I remember the pattern and ridges stamped into our kitchen linoleum. It was shiny and holding its own against the scrapes of chair legs, metal toys, and fallen pots and pans, but nobody was fooled into thinking it was expensive, imported, Italian stone. I remember thinking my life was shiny and holding up under the pressure. I was keeping up the appearances of a good life, but feeling like a cheap imitation.

Jack walked past us without saying a word. So much for my planning and effort. Tired of asking questions that wouldn't be answered, I determined to let him be the first to speak.

When supper was ready, Paula offered to deliver the courtesy knock on our bedroom door. I told her to take her seat instead. From the prayer before our meal to the last bite of my semi-famous loaded oatmeal cookies, our conversation centered on Daddy.

I saw in Robbie and Paula some of the behaviors and comments one would expect of battered or abused children. They asked why. I had no answers. They made excuses. Just like I did. One of them would say, "His back hurts."

The other would agree, "He works too hard."

It was obvious they wanted their old Daddy back. Whatever it was between me and Jack had already affected our children. A new determination took over. I would not stand by while . . .

The words needed to finish that thought wouldn't come. As much as I tried, I couldn't figure out what it was that I wouldn't stand for.

Tears welled up in my eyes during worship at church and even during Bible study. I felt like an explosion might bring relief, but I had nothing to ignite a fire. This was not the kind of problem discussed in my church ladies group. Other women had that sort of problem. Not me.

I didn't know what to ask for in my prayers. If I couldn't define my problem to Jesus, how could I explain my need to a mere friend? Another Christian book, Bible study, or conference was not the answer. How many times had I purchased new *gear* and planned for a life-changing mission that didn't happen?

Using the concordance in the back of my worn King James

Version, I searched for a short little verse learned in VBS—the one about casting all our cares on Him. I wanted to read it in context. The words had been the benediction for all my prayers of late, but I needed to remind myself of who said them and why.

I found the verse: "Therefore humble yourselves under the mighty hand of God, that He may exalt you in due time, casting all your care upon him, for He cares for you" (1 Peter 5: 6–7).

My frequent and fervent prayer was for God to change Jack in some miraculous way. I wanted for Jack to rest in the fact that he was loved by a mighty God who knew him intimately and cared about his troubles. Some of my Bible study friends might have been quick to recognize I ought to be praying for a change in me too, but I was not yet able to seek the comfort and counsel of even godly friends.

How much my parents gleaned about what was going on in our home, I didn't know. Passive-aggressive comments about Jack from me, and even the kids, had to give them a clue, but they waited for me to talk, and I didn't know how or where to start. Robbie and Paula were always close enough to hear anything said about their father.

Five or six times, I planned for time at Mom's kitchen sink or table. But Jack must have known when I was close to my breaking point, because his mood would change, and there would no longer be a need for counsel or comfort.

I did call one time, asking them to come get the kids for a while.

The house was cluttered. Piles of dirty laundry were in the hallway waiting for a turn in the washing machine. Dirty dishes filled the sink and covered the counter. Jack demanded, loudly enough for the neighbors to hear, that the house be "spotless" before I went to bed. He was right. I was a "lazy slob!" This wasn't the first time our home had been in disarray. My journey toward becoming a Proverbs 31 kind of woman had taken a detour somewhere between college coursework and volunteering at church. Pregnant or not, a Proverbs 31 woman wouldn't have let it come to this. I was at fault, but too tired to care.

Jack grabbed a half-empty glass of grape juice and threw it hard against the kitchen wall. Now my mess looked more like a disaster.

In front of the kids, he grabbed a guitar he had been building and smashed it against the brick fireplace.

I didn't trust the neighbors to hear his threat of personal violence and come to our rescue. Without hesitating, I dialed my parents.

Dad and Kevin were at our door within a few minutes. The yelling stopped immediately, but both of us were visibly shaken. I don't think Kevin said anything, but he showed a readiness to defend his sister and her kids. They had heard Jack ranting during the very brief phone conversation. Both of us had been yelling. I remember telling Jack to calm down by screaming so loud my eyes hurt. If it had not been so painful, it would be a hilarious memory.

I expected Dad to be a loud kind of angry. He was controlled and empathetic toward both of us, but his right hand trembled. He acknowledged that Jack deserved to come home to a tidy house, and that I would have more energy to take care of the house if Jack would help with the kids some evenings.

Robbie and Paula were hiding in their beds by now. Dad suggested they go with him and Kevin. He offered a bed for me too. Jack was quiet and controlled, so I thanked them for coming, but thought we would be all right. It would be better for the kids to sleep in their own beds.

Dad turned his attention toward the Humpty-Dumpty pieces of the guitar. Jack rationalized that his varnish job was sloppy and he didn't have the time to start over. That wasn't true. They hadn't seen him sand and polish until his fingers ached. They weren't watching when he opened the package of ivory tuning keys and made Robbie wash his hands before touching.

Dad and Kevin hadn't seen Jack's face or his white knuckles when he threw that glass, but I think they knew he was lying about wanting new wallpaper. I really liked the yellow-checkered pattern. Dad took the soapy rag from my hand and began to wipe.

"I think this might just come off," he said.

As it turned out, that wallpaper was of excellent quality. Spots of grape juice, noticed weeks later, disappeared with a little soapy water and mild elbow grease.

Dad gave Jack a restrained, yet stern, warning before they left. "Things can be repaired or replaced, but a wife and children can be gone in one regrettable moment of violence."

He mentioned my pregnancy and the fragile nature of an unborn baby. Jack's shoulders relaxed, and his demeanor softened. I could sleep that night for knowing how quickly Dad and/or Kevin would be there, if I called again.

Jack didn't attend church after our big fight. He avoided Mom's home-cooked Sunday dinners as well. I understood his reasons and figured he would resume church and family activities when he was ready, so every Sunday morning I left him with an "I wish you were coming with us." If cajoling, nagging, or threatening in order to get Jack to join us for a half-day on Sundays, meant risking family peace the other six and a half days of the week, it wasn't worth it, and Jack was not one to be manipulated.

A few weeks after that incident, I went forward during the final hymn on a Sunday morning. I knew God was already hearing me as I stood, gripping the pew in front of me, but there was something symbolic about letting go and taking that first physical step. My intention was to kneel at the front pew and continue with my private prayer. *So why now? How could I let my emotions overwhelm me? In front of all these people? Jack should be with me. This was our problem. Not mine alone.*

None of those things mattered once the pastor caught a moment of eye contact, and he saw my pain. He knelt beside me and prayed quietly. My tears began to flow.

When the hymn was done, the pastor took my arm and guided me through the crowd in the sanctuary and toward his office. As we walked by them, I heard Robbie and Paula saying, "Is Mommy all right?" "Is Mommy okay?" "What's wrong with Mommy?"

Our pastor, on top of his divinity degree, had a degree in psychology. I would have confided in him earlier, but my problem was humiliating, and Jack had warned me, "Don't take our problems public, especially to the preacher."

What would our pastor be able to offer me anyway, other than advice to pray and read my Bible? I didn't want our pastor to judge Jack's and my entire relationship by telling him about our most recent fight, because I knew the fight was a symptom and not the problem.

"Jack and I need marriage counseling." Saying those words aloud was my second step toward letting go. "But he refuses to talk to anyone. In fact, I'm here against his direct instruction not to talk to you about our problems." At that point, I had committed to casting all my cares—on anybody who could handle listening.

"Let's pray." I don't remember one word of his prayer. I was busy formulating my own opening statement. I do remember him telling me that what we talked about would be held confidentially, but that he would be willing to call Jack and ask him to join us.

"He wouldn't come, and that would probably make things worse. And don't tell me to read my Bible and pray. I've been doing all that. I'm all prayed out."

"Rita, is this Jack's baby?"

Like my doctor, he went for the direct answer. I didn't mind. How could I respect him if he avoided the hard stuff? Wasn't that what a pastor is supposed to do?

"Of course it's his."

"How certain is Jack that this is his baby?"

I answered with an abbreviated history of my high-risk pregnancy, including the part about Paula's prayer. We hadn't talked, but he knew some of the facts secondhand.

"Did Jack want you to have the abortion?"

"No. We both want this baby."

He rested his forearms on his desk, where a notepad and pen rested next to his Bible on a stack of paperwork. I hoped he wouldn't use the Bible to give me a verbal lashing. I already felt vulnerable and unsure about my unplanned and emotional decision to talk about our problems.

"Has either of you been unfaithful?"

"Jack is my first and only love. My feelings for him have not changed. I'm pretty sure he would say the same about me, although sometimes he makes me wonder."

I confessed to the snooping and how I'd found nothing to explain Jack's mood or behavior. Part of my investigation had been to count his leftover pain pills. No problem there. I had no reason to believe he was using alcohol or illegal drugs, even though he had commented that he'd thought about it.

Our pastor had officiated over John's funeral, and was aware of Jack's grandmother's recent death. We discussed how lingering back pain might affect Jack's ability to cope.

His next question knocked down the wall holding back another flood of tears.

"Do you feel like you and the kids are safe?"

"I don't know what I did to set him off. I don't know how else I could have responded. My own temper can get the best of me, but other than that fight, we've been getting along fine."

My attempt to redirect must have answered his question. Rather than scold, preach, or force an admission, he asked, "Did Jack have a difficult childhood?"

The man I'd come to respect and admire for his quick answers to complex theological questions listened for the two minutes it took to summarize Jack's story—one thumb supporting his jaw, and a finger against his left temple. When I finished, his face dropped into his open hands, like a heavy weight. Both thumbs supported his jaw now, and his fingers pressed hard, massaging his brow. I couldn't tell if his eyes were open or closed. The silence that followed was most uncomfortable.

Pick up the pen. Write something. Pick up the Bible. Read something. Look at me. Say something.

If God could use this man to speak and change a congregation, surely He would give him a word for me. My next breath depended on his answer.

It was not what I expected, or anything I could have imagined I would hear, but at least another adult knew about the goliath living in our home, and I felt permission to exhale.

"Jack needs to see a psychiatrist who can prescribe medication. He has a mental *illness*. This isn't a phase or an emotional or spiritual problem. This is more than a sin problem. This is a serious illness. I'm a psychologist. I can counsel one or both of you, but I can't prescribe the medication that will help Jack. He needs to see a psychiatrist as soon as possible."

We prayed again. I thanked him and walked out of his office with the names and phone numbers of two local psychiatrists. The heaviness that had been on my shoulders for weeks was beginning to lift by the time I opened my car door.

Mom had saved a plate for me. She packed a lunch for Jack, the way she had been doing for the past few Sundays. My parents were surprised the pastor thought Jack needed to see a psychiatrist, so I let them in on the severe depressed behavior we had been living with.

Robbie pretended to be distracted and not listening to our adult conversation before chiming in. "Dad stepped on one of my Hot Wheels cars and went to bed until morning. He gets sad real easy."

I had not yet decided what to tell Jack when we walked in the door. The kids wanted to finish their Sunday afternoon outside. Good idea.

Jack warmed up the lunch. "Tell your mom thanks. Maybe this will help me put back the five pounds I lost last month. I haven't had much of an appetite the past few weeks."

He pulled me to his side, pressed a hand against my growing tummy, and said, "Looks like your appetite is good."

This was not the same man who had crawled into my bed last night. He *looked* like the man who wouldn't get out of bed to watch his son's new bicycle stunt yesterday, but who was this guy?

Some women might have pulled away, offended by a comment about their pregnant belly. I took his face in my hands and kissed him on the forehead.

"You could use a haircut."

He nodded. He'd passed the test. A week ago, that comment would have turned into an argument or sent him to the bedroom to pull down the shades. *Could God have answered my prayers?*

"I talked to the pastor today."

No warning. The words spewed without permission. I took in all the air my lungs would allow and waited for Jack's response. I loved him, and I knew he loved me, but I wondered if this could be my last breath. I'd seen his hands, cupped and ready, within inches, to choke the life out of me. I never wanted to be in a place like that again.

Jack asked, "What did he have to say?" Then he took another bite of his late lunch.

I didn't fully exhale. "He thinks you should see a psychiatrist. He thinks you might be depressed."

"I wonder if my insurance will pay."

I exhaled and took in a breath of relief. It had to be God. Aside from divine intervention, this calm, non-emotional conversation could never have happened.

During supper the next day, I said, "I looked at your policy, and psychiatry is covered."

Another slow response. "Make an appointment."

I made the appointment for the next afternoon.

We arrived fifteen minutes early. I picked up a magazine. Jack alternated between sitting next to me and standing to look out the window overlooking the parking lot. Several times, I thought he might walk out, but he returned to his seat each time.

"Make yourselves comfortable," the psychiatrist told us upon entering her private office.

Jack and I looked at each other with a silent *Yeah, right*. I knew how far out of his comfort zone Jack had stepped, and I loved him as much as ever in that moment. We were in this together.

The psychiatrist looked to me. "You made this appointment based on your pastor's recommendation?"

The rest of her questions were directed to Jack. His medical history was covered in less than a minute. The back injury and surgery were his only medical problems worth mentioning. She asked about his pain management. He hadn't used pain pills in months.

"What brings you here today?" She leaned back, reclining her chair a little, and twirling her pen, like a baton, between her fingers. I had the impression she was a woman in her fifties, and had been twirling that pen for a quarter century or more.

Jack tilted his head and rolled his eyes toward me. "She says I'm depressed. I don't know. I've been sleeping a lot and spending time alone. She doesn't like it. She thinks I should come home from work every day and work another eight hours."

His words and tone caught me off guard. *Great! He's blaming me for our problems.* I opened my mouth, but I wasn't offered the opportunity for rebuttal.

"Jack. Rita told my receptionist that both your father and your grandmother passed away, and that's when she noticed a change in your mood?"

She posed a question she already knew the answer to. Jack stated questions that way, but resented it whenever I tried to do the same.

I wanted to fold my arms and lean back smugly. *Good luck getting an essay answer.*

Jack began to provide his standard summary of what his father did for a living and how his grandmother was a pillar of the community. All true. I'd heard it all before, and did any of that matter? *Get to the important stuff.*

She was more patient than I would have been, and waited for Jack to finish before asking her next question. *"Paid by the hour"* I thought. *"That explains it."*

"What about your mother?" Now, I thought she was going somewhere.

Then her questions came hard and fast: Is she still living? At what age was she diagnosed? How old were you? Was there abuse in the home? What about your relationship with your mother now?

They were questions I could have answered in Jack's absence. No surprises. Yet I remember the frustration I felt as Jack responded to her prying questions without sarcasm or attitude. Something he wouldn't have done for me.

Using the same tone of voice, but without eye contact, she asked another question. "Have you ever had thoughts about taking your own life?"

"Yes."

This time I wasn't smug. I wasn't surprised by her question, but Jack's answer changed my life. *Who was this goliath living in our home?*

Our session was over after a few more questions and comments. She walked with us to the receptionist and instructed Jack to return in a couple of days and both of us in one week. She ripped her handwritten prescription from the pad and held it out. I reached for it, but Jack nudged my hand out of the way. He took the little square of paper himself, folded it once, and tucked it into his shirt pocket.

He took my hand as though we were on our merry way to a happy place. Was that relief on his face? I thought the gesture was partly for appearances—until his fingers tickled mine as he opened my car door.

But I wasn't over the visit. "I can't believe you talk so easily to her about those things. Why don't you talk to me like that?"

Forgot to pray before that came out. Jack practiced some prayerful restraint himself by not responding. I didn't ask what else he would tell her that he couldn't tell me, or if he planned to keep the next appointment.

Jack did keep his next appointment. After a fifty-minute session, I hoped he'd have more to share than, "She says I have manic depression."

"That's it?"

But it was something. Something big. Our goliath had a name.

I pulled one of those thick nursing textbooks from my bookshelf. Our goliath had a scary definition.

Jack listened as I read aloud and then took my book to read for himself:

> **manic depressive**. a person with or exhibiting the symptoms of bipolar disorder.
> manic-depressive psychosis. See bipolar disorder.
> bipolar disorder, a major affective disorder characterized by episodes of mania and depression. One or the other phase may be predominant at any given time, one phase may appear alternately with the other, or elements of both phases may be present simultaneously. Characteristics of the manic phase are

excessive emotional displays, excitement, euphoria, hyperactivity accompanied by elation, boisterousness, impaired ability to concentrate, decreased need for sleep, and seemingly unbounded energy, often accompanied by delusions of grandeur. In the depressive phase, marked apathy, and underactivity are accompanied by feelings of profound sadness, loneliness, guilt and lowered self-esteem. Causes of the disorder are multiple and complex, often involving biological, psychological, interpersonal, and social and cultural factors. Treatment includes antidepressants, tranquilizers and antianxiety drugs, or the use of electroconvulsive therapy for persons who present in immediate and serious risk of suicide, followed by long-term psychotherapy. Careful nursing observation is important during depression, particularly during the recovery from depression, because of the possibility of suicide. (*Mosby's Medical and Nursing Dictionary* (1983). The C.V. Mosby Company: St. Louis, Missouri.)

Our goliath had a name. We had a doctor. Surely, all we needed was the right stone. So we prayed.

21

KICKING AND SCREAMING

"This baby doesn't seem to be moving as much as my first two."

I offered my obstetrician what I thought was a good reason for a repeat sonogram. True, this baby wasn't as active as my first two, but I thought a sonogram might prepare my heart for the day I would hold a sick and grossly deformed baby. There wouldn't be another sonogram. Nothing had changed, other than an appropriate amount of weight gain and a few more centimeters around my midsection.

Nothing could be done, even if a sonogram confirmed the expected.

Iodine pills, commonly used to treat hyperthyroidism and known to be "harmful to the fetus," were necessary for my health and ability to carry "the fetus" to term. I was taking the lowest possible dose to keep my thyroid from running wild while minimizing any harm to "the fetus."

When we first found out about the pregnancy, it was a baby, *our miracle baby*. Now, at five months along, "fetus" felt like the more appropriate term. Paula was with me. She sat in the same chair, in the same corner, during each of my visits. She watched the doctor's every move.

With her listening, some of my questions would never be addressed, but what did that matter? It seemed I had no control in this or any other situation in my life.

"Are you still feeling those heart palpitations?" the doctor asked.

I was.

"Are you keeping your vitamins down?"

I was.

With one hand on the door handle, like doctors do, he was ready for his exit when Paula spoke from her chair in the corner. "Is our baby all right?"

His face softened, and he put aside his medically cautious jargon. "I think your baby is fine."

To celebrate another month without bad news, and as a reward for her good behavior, we stopped for burgers and milkshakes on the way home. Robbie's typical after-school dawdle became a sprint toward home when he saw we had fast-food containers.

Jack came through the kitchen door a few minutes later. He had a smile on his face, even before noticing his vanilla shake.

"I'm getting a worker's compensation settlement for my back. We need to go talk to the lawyer next week."

The rest of the evening we talked about what we could do with this unexpected lump sum of money. Jack insisted we do one thing: I needed braces. My overbite had never bothered him, but he knew it bothered me, and now it was becoming a matter of dental health and not just a vanity issue. We settled on a plan that included braces for me, paying off the family car, and depositing the rest into our anemic savings account.

Our conversation was interrupted by a phone call.

"Wrong number." I lied.

It was a car salesman following up on a show room conversation. The call explained why Jack had been over thirty minutes late getting home from work. Talking about a new car, even if we could find a way to manage the payments, wasn't on my agenda.

We had a good day. A normal, happy day. From the outside looking in, who would have expected to see a couple, with our issues, sitting tucked into opposite corners of a comfortable sofa, bare feet teasing each other on a coffee table, and smiling children playing in front of a fireplace?

We'd never see our old "normal" again. Less than twenty-four hours later, the two of us were sitting in the professionally decorated office of the psychiatrist for our second appointment. The goliath, who had been messing with our lives from some sort of shadow, stepped out into full view.

My shoe-clad feet, attached to my petite frame, stuck out like those of a child in a grown-up's chair. Jack sat up straight, the way he'd sat in the minister's office for our pre-marital counseling and in the bank when we applied for our mortgage. A mahogany table separated us. With its massive pedestal, it spoke of wealth, but dust and furniture polish had settled in the deep crevasses of its ornate carvings.

I imagined the matching mahogany desk provided a solid barrier between the doctor and some of her more unstable patients. This was not a place where happy children played. We came, or at least I did, expecting to hear a plan for saving our marriage.

After some small talk and a description of how great life had been over the past few days, she gave us three options. Jack, she said, could not be responding to the medication so quickly. His behavior had to be the beginning of a manic phrase.

Our options were just as breathtakingly stark as her diagnosis. Jack could sign himself into inpatient treatment, I could sign a document to commit him for thirty days, or she would sign a court order for him to be committed for an amount of time to be determined.

I protested. "This is not a manic phase. The past few days have been the real Jack, the normal Jack."

Mosby's definition aside, I loved Jack's energy. He was "boisterous" when he wrestled with Robbie on the living room floor. Wasn't that normal?

"Other people might have delusions of grandeur, but not Jack. He is humble and nearly always too cautious. This can't be."

But Jack wasn't helping my cause. He was silent for a while, then confessed were it not for a salesman suggesting "Bring your wife in. Take her for a ride," he would have signed a contract accepting forty-eight months of debt for a fast and shiny blue sports car that could accommodate the driver and one passenger.

I could be more specific, if that's what it took to convince her. Jack's mood shift was because his physical pain was more tolerable and we were about to receive a nice sum of money. I reminded her that our baby was a month older and still alive. Things were turning around for us.

"I've been feeling better and kept up with the housework the past few days. I've felt like cooking, and what man doesn't want a car like that? He didn't actually buy it."

But the car salesman might still be waiting for Jack to bring me in for a look and a ride. I knew the truth. There wouldn't be a fourth option.

Outnumbered and less informed than the other two people in the room, I was kicking and screaming on the inside, using every ounce of adult restraint to keep from dropping to my knees and pounding my fists against the floor.

What I heard next was a convincing rationale for inpatient treatment, and her plan for saving not only our marriage but our lives.

First, the degrees of mania and depression could vary widely among people and between phases. Second, Jack had considered two different scenarios for suicide. Third, the most recent scenario had involved him taking my life, the lives of our children, and then his own. He had been having those thoughts for over a year. He'd told her all about it in his solo appointment a few days ago.

This was news to me.

Jack had owned a pistol, but he sold it within days after the fight that brought Dad and Kevin to our doorstep. "Isn't that a good thing?" I asked, hoping for something positive.

"That is a good thing, but it's not enough," she said. "It's during the manic phase that Jack is at most risk. During the depressed phase, he has little energy, generally not enough to follow through with his ideations. Going into the manic phase, there seems to be a burst of energy—physical, mental, and emotional. It's best, for everyone's sake, that he be admitted while we adjust his medication."

I looked to Jack and knew she was right. He was wearing his "big boy" face.

After stopping at home long enough to pack from a list of what he could bring and what was prohibited, I drove him to the hospital. He signed himself in.

Whatever I told the kids would be repeated to any child or adult who asked and to some who didn't. The psychiatrist's suggestion sounded oversimplified, but we used it. "Daddy went to the hospital because he isn't feeling well, but he will feel better soon."

The kids didn't ask for clarification.

Our situation wasn't going to go away, and I didn't like guarding secrets, but I shared only the basic information I'd given to the kids whenever anyone asked about how Jack was or where he was. Protecting his privacy wasn't an easy task, but it was necessary if I wanted to keep his trust and our marriage.

The rumors were more creative than Robbie or Paula could have generated. It must have been a curious soul, lacking in courage, compassion, and integrity, who fabricated a story about Jack leaving me and the kids. *And of course, he had good reason. The child she's carrying is not his.* Isn't it ironic how the truth is many times more interesting than a falsehood?

Forty-eight hours later, Jack was allowed visitors. We stepped off the hospital elevator with our bag of goodies, including a new electric shaver. Razors with blades were not allowed. The mandatory search for contraband was unnecessary. Between Robbie and Paula, every item in the bag was described in detail, even to the exact purchase price of the new electric razor.

The visit took me back to when I used to go with my parents to a nearby psychiatric hospital. Mom, Dad, and other church members used to minister to the patients with Bible stories, music, and food.

Jack, I felt, didn't belong there. He didn't drool from the corners of his mouth. Jack didn't chain-smoke or drown himself in cheap aftershave. Jack wore brand-name jeans and ironed shirts. He combed his hair. He had never approached a stranger for vending machine money or to bum a cigarette. Fearing Jack's future was represented in the people meandering in that long hallway, I wanted him out of there. Robbie and Paula were fascinated to the point of being entertained. I was embarrassed for them to see their father in that place, and among those people.

Robbie, Paula, and Jack smiled and played checkers while I pretended to enjoy their talk of strategy. Jack and Robbie's "strategy" was to let Paula think she was winning.

A nurse carried a tray into the rec room where we were visiting, and most of the patients lined up to take pills. Not Jack. He took his "with meals and at bedtime." He had started a couple of medications, lithium being one. I noticed other patients with hand tremors, nervous twitching, fast and disconnected speech, or an apparent disconnection to the people and things around them. I didn't know whether these were symptoms of the diseases being treated or adverse effects of the drugs used to treat them.

I told myself it would take weeks for the drugs to stabilize his mood and for side effects to show. *"Just enjoy a little rest, and let the kids see their daddy while he feels good. And remember what the doctor said. Lots of people take these medications without ill effects. I'm seeing these people at their worst. Jack won't be like that. He only has manic depression. These other patients are really sick."*

A lady, old enough to be a grandmother, and with a dark red color outlining her lips and cheeks, approached me. She carried a paper bag filled with sample-sized colognes and reached in to spritz the air around her each time someone entered or exited the visiting area. Her blend of scents didn't hide the fact that she, and most of the people in the room, were addicted to nicotine. Her hair, except for the two inches of gray framing her face, was a beautiful shade of auburn. I wondered if Jack had noticed the resemblance between her and Margaret. She touched my belly without asking permission.

"You're pregnant, aren't you?" she asked.

"Yes."

"It's a boy."

"You think so?"

"You just found out you were pregnant, didn't you?"

"No. We've known for a while."

"I can tell you things the doctors can't. I'm gifted. You come back when you're farther along, and I will tell you how many contractions you will have and how much your baby will weigh."

It took a deep breath, and clinched teeth, to keep my thoughts from turning into words, and my facial expression from spewing a sinful kind of ugly.

I fought my fears and feelings, but was losing to the awareness that this was a forever illness, and we might be visiting Jack many more times in a place like this. Our children would be raised in the uncertainty of a sobering mental illness. Jack had hinted that I should leave him, the way his father had left his mother. I was better than that, I thought. I loved Jack more than that.

Frightening scenarios bounced between conflicting emotions. My stomach began to churn, and I bolted into the hallway. My heart was beating fast and hard, racing with my thoughts. The restroom door closed behind me, and I pulled my hair away from my face just in time for the eruption.

While bending over a public toilet, my self-talk became a prayer: *If Jack is going to take his life, let him do it sooner rather than later. Save him from the suffering, and save us from living every day of our lives in fear of the next day's disaster. Don't let him hurt my kids.*

Shame and guilt for what I had prayed stared at me as I looked in the restroom mirror and wiped my face. I prayed again. This time confessing. God forgave me during that breath, but I wouldn't forget. Words from Scripture washed over me as I walked the hallway, returning to Jack, Robbie, and Paula. *I have plans for your good and not for disaster, to give you a future and a hope.* They weren't words I had memorized. I wouldn't have been able to say where in the Bible to find them, but I trusted God's word to be true.

The weight of Jack's illness wasn't ours alone. As I drove the kids home that day, I reminded myself that yes, this was a lifetime illness, but we were loved with an everlasting love, by a God with unending care and patience for people like me. We had an open, and standing, appointment with the Great Physician who specializes in wounded people with extraordinary need.

Bible verses memorized in Sunday school, VBS, and GAs

reminded me who I was, how much I was loved, and that I was not alone. Verses, perfect for my current situation, came to my mind and answered my immediate need. The words "Holy Bible" are branded into the covers of many Bibles, but that's not what told me it's a holy book. It was the way God's words had been pressed into my heart, and rescued me.

Over the weeks while Jack was hospitalized, I prayed not to say or do anything to add to our troubles.

Isaiah 41:10 told me not to fear, that God was with me, he would hold me with his righteous hand. When I tired of waking up to the same problems and wondered why God hadn't cured Jack's illness and taken away our pain, I was reminded in 2 Corinthians 12:9 that God's grace is sufficient and his strength made perfect in my weakness.

I had questions. Whether I was talking to family, friends, Robbie, Paula, or Jack, I didn't trust my judgment regarding what to say or how to say it, but I knew that somewhere in the New Testament (James 1:5) I'd read to ask God for wisdom whenever—that he would give it liberally and without scolding.

How would we pay the bills if Jack didn't get back to work soon? My God would supply all my needs according to his riches. Philippians 4:19 was right. Jack ended up being discharged before all his paid sick days were used.

Why would God put an innocent and delicate life inside me now? Why couldn't He have waited to answer Paula's prayer until Jack was better? God took me to Psalm 139:14. "I will praise You, for I am fearfully and wonderfully made; marvelous are your works, and that my soul knows very well."

Jack spent the remainder of his time reading in his room, going to group sessions twice daily, and eating food he claimed was "not so bad." I offered to call his doctor and ask for an early release, but Jack wanted to get better. If staying put for a while meant he could get his old life back, it would be worth it. I visited Jack every day possible, taking the kids at least twice a week. His roommate would go to the lounge to allow us privacy. Other than a couple of slow, tight, hugs and quick kisses, our interactions looked like a hospital visit between two friends. After a few minutes, we would run out of things to say, and I would leave.

When I wasn't at school, visiting Jack, or sleeping, I was dealing with the routine kinds of things wives and mothers do. I don't remember the exact criteria used to determine Jack's readiness for discharge, but it had something to do with drug levels in his blood, how he responded during group sessions, and the opinion of his psychiatrist. No one told me so, but I knew my role in Jack's discharge plan was to keep our home running smoothly while he was away.

By the time he was ready to come home, friends and neighbors had quit asking where he was and how he was doing. The kids and I had adjusted to a new routine—a routine that included either Robbie, Paula, or both of them sleeping with me at least part of the night. My explanations for mysterious middle of the night noises were never as satisfying as Jack's. Neither were my flashlight and baseball bat walk throughs. We had missed Jack, especially after dark.

Our backyard had just the right amount of shade for a late afternoon picnic on the day I went to pick him up from the hospital. According to the weatherman, the rainstorm headed our way wouldn't hit us until morning. Paula helped me prepare the picnic table for a welcome home dinner. Robbie wasn't with us to engage the nurses during the discharge process, so in her brother's absence, she told them about out picnic plans and said, "Thank you for making my daddy feel better."

Jack said his good-byes to the female nurses, staff, and other patients. I watched as they gave him encouragement, handshakes, and long hugs. He had told me about many of them during our visits, and it was wrong to be jealous, but I was. I felt like an outsider in my husband's life. It didn't seem right for strangers to have heard intimate details of his life, or for another female to have given him emotional support he wouldn't or couldn't accept from me.

Each of us needed a nap after our anxious morning. Paula slept at the foot of our bed. Jack and I lay still on our backs, arms across our chests. I don't know what he was thinking, but my thoughts turned into a prayer of confession that I was lost and helpless in this relationship and needed Jesus to abide with us.

The word "abide" was a bit old-fashioned for my everyday vocabulary—even my thought vocabulary. I had heard it most often in songs that older people enjoyed, but I knew an invitation for Jesus to abide meant much more than an invitation for him to hang out until I needed him. I knew it was an invitation that had never been declined.

Jack spoke first. "I missed you."

"I missed you too."

"Was that the baby kicking?"

He placed a hand over where our baby had caused a slow but definite wave in my belly. We fell asleep marveling at how strong a baby must be to move around in such a confined space. I woke up with a few minutes left to work on our picnic before Robbie would get home from one of his last school days in 1984.

The house was immaculate. Burgers were ready for the grill. Fancy paper plates waited to be carried outside. Jack's favorite soft drink was cooling in the fridge. I looked around for something to make this meal more perfect and could find nothing. The weatherman was spot-on. It was a lovely evening to eat outdoors.

Jack was not depressed. He was definitely not manic. The old Jack was almost back when the kids were around, and it was comfortable, but it was as if some sort of curtain was between us when we were alone. We were both different people. The separation and the disease had made us intimate strangers. He was romantic, but it seemed artificial. I hoped I was a better actor than he was.

Eggshells crumbled under our feet and made their way between our sheets.

He went back to his job and resumed working out. Names and personalities from the hospital psychiatric unit would surface, reminding me of where he'd been, and that he had opened his heart to mere acquaintances in a way that was impossible with me. He had bonded with some of the other patients, and he kept their stories in confidence. When I asked, he promised he had only said good things about me. Every day for a week he thanked me for visiting and being there for him, comparing me to some of the other spouses.

I wished there had been some sort of class or counseling for me. I could have used some guidance on how to live with this illness. Jack's medication hadn't made it go away; it helped only to manage the disease. Some days, maybe most days, that meant no depression and no mania, but a middle of the road, what-kind-of-life-is-this Jack. No prescription for me. No pill to help me think or cope with my feelings.

We waited for the period of adjustment to end. Meanwhile, the stigma of mental illness was ours to own. Jack felt it at work. He spoke of the looks and innuendo. Until I stood in front of the cash register of our local pharmacy, I wondered if the stigma was real. As the pharmacist reviewed the side effects and cautions related to Jack's new medications, he offered a look of sympathy, or maybe it was pity. Jack carried the heaviest part of this burden. Dealing with the pharmacist was just one way I could lighten his load.

Medication might have been the stone God provided, but if a tangible bag of stones had been available, my fingers would have reached into that bag several times daily, feeling around for a bigger, smarter, and kinder weapon.

I managed to read from the Psalms and the Proverbs most days. It was a nice break from nursing textbooks and more uplifting than all the research on manic depression, manic-depressive psychosis, bipolar disorder, every combination of those terms, and the drugs used to treat Jack's incurable disease.

One night, Paula requested a second bedtime story. I sent her back to her room to pick out "a skinny book." "Mommy is tired."

She returned with *The Story of David and Goliath*. We read about how the Lord was with David when he fought against a lion and a bear. When we turned to the page with the picture of Goliath, standing with chest puffed up and arms as big as tree trunks, Paula always pretended suspense, even though she knew who would win the battle and how it would be won.

She hadn't fought a lion or a bear, let alone a goliath, but at five years old, she was already learning where her strength came from.

"That's your favorite story, huh, Mommy."

"Yes, honey, that's my favorite story."

As I read, I wondered if our current circumstance might be like the lion and the bear, merely a warm-up. I didn't want to look for trouble where there was none, but I couldn't shake the feeling that we were living too close to Goliath's Mountain.

I prayed for the curtain in Jack's and my relationship to be lifted, and for the eggshells to find their way to the trash. My kicking and screaming settled down for lack of reward. The old Jack was gone and I missed him, but this new guy was as handsome as ever. If I was stuck on Goliath's Mountain, I wanted it to be with him. I loved it when he called me "Sport," and I still felt like a Cinderella when he touched me.

22

NESTING

We made it through the second trimester. Our baby was active, and my monthly checkups were going well. Nesting set in.

According to me, and not necessarily Merriam-Webster, nesting is a natural phenomenon that occurs in expectant mothers whereby they are motivated to prepare a safe and comfortable place for a delicate newborn to live. Like a latent virus that reactivates after years of inactivity, nesting can also be observed in expectant grandmothers. It must not be a biological disorder because adoptive mothers suffer too. The onset of nesting is generally characterized by anxiety and excitement. Expectant fathers and grandfathers attempt to stabilize the condition. They fail. The onset of birthing pains may or may not halt an exacerbation of the condition.

There is no vaccine.

It wasn't as though one day I woke up and remembered we had sold or given away all our baby things four years prior. It was more about final exams being over. Jack was expecting a cash settlement for his back injury, he was stable on his medication, my thyroid was behaving, and the doctor encouraged me by losing the term *fetus*. He was now referring to Robbie and Paula's little brother or sister as "Baby." We also had a sizable income tax refund arrive on the same day as a department store advertisement for baby things.

I bought the basics, everything gender neutral. Paula offered to donate her pink sweater for the cause. We explained that it might be a baby boy. She kept insisting she had prayed for a baby girl.

Her exuberance made it easy to set up a nursery that occupied half of her room. She fell asleep, many nights, talking about the things we had ready for when her "real baby" arrived. Any disappointment with her gifts under the tree in 1983 was in the past. I could visualize the caption "Christmas 1984" under a large photo of Paula sitting in front of a Christmas tree, holding a three-month-old baby swaddled in red and green wrapping paper. The gift tag would read, "To Paula. From God." I knew the sex of our baby had already been determined, but I found myself praying for a girl.

A few weeks after he was discharged from the hospital, Jack resumed church attendance and Sunday dinners with family. We had a couple of conversations about family planning. I thought maybe I should be the one to have surgery this time. Jack was undecided and leaning more toward letting God determine our family size the natural way.

He had not followed through with our doctor's suggestion to see a urologist, and my nesting instinct had me in the mood to clean up unfinished business, so I dialed the number and made the appointment. We went together. A simple test labeled us an infertile couple.

The urologist indicated, by pointing to what was now undeniably a baby bump, that what he was about to say wasn't exactly trustworthy. "Men with your count don't father children."

He offered a couple of explanations as to the why and how of this conception, reiterating with each possibility, "it only takes one."

An offer to do an exploratory surgery with a possible redo was declined. (I thought I saw a vision of a lawn mower dance through Jack's head.) The urologist praised him and shook his hand as if to welcome him into an elite male fraternity. Jack's shoulders got a little wider and his chest a little bigger when he looked at my belly. He was on par with Superman in his mind and my heart.

I loved the perfect smile that accompanied Jack's masculine pride, so I successfully resisted the urge to let the urologist in on the whole story. Why spoil Jack's moment? Sure, it was a God thing, but Jack knew our little miracle happened in his body first. My body was only carrying the evidence.

I breathed a sigh of relief as we fell into bed that night, content. Our baby would be welcomed into a comfortable and safe home. A couple weeks had passed without tears or worry. The threat of a sick baby hadn't dissolved, but I would worry about that later. I checked my pulse. A little fast, so I closed my eyes to pray. Three deep breaths shy of amen, and I was asleep.

Rest gave me energy for the morning. I pretended it was an accident that I woke Jack, and he pretended to listen as I recited items checked off my "prep for baby" list. He interrupted my monologue to ask what I wanted for my birthday.

"I just want a healthy baby. It would be nice to deliver before my birthday so I can eat cake at home."

Jack was never good at holding gifts until the occasion for giving. About a week before every Christmas, he would pull one gift from my hiding place to give the kids an early thrill. Even so, I was surprised to see him jump out of bed to retrieve a small box from the back of his closet's top shelf.

"It's a thank-you gift, for having my baby."

"The baby's not due till September. It's still June."

"I want you to wear it now, before the baby comes—in case something happens."

It was a necklace, with a small round sapphire, to match the ring he had given me on the day our baby was conceived, and the same sapphire blue as a two-seater sports car that was still sitting on the showroom floor of our local car dealer. When I saw the date on the receipt for the necklace, I thought, *Some car salesman's loss is my gain.*

I've never met an expectant mother who hasn't had at least a moment or two of fear. I wore my new necklace every day. It reminded me not to be afraid. It reminded me this baby was a gift. I prayed again, for a girl.

23

READY OR NOT

Goliath found us in June of 1984.

Anyone with air-conditioning was inside. Little old ladies in the neighborhood avoided the hotter-than-usual midday sun. They came out to sip iced tea on their covered porches just in time to complain about the mosquitos. The kids and I spent many mornings at the community pool or under a lawn sprinkler.

Jack was in and out (mostly out) of the air-conditioning all day at work, which was what got the blame for his summer cold. He came home from work, three afternoons in a row, with a terrible headache and went straight to bed. He managed to wake up in time to eat a little supper and spend a little time with me and the kids, but after about a week, his cold was looking more like the flu. Now he had no appetite.

He missed a dose of his medication one morning and felt better that afternoon. Off the medicine, he had no nausea, and he felt less sluggish. Without me knowing, he skipped another day. Then another. I assumed he was over the flu.

Something in him prompted this confession: "I flushed all my pills down the toilet."

Wasteful, impulsive, childish. I thought a lot of things, but I asked, "How many days ago was that?"

He couldn't remember if it was a Monday or a Tuesday. "It could have been a Saturday?"

I started to panic. I wanted to be angry, but a couple of memorized verses called me to "a perfect peace" and cooled my hot temper.

"Where are the bottles?"

"They went out with the trash."

Jack began apologizing, profusely and sincerely, admitting he had made a rash decision. A year earlier his apology might have been met with sarcasm, but this was a Friday, and his psychiatrist would be walking out of the office to start her weekend in ten to fifteen minutes. We couldn't afford to waste any time arguing.

A year earlier, I would have been the one to talk to the doctor, to offer an explanation and maybe an excuse. Not that day. I looked up the number, dialed, and then held out the phone. Like a remorseful teenager, ready to accept consequences, Jack took the phone and waited for an answer.

He told her what he had done, repeating his apology.

Jack held the phone away from his ear, just enough so that I could hear the calm in her voice. She explained that excessive perspiration, along with not drinking enough fluid, would cause a more concentrated level of medication in his bloodstream, and that could be the reason for the nausea, loss of appetite, and lack of energy.

She stressed the importance of adhering to his schedule and avoiding dehydration. She would call in another prescription for the lithium right away. Their conversation lasted another minute or so. I heard her use the word "essential" at least three times. Jack listened and added an occasional "Okay."

"She was pretty nice," he said. "I guess that happens a lot."

With that, we went to the pharmacy. On the way, Jack opened the sunroof and sang along to rock-n-roll. Even as I pulled out my wallet and paid for replacement medication, he was smiling. I sang along on the way home, for the sake of the kids.

Because it was a Friday and this was the best hope for a good weekend I'd seen in a while, I followed Jack's lead and decided to be happy. I tucked Robbie and Paula into bed the moment the sun went down. The fan on the air conditioner was still on high, and the hum of the dishwasher would have been annoying, except it announced the end of my workday.

I sat at the piano, waiting for Jack to finish his shower. As I skipped through a songbook, stopping for the easier tunes, I wished I could play like Rhonda. My younger sister's natural musical talent had made my own piano practice sessions seem futile. I had quit piano lessons in order to avoid an upcoming recital.

As I struggled with the fingering of what should have been an easy song, my mind wandered from the notes to my life—specifically my spiritual life. I'd been frustrated seeing others doing the Christian thing better than me, with what appeared to be less effort. Prayer and Bible study felt like piano practice, and they never brought me to another's level of faith. Sometimes I wanted to quit, but I knew something comparable to a recital would eventually take place, and I would not be able to avoid center stage.

Between songs, I realized why Rhonda had been the highlight of many music recitals, and why I had been struggling to grow my faith beyond the ordinary.

Rhonda played so beautifully because she practiced, and she practiced for the love of music. Most of my life, I'd been practicing the Christian disciplines more out of duty than my love for God. I'd been preparing for a dreaded recital when I could have been enjoying the music.

By the time Jack had finished his shower and came out of the bathroom, I had repeated the verse and chorus enough that my fingers could find the right notes without hesitating:

> *Pardon for sin and a peace that endureth,*
> *Thine own dear presence to cheer and to guide;*
> *Strength for today and bright hope for tomorrow,*
> *Blessings all mine, and ten thousand beside!*
> *Great is Thy faithfulness. Great is Thy faithfulness.*
> *Morning by morning new mercies I see.*
> *All I have needed Thy hand hath provided.*
> *Great is Thy faithfulness, Lord unto me.*

I reached to turn the page in the songbook, but too late. Jack lifted it from the stand and laid it open, but upside down on top of the piano, marking my spot for when I returned.

He asked me, "Do you love that piano more than you love me?"

"You know I don't, but I do love that song."

"Me too, but it's time for bed."

Nothing about our weekend stands out as remarkable. That was a good thing. We never felt the need to be the social, party-going type. By starting our married life away from family and old friends, we had learned to entertain ourselves with simple pleasures. As hard as I try, details of that Saturday, Sunday, and Monday elude me.

No one called out, "Ready or not!"

I'd played the game of hide-n-seek from the time I was a child. I played along with my own children. So I knew that even if the seeker cheated and started the hunt before the countdown was over, I wouldn't be found until I heard that clear and loud warning.

We trust ourselves to be prepared as though we'd know what to do when trouble finds us. We expect to be treated fairly, according to our definition of fair. We believe, to our detriment, that we'll recognize a final warning—and have time. But life doesn't work that way.

Anything that happened before 7 p.m. on Tuesday, June 26, 1984, is lost to my memory along with the previous three days. I suppose Jack went to work, and I spent at least part of the day preparing for a Baptist Young Women's study while Robbie and Paula scattered toys or otherwise did what eight and five-year-olds do.

The women's group had become a regular part of my life. My routine was to prepare a simple supper, eat fast, take a quick shower, and remind Jack of where I was going before I ran out the door, with my hair still wet, at five minutes before seven.

Our group of about twelve met monthly. We were teachers, leaders, or choir members at church. Some of us were all three. We saw each other often, celebrated birthdays, had fun being secret pals, did missions projects, and prayed together. Some of us had been friends since our teen years. Any, or all, of these women would have prayed with me anytime, if I had asked.

Most of us had kids to put to bed, but we tried to spend at least a few minutes chit chatting and staying connected before returning to our homes. Some of the husbands played in the church softball league and wouldn't be getting home with the kids until after nine. Jack didn't play softball, so I left a little early and went to the local convenient store to pick up ice cream treats for the four of us.

Robbie and Paula were still playing in the driveway. None of the bikes or wheeled toys had been stored for the night. The driveway looked like a regular playground. I flashed the box of frozen treats to encourage a quick cleanup. It worked.

I put Paula in the tub and gave Robbie his treat, then went back to give Paula a good scrubbing. She could get as dirty as any of the boys. I used a towel to protect her clean pajamas, handed her the ice cream on a stick, and sent Robbie to the tub. It was my turn for just a few minutes, so I grabbed my own treat and turned on the television to catch part of my favorite detective show. Like a lot of mothers of eight-year-old boys, I had learned to multitask by yelling instructions.

"Be sure to use soap!" I never expected a response, but a pause seemed appropriate.

"Brush your teeth, and I'd better smell the toothpaste when you're done!"

"Don't fill the tub too full, and don't splash!"

Those were my basic commands, but I rotated others into our routine in order to break up the monotony and let Robbie know he wouldn't fool me with any of his shortcuts.

"Wash your neck real good!"

"Be sure to wash between your toes!"

I realized that I hadn't seen or heard Jack since coming home.

Paula was still at the table eating ice cream. "Paula, where is Daddy?"

"I think he's sleeping."

I mumbled under my breath, "Well, isn't that wonderful."

She must have sensed my sarcasm and came up with another possibility.

"He might be running at the track."

On the way to our bedroom I chose not to be angry. I would just let Jack know his ice cream treat was in danger of disappearing.

The door was unlocked, and Jack wasn't there.

"Robbie, where's your Dad?" I asked through the bathroom door. "Is he at the track?"

"He's probably still in the garage."

A huge lump in my throat pulsed, and my heart sank. I went back to the bedroom to look for his keys. No keys. I went to the mantel and saw his wallet, but no keys.

I knew. I just didn't know how.

As sternly as I possibly could, I instructed Paula, "Stay right here. Don't move."

She followed me anyway.

I raced to the garage, telling Paula once again to get back inside the house. She clung to me. The side door was locked, but I could see his car and noticed it wasn't running. I banged on the door. No answer. I went back to the heavy overhead door.

Adrenaline boosted my strength, and as I lifted it, the door flew up fast and out of my control. Because her five-year-old eyes came only to the level of my waist, Paula saw her daddy first, and she was leaping into my arms before I saw what Jack had done. I jerked the door back down so hard it bounced off the driveway floor before it closed, but it was too late. The wide-eyed wonder on Paula's face turned to an empty stare.

I held her tight and ran back inside the house, where I pulled her clinging arms from around my neck and dropped her onto the sofa. She was in the same position when I returned dragging her dripping wet brother from the bathroom. He was pulling pajama bottoms on with his free hand as I grabbed Paula again, and ran outside to the car. Every light in the house was on, and the door was left wide open.

Robbie was asking questions even after we got into the car. "What's the matter? What's the matter?"

"Just buckle your seat belt!"

"But Mom, I can't. You're going too fast! What's the matter? Where are we going?"

"Just do what I say. I'm going to the fire station for just a minute. Then I'm taking you to the ball game to be with Grandma and Grandpa."

"Is our house on fire? Will it be there when we get back?"

I adjusted the rearview mirror in order to see Paula. She sat quiet and motionless. Huge tears were dripping off her face.

"Where's Dad?" was Robbie's last question before he too was silent with tears. I didn't answer. There wasn't time. I couldn't. Maybe it wasn't so.

The fire station was five or six short blocks away. I pulled up close to the door, left my car running, my car door open, and ran in.

"My husband just hanged himself! In the garage!"

Without pause, I yelled out our address and ran back to the car. We heard sirens as I backed out of the fire station's driveway. Once we got to the park, I carried Paula and ran toward the bleachers where Mom and Dad were watching the game. Robbie ran beside me. Someone must have seen us coming and warned them, because Mom and Dad were already at the bottom of the bleachers when we got there. No explanation. I told Mom to take the kids to their house and Dad to come with me. They didn't hesitate or question.

There were more sirens now. My whole body, but especially my heart and lungs, was telling me I had better slow down, but I couldn't.

Dad took my keys. Neither of us spoke until both car doors were closed and the car was in gear. He knew to speed as I told him what Jack had done. Stop signs served as cautionary reminders, even after he knew I had already notified the rescue squad. He asked me if I was sure it was too late. I told him what I had seen. I knew, from watching old westerns.

"He wasn't swinging, Dad."

I wanted desperately to be told I was wrong, for Dad to debunk what I'd learned from old Hollywood movies, but he was silent.

We couldn't park in front of the house because of all the fire and police vehicles. The block was lit with red, white, and blue flashing lights. Neighbors lined our driveway and the street in front of the house.

An empty gurney waited outside the door of the rescue van. One of the firemen stopped me from lifting the garage door. "You can't go in, ma'am."

"But that's my husband in there."

"Ma'am, they are working on him right now. You don't need to see that."

"Is he alive? He wasn't moving. I thought he was gone or I wouldn't have left. I had to get my kids out of here. I couldn't let them see. But he's my husband!"

He guided me into my own home. Police officers were already looking around.

"This is the wife, and this is . . ."

". . . my dad."

The questioning began. Where had I been? Who was I with? Who had Jack been with? What time this, and what time that? Was anyone angry with Jack? Where did he work? Where was his wallet? His keys? Did we rent or own? Which car was his, and which was mine? I tired of the questions and tried several times to get off the sofa and go check on Jack. Each time I felt Dad's hand on my shoulder keeping me in place.

I'd seen an officer standing close to him and talking. *What did Dad know that he wasn't telling me?*

I saw the rescue truck pull out of the driveway. No flashing lights. No siren. I asked if I should follow them to the hospital.

"No, ma'am. That won't be necessary. Do you have a preference for a funeral home?"

One officer questioned, leaving no time for thought or to absorb the impact of my answers, and his questions became more personal in nature. I protested by adding sarcasm to the obvious answers. I asked some questions of my own. I wanted to know where they were taking Jack. I needed details of his condition. When could I see him? Instead of answers, the officer continued with his agenda. I wondered, had he memorized his questions, or was he making them up as he went along?

Dad told me the questions were "standard under the circumstances," but he began to either answer for me, or defer the questions all together. He must have been feeling the fatigue himself. "I think you've got all the information you need for now." He stood and directed that particular officer toward the door.

Another officer stepped forward, in charge now. He explained what should happen that night and the next day. As he instructed us, a couple of other police officers opened every door and closet. They rifled through drawers. They checked inside the washer and dryer and under the sinks. Our trash was searched. They looked in toy boxes and the baby's dresser.

"What do you think they're looking for?" I asked.

Dad wasn't sure. We waited in helpless silence until two of the officers came out of our bedroom.

"Is this your husband's handwriting?"

They handed me a paper tablet, and I read Jack's apology for what he was about to do. His note said it wasn't my fault, that he loved us, and that he had no other choice. He left instructions. It wasn't dated.

"Yes, that's his tablet. His writing."

They took the tablet from me, and I never saw it again.

Did Jack actually think words on a paper would make me feel better right about now? Was there one moment when he had a second thought between the time he wrote the note and the time he closed the door to the garage? When did he write it? He must not have loved me enough to stay with me. I wasn't the perfect wife, but I loved him. Did he know how much I loved him?

Why? Why did God let this happen?

None of my questions could be answered, but they raced through my heart and brain, rapid-fire, with new ones slipping into the cycle. Some of them would soon become tools of the devil, especially one. Had Jack sensed the prayer I'd uttered during a weak and vulnerable moment? What had I done? Of all my prayers, why would God answer that one? *I took it back, God. You know I didn't mean those words. You're supposed to be forgiving and just.*

No doubt, this was a goliath—the kind of goliath Dad talked about when I was a little girl. I should have seen this one coming. Where was my arsenal of stones? Why wasn't I prepared to fight? I felt a goliath-sized spear pierce my heart, and the unanswered questions that followed were like having a giant stand over me, mocking what I had done with my life, defying me. Defying my faith.

"Ready or not" didn't work the way I thought it should.

I wish I could state that, like David the shepherd boy, I slew a giant. But I can't. I was knocked down, with no strength of my own and no desire to get up. What I did have was a network of family and friends who held me and a familiar voice promising to never leave or forsake me. I needed that voice more than anything. It was hard to listen through my pain, but that voice was (and still is) with me.

24

STAGES OF GRIEF

"The baby hasn't moved since last night."

It was mid-day, and friends had come to drop off food and offer condolences. At my casual report, Mom announced, "I'll take you to the doctor." Off we went, without a thank-you or goodbye for our visitors.

The only time I've ever seen my mother get pushy or demand special attention was the day after Jack died. She insisted I should not be expected to remain in the waiting room but be "seen by the doctor immediately."

The nurse took us to an exam room before we had a chance to take a seat. The doctor listened. "There's a good strong heartbeat."

I cried hard. Mom's not a crier. She had a tear, but she didn't let it fall. The obstetrician provoked my baby to move by applying what felt like an enormous amount of pressure to my round belly. He prescribed a mild sedative, with instruction to take one nightly for the next three nights. It would help me get some sleep.

"Don't expect much movement over the next few days."

The nurse led us to the parking lot through the employee exit. Our privacy was preserved, and the women and children in the waiting room wouldn't see another expectant mother in crisis and wonder if whatever the doctor did to me, he might do to them as well. I wasn't sure whether the emotion was from relief because our baby still had a heartbeat or from knowing this baby would need more than I had to give.

Jack's note instructed there should be no funeral and no cemetery. I didn't like it, but I wanted to follow his wishes. Someone, possibly our pastor, suggested a memorial service for mine and the kids' sake. It would help us grieve and bring closure. A memorial service was planned, but I kept his wish for cremation.

With all the profound and comforting words spoken in the midst of a crisis, I doubt I'm alone in having the clumsy words of a well-wisher seared in my memory. One woman hugged Robbie as she challenged him to be the "man of the house" and to take care of his mom and sister. He was eight years old.

The presence and protection of a good friend sticks with you, as well, even if their exact words of comfort get lost in all the grief. One such friend sensed Paula's discomfort and discreetly rescued her from an inappropriate conversation on the other side of the room, taking Paula's hand and bringing her to me as I was in a long line receiving condolences.

Another friend hugged me tight and, without a word, invited a whispered confession of my selfish prayer, the one prayer I wished I could take back. She wasn't a psychologist or a psychiatrist. She didn't have a college degree. We were just prayer partners. But she knew what I needed to hear.

"Sometimes we pray a prayer from our heart without running it by our head, and sometimes we say a prayer from our head without it passing through our heart. Your mind could have been preparing for what your heart wasn't ready to handle," she told me.

She explained anticipatory grief in a way I could understand, and would follow up, months later, with some comments during a group discussion. We were learning about Job. She addressed the entire group, but I knew she was thinking of me and my feelings of guilt when she suggested we look at the story from the perspective of Job's wife.

Her wise and compassionate explanation went something like this:

"We typically think of Job's wife as a hindrance to Job's faith, as a negative, but consider Job's wife as a woman who'd lost everything along with Job and was watching her husband's extreme suffering. When she tells Job to 'curse God and die,' she was asking for release from extraordinary pain. We judge Job's wife based on a few words uttered on the worst day of her life. Anyone else we would forgive, but we somehow find it hard to offer grace to her—and to ourselves."

Through his tears, Robbie fired pragmatic and earnest questions. I answered where I could and told him "I don't know" when I didn't have an answer. When I just couldn't bring myself to give an honest answer in front of Paula, I would tell him, "We can talk about that later." Some of the answers made him angry, but the truth was important. It would take some time before all my answers were believable, not just for Robbie, but for me.

"Daddy loved you and Paula very much. He loved me too."

"Then why did he do that?"

"I don't know for sure, but he had a disease that made it hard for him to think straight. For some reason, he thought he was doing the best thing for all of us."

"How did he get the disease?"

"I think he inherited it from his mother."

"Do you have manic depression?"

"No. I don't."

It wasn't the end to his questioning. Over the next few months, he would ask teachers, aunts, uncles, and any stranger who appeared willing to talk. Once in a while he would come back to me for clarification of someone else's answer. When I noticed him asking questions about how to complete household chores that had been Jack's responsibility, I wondered if he wasn't taking being "the man of the house" to heart.

"Grandpa, I need to know how to change the oil in Mom's car."

"I can show you," Dad said. "But I've been thinking about taking the cars to the garage and letting someone else deal with the mess. You want to go with me?"

Paula asked one question that first night and repeated it several times over the next few months. "Mommy. Who will we live with if you go to heaven to be with Daddy?"

I had a question for Paula. How much had she seen? She didn't, or couldn't answer. I never asked again, and I prayed no one would ever ask that question of her.

Although I wouldn't appreciate it immediately, a five-minute phone conversation with Jack's psychiatrist gave me comfort. "Nothing you could have done would have prevented what happened, and nothing you did could have exacerbated John's illness or hastened his death."

There was some comfort in knowing he had mentioned, several times, how much he loved us and that Robbie, Paula, and I were the reason he sought help for his illness in the first place.

It helped to have a psychiatrist agree that my answers to Robbie and Paula were appropriate. She reminded me that although bipolar disorder has a hereditary component, children of mothers with the disorder were about twice as likely to have bipolar tendencies as children whose fathers had the illness.

"The best thing you can do to prevent mental illness in your children is to be a healthy and loving mother. Call me if there is anything I can do. Take care."

I considered how difficult it must have been for her to pick up the phone and offer condolences to me, but she was a professional. Her patient's name was John. My husband's name was Jack. I was thankful for the information she offered, and I didn't blame her for what Jack did, but it was fine that I never heard from her again.

To think that someone might approach one of my children for information made me cringe. Managing the comments and questions of friends, neighbors, and acquaintances was difficult enough for me. We would discuss the word *suicide*, but not yet. For several nights, it was *not tonight*.

Mom rocked Paula through the night. Robbie rested on their love seat, and I had the sofa. Sleep came in two to five minute increments, but one of us was always crying. I was aware that my sobbing could be heard throughout the house, or by anyone who might be ready to ring the doorbell. I've never seen an academy-award winner portray the kind of sobbing we experienced, and it continued off and on for days.

Audiences might be drawn, out of empathy and even curiosity, to sit with a crier for a little while, but it takes someone who has given part of their life to the mourner to stick around until the sun rises and through the days and nights of crying that follow. My mother was that person for me.

I went to church the next Sunday, in search of comfort and because it was my habit. We walked in at the last minute to avoid conversation. I sat through the announcements and a prayer, but my sobbing resumed when the music started and the flowers, still in place from the memorial service, caught my eye. I took the kids by their hands and left. Mom followed.

I learned to quiet the audible grief, but I could only stuff so much emotion before the tears would return. Heartache or heartbreak can create an actual physical pain—not imagined or psychosomatic, but real pain. It came from the left side of my chest and rose to my neck as a lump in my throat. It was a deep and unrelenting ache.

The medical name for what I experienced, *Takatsubo cardiomyopathy* (Broken Heart Syndrome), wasn't in any of my textbooks at the time. The pain mimics a heart attack so closely that it sends people to emergency rooms, but typically older people, not twenty-eight year old pregnant women.

My rapid heart rate concerned me, but I understood that treating my thyroid more aggressively meant increased risk for my unborn baby. The physical ache on the left side of my chest worried me, but for the baby, not for me. It lasted for a few weeks. The lump in my throat returned any time I thought of Jack. I noticed it well into 1985.

For me, the kind of emotional pain that inspires poets and songwriters never has gone away, but with time, it lost the ability to paralyze my thoughts and decisions. Years have passed, and the times I think of Jack with sadness still outnumber the times remembered with a smile. I've been through every stage of grief.

The stages of grief are universal and inescapable. Yet, we all grieve our own way, in our own time. Some of us fast-forward through a stage, making it hard to recognize, but we all go through at least five—denial, anger, bargaining, depression, and acceptance.

Grief hurts. It places our emotional, mental, social, spiritual, and physical well-being at risk. If one of those areas is already weak, I think that's where grief hurts the most and lasts the longest.

I sold Jack's Pinto. It marked my transition from acute mourning to ordinary grieving, the chronic phase. I didn't want to sell the car. It was a necessity.

Most of us make it through the mourning phase, what employers call the bereavement period, intact, having experienced at least a little denial, anger, bargaining, depression, and acceptance. The chronic phase is when we begin again. We all miss something the first time through the cycle to acceptance, and probably the second and the third. The chronic phase is where we choose to deal and heal or give in and give up.

Having two kids and another on the way forced me to deal and heal. With kids to raise, I couldn't hide or avoid the inevitable. Many people are alone in their grief. I wished to be alone some days. In the short term it would have been easier, but I was blessed with three long-term solutions.

I gave Jack's clothes away and rearranged our closet. I cleared things from his bathroom shelf and loaded it with baby stuff. His latest bottle of cologne was nearly full. It would have been a shame to throw it away. I tucked it into a box, along with his wallet, his Bible, and the other things from his dresser. When the period of mourning was over, the scent of his cologne when I opened that box heightened the grief, but I couldn't help myself.

I knew that Robbie had been rummaging through the box marked "Jack's Things" when I found items intended for safekeeping askew. I scolded him when the lid to the cologne went missing. Jack's cologne would last a year or two.

We all grieved differently. Dad went to his guitar. He would play and sing through a variety of songs. His repertoire stretched from hymns by Fanny Crosby to Elvis or Johnny Cash. The song before he returned his guitar to its place in the corner was always a song of encouragement. Dad may or may not have realized the therapeutic effect of his singing and playing, but it helped him cope, and even though we didn't feel like singing along, the words to the familiar songs had a way of drifting through and changing the atmosphere.

Mom spent time in the kitchen preparing our favorite foods. Robbie, Paula, and I had no appetite for several days, but someone was always available to eat her therapeutic Southern cooking. She was also the one to take care of business. She guided me in dealing with essential tasks and legal paperwork. Without her, I would have missed appointments, bills would have gone unpaid, and bedsheets might not have been changed. Mom shows affection by getting things done. She heaped a lot of extra love on us during those days.

Mom and Dad made long-term room for us in their home. The kids had comfortable bedrooms of their own when they weren't crawling into bed with Grandma and Grandpa. They set up a twin bed in the family room for me. I went back to Bellaire Street every day to pick up things as we needed them, and I stayed just long enough for a memory or two and a healthy cry.

On the Fourth of July the kids asked, "Can we go to the fireworks with Grandma and Grandpa?"

"Sure. That's a good idea."

"Are you going?"

"No. I don't think so. I need to stay home where it's cool."

Five minutes after they were out of the house I was angry. They would be out celebrating when their Daddy had died less than ten days earlier.

Robbie got sick after eating a hot dog, but he begged not to be taken home because he wanted to stay for the fireworks finale. At first, I thought he must have been avoiding coming home to me and all the crying. When he didn't have a fever or any other symptoms, I thought his upset stomach was grief manifested physically. Paula got clingy, but over the first few weeks she clung to her grandma more than to me.

Denial is commonly known as the first stage of grief. I suppose it's a defense mechanism. There wasn't a lot of room for denial in our situation. The lights, the sirens, the memorial service, and the mark from the rope on the rafter in the garage all pointed toward our harsh reality.

I would, with no provocation, hear Jack's voice or breathe in the scent of his soap as I felt him brush past me. A pleasing touch to my face or shoulder would startle me, but within the same second, reality would spoil the moment, and he wasn't there.

I hadn't seen him on the gurney or in the casket, which allowed me to imagine an elaborate hoax. I fantasized that Jack was in the hospital, refusing to come home until after a full recovery. Maybe that was his Pinto pulling into the driveway? Or maybe that was my version of denial.

Imaginary endings to our unfolding story came to my mind every night. Maybe the psychiatrist realized a misdiagnosis and discovered a small, operable, benign brain tumor. Maybe I came home half an hour earlier. Maybe a bolt of lightning or loud clap of thunder made Jack come to his senses just in time.

My imaginary stories didn't include Robbie and Paula trying to understand what happened to their daddy while I struggled with the truth. The word *suicide* was not part of my storylines. Maybe I'd realize I'd been dreaming. But all my imagining was dispelled when I opened my eyes.

Another form of my denial wasn't so easily recognized. It looked like strength, fortitude, and a solid faith. Some people are strong. I wanted to be one of them, so I pretended. That too was denial. I couldn't deny that Jack was gone, but I could deny that my life was in shambles, and I needed help.

The anger stage gets complicated. Most everything I've read about grieving teaches the stages of grief as fluid, having no distinct starting or stopping points. I learned that to be true. Anger comes out or gets stuffed differently depending on personality and circumstances. Robbie and Paula didn't demonstrate anger the way I did, but every stage of grief has smacked them too.

Robbie worked through the acute stage of anger within the first few months, but chronic, lingering anger caused him to rebel against my authority for the next couple of years. He struggled to concentrate on schoolwork. If I pushed, he pushed back. If I relaxed, he took advantage.

Paula was the close-to-perfect child. Smart, pretty, polite, and passionate, she had a temper, but it was seldom seen, and mild compared to mine and Robbie's. I recall one out of the ordinary temper tantrum, but during the year that immediately followed Jack's death, Paula gave me little cause for concern.

No one told me how to recognize the stages of grief in a child. What I knew about the stages of grief, I learned from a section of a chapter in a nursing textbook. I supposed that was enough, and that my motherly instincts would make up for any gaps in my understanding. It's only in hindsight that I see how much I missed. Either motherly instincts are for pets and wild animals, or mine were numbed in my own grief. It's also possible that young children use denial as a coping mechanism, and use it more skillfully than some adults.

I still loved Jack. Perhaps out of courtesy to me, no one other than me verbalized direct anger toward him, but it was there nonetheless. Exposing it brought on feelings of guilt and shame, so I redirected my anger to easier targets.

Ginny hadn't returned for the funeral. A six-hour drive or a short flight, and she didn't feel like she could ask one of her adult children to drive her. A flight was "out of the question." I legitimized my anger toward her with facts—facts that no one could or would dispute—but the bottom line was that Ginny was no more to blame for Jack's suicide than I was.

God got the silent treatment except for an occasional *why did you do this to me?* I didn't bother to open my Bible to find answers. *Why should I?* I'd been raised in the church. I already knew the answers. It was over a year before I found any solace in reading the sympathy cards, and even then, it was seldom the words penned by a professional poet, it was more likely the personal note and the signature that gave me comfort.

In the past, I'd found solace at the piano. The first time I went back to the house after the memorial service, I picked up the songbook

Jack had turned upside down to mark my place. The music came from my heart and through my fingers. I thought, for a moment, I might be feeling what Rhonda felt when she played. I didn't need the music once I started singing the words:

> *Great is Thy faithfulness. Great is Thy faithfulness.*
> *Morning by morning new mercies I see.*

I couldn't go on.

With fists in the air I called out, "God, is this what you call faithfulness? Where was *my* mercy? Put *that* in your hymnal!"

The songbook flew across the room. I collapsed onto the keyboard, but the sound wasn't angry enough to match what I was feeling inside. I tried again. The result was a bruised elbow and a startled neighbor. She had seen my car in the driveway, and was poised to knock on the frame of the screen door when the discord between my arms and the piano keys made her think that perhaps she had come a bad time.

I picked up the book after she offered condolences, then went back to the piano. I had to make myself read the words:

> *Great is Thy faithfulness, O God my Father.*
> *There is no shadow of turning with Thee.*
> *Thou changest not, Thy compassions, they fail not.*
> *As Thou hast been, Thou forever will be.*
> *Great is Thy faithfulness.*
> *Great is Thy faithfulness.*
> *Morning by morning new mercies I see.*
> *All I have needed Thy hand hath provided.*
> *Great is Thy faithfulness, Lord, unto me.*

It would become my favorite hymn, but not that day.

The person I was most angry with was me. I should have seen this coming. I should have recognized the signs. I nagged when I should have understood. I should have told him I appreciated him more often. I should have been a better housekeeper. I should have been more vivacious in the bedroom. I should have concentrated more on our marriage and less on nursing school or church. I should have looked for Jack as soon as I got home that evening. I should never have prayed that prayer.

Dad brought me a bag of furnace filters from the hardware store one day and volunteered to show me how to change them. Trouble is, he used the word "should" when he mentioned the frequency with which the filters ought to be changed. I blew up. Dad, who is almost never speechless, had no words to answer my loud and long tirade about hating to be told what I "should" do. I used words like "always" and "constantly" to add some drama to my tantrum. He hugged me tight until the crying stopped. I apologized. He forgot about it, but I didn't. I still remember the day my father, a strong man, absorbed my anger and didn't back away.

Jack had liked my long hair. He wasn't around to hear me yell or to take a punch, so I cut my hair. The next morning I cried over what I saw in the mirror and blamed him. I had an appointment to get braces on my teeth and wanted to cancel. The haircut with the braces was a bad decision. I would look horrific. This was Jack's fault.

Why did you let me do this? Why am I yelling at you when you're not here? Why everything!?

Mom tried to make me feel better, in part, to avoid the drama that accompanied my anger. She was a great one for activity and family meals to keep us distracted. On the occasion of my first birthday after Jack's death, she prepared a special meal and get-together and gave me a very nice onyx necklace and matching pair of earrings. She spent more than usual. The setting was similar to the sapphire necklace and earrings Jack had given me. I felt Mom's attempt to replace Jack as a giver of special gifts. It didn't hurt, but it didn't help either.

I'd lost my husband, my best friend, my lover, the father of my children, our family's breadwinner and mechanic, the person who changed furnace filters and could reach things on the top shelf. Jack was the person who finished my sentences and didn't mind when I finished his. I lost the man who ate the last few bites of leftovers in order to save space in the refrigerator. The onyx jewelry showed that Mom cared, and it put off my anger for an hour or two.

Mowing the lawn of a grieving, pregnant woman, might have made someone else feel charitable, but I refused all offers. Is there a better way to let anger out in public, than to yank on a lawn mower's cord, bounce it over rocks and twigs, jerk it around corners, and use it (along with some cutting words) to knock down innocent blades of grass? With the noise of the mower drowning out everyone else's voice, it was just me and the Lord. Whether my lips were moving or not, did I ever let him have it!

Why do I have to be the one who takes out the garbage, plunges the toilet, clears hair clogs from the drains, cleans out the fireplace, fills the gas tank, moves heavy furniture, and changes the furnace filter?

He listened to more—things I would never have been able to say to another soul. Then, as I showered off the sweat and grass clippings, God seemed to give me peace and rest from the anger. I know it was him. Anyone other than a true friend would have sent a humongous bill for such intense therapy sessions.

The saying that "a soft answer turns away wrath" is a trustworthy teaching from Proverbs 15:1. God demonstrated that to me. The loudest of my angry questions was not enough to block the softest of God's answers. Other verses of comfort and instruction came out of the blue with surprising frequency. I wasn't opening my Bible—He had to interrupt my thoughts with verses and themes I'd learned years before.

Because of my pregnancy and the kindness of family and friends, my responsibilities during the first few months after Jack died were pretty much limited to signing a few checks and managing my own personal hygiene. For those, I needed an occasional reminder. Mom and Dad took care of Robbie and Paula. I may have given them a bath on occasion, prepared a meal, or washed a few loads of laundry, but nothing was expected of me. My high-risk pregnancy shielded me from the day-to-day reality of others' anger.

Of the five stages in the grieving process, anger was the longest and the most pervasive for me. I'd been taught not to let anger lead to sin (Ephesians 4:26), but self-control wasn't one of my strongest qualities. My angry words brought release, albeit temporary and with regret.

It would be a while before I picked up my Bible for anything other than to complete a going-to-church look. I had no energy. My mind could not focus. I had no desire to commune with the one who had allowed this course in our family's history, except to quickly vent anger, assign blame, or accept a brief comfort.

The bargaining stage started when the lights and sirens left on that Tuesday evening. No, I didn't get down on my knees and beg, but I did promise God I would do my best to raise my children to know him and teach them his ways, if he would just somehow take care of us.

My first thoughts were of Robbie, Paula, and the baby still inside me. I didn't have the resources or the strength to raise three kids alone, and I knew it. What I did have, was the potential to really mess up. Foxhole promises don't always take place in real foxholes, and bargains made with God aren't always forgotten as soon as the crisis is over. Sometimes they stick for a lifetime.

I'm smarter than to attempt a deep theological discussion about right or wrong when it comes to bargaining with God. All I know, is that God took my attempts to bargain and turned them into comforting conversations where I was reminded of his already established promises.

Some of my bargaining attitude came from a place of doubt. Would God really have allowed this to happen if I were truly his child, and he loved me? I was bargaining for proof, not that God existed, but did he hear my prayer when I was six? Had that been real? Was God so angry with me that he changed his mind, and if so, what had I done to stir his anger?

It didn't take a meeting of seminary professors to get my answer. It was a verse, I'd memorized, that reminded me I was God's child:

"For I am persuaded that neither death nor life, nor angels nor principalities nor powers, nor things present nor things to come, nor height nor depth, nor any other created thing, shall be able to separate us from the love of God, which is in Christ Jesus our Lord" (Romans 8:38–39).

From a Bible story, a song, or maybe a public prayer, I'd heard something about a hedge of protection. I asked for it. I begged for it to be placed around my children, and he gave it.

I'm not saying I heard or felt that God would alter history because I begged or made a promise. I am saying, He reminded me of things He has been promising persons of faith since the beginning.

"Blessed be the LORD, Because he has heard the voice of my supplications! The LORD is my strength and my shield; my heart trusted in him, and I am helped; therefore my heart greatly rejoices, and with my song will I praise him" (Psalm 28:6–7).

I made several attempts to bargain with God. I'm a little embarrassed to admit our financial well-being was at the top of my mental list of stuff to worry about, but in all fairness, I had lost our family's health insurance along with our breadwinner. I was pregnant and would need some sort of treatment, probably surgery, for my thyroid problem after the baby was born, and the kids only had clothes to fit for the current season.

God knew the value of my promises, but He was gracious. In spite of those things, I was able to give a tithe through my church every week. He took care of our immediate needs through the generosity of loving family, friends, and a small amount of life insurance. We got through some lean years with a car that survived far beyond anyone's expectations, a debt-free home, and survivor's benefits from Social Security. He allowed me to continue with school through grants, scholarships, and student loans, then provided me with not just a job, but a career.

The denial and bargaining phases were brief. Anger crept in often. Never in a million years would I have admitted to depression, but it was eager and ready to take me down.

Sometimes depression was disguised as a feeling that all I needed was a short break. Others had to wait while I took my time making decisions or neglected to follow through with commitments altogether. Depression was (and is) a sneaky demon. Days would go by when I could barely get out of bed. My children were seeing in me some of the same behaviors they had seen in their father. At times, that hedge of protection I wanted for my kids was actually protecting them from me.

My depression looked different from Jack's. What I would have given to feel a manic phase, but it wasn't in me. The consequences of my depression were the same. I became, for a time, the absent parent my kids had to see every day.

I was still Rita. My personality hadn't changed, but I was different. No one asked me if I was depressed, or I might have recognized it sooner. I might also have slugged them, which is probably why no one asked. At first, it's not depression, it's sorrow. Then it's not depression because it's coping with stress. Asking when it becomes depression is like asking where blue turns to gray, or how much is too many pennies.

Were it not for the kids, though, I might still be in bed. They motivated me more than anyone or anything. When I succeeded, they praised me. When I failed, they encouraged me. I needed them as much as they needed me.

They say the final stage of grief, acceptance, comes after the other stages have been worked through. By definition, the term acceptance implies an ending, but after experiencing personal grief and years of observing others, I know that grieving never ends. I see acceptance as another transition, a change in the way we grieve, and a lessening of the intensity of emotion that comes with the thought or the mention of who, or what, we grieve.

When someone dies, they take more than themselves away from us. They take things like opportunities, lifestyles, and dreams. Just when we think we've accepted the loss of a loved one, we're reminded of something else we've lost, and the grieving process begins again. Maybe for only a day or a few minutes, but we grieve again.

When, five years after Jack died, a coworker's husband took his life, friends suggested I be the one to deliver the card and donations collected by our group. I trembled on the inside, but I was able to express our sympathy, hand her our gift, and let her know she would be in our thoughts and prayers. When she cried, my tears followed. As I backed out of her driveway, I realized I had begun to accept my own loss. The tears I wiped from my eyes were for my friend and her children, not for me and mine.

Jesus said, "Blessed are those who mourn, For they shall be comforted" (Matthew 5:4).

I misunderstood that verse. I was someone who mourned, yet I didn't always feel "comforted." I didn't know then what I understand now. Comfort, like joy and contentment, is found in relationship with Jesus Christ. I was comforted in spite of and through my grief. To understand that kind of comfort, I had to experience it.

25

JOY COMES IN THE MORNING

Dad wasn't one to take walks without some place to go, but he took me for evening walks. I had the feeling he wanted to tell me something, but he didn't get around to saying it until about a month into our evening routine.

"Rita," he said. "I never would have thought Jack would do what he did, but now that I think about it, there were clues."

"What kind of clues?"

"Well, nothing specific. Just clues. He bragged on you, Robbie and Paula. He told me the three of you were smart and could get along fine without him."

"But Dad..."

"I know. I feel like there must have been something I could have said or done, when there was nothing. Same goes for you. There was nothing you could have said. Nothing more you could have done."

Our walks gave the rest of the household a break from my moaning and complaining. Sometimes we stopped along the way to wait for a pain to subside, and sometimes I walked in spite of the discomfort. Near the end of August, when the heat and humidity gave everyone with any sense (and half a brain) an excuse to stay inside, Dad insisted on walking. I'd collapse on Mom and Dad's sofa after one of those walks. Dad would pour himself a cup of caffeinated and hot coffee, but not before bringing me an icy cold drink.

"Water. Here's some water."

I must have heard his lecture about the evils of sugary beverages fifty times. I was ready for his lecture to end, and for this pregnancy to be over. The baby squirmed into a new position after most of those walks. The waves of movement from inside my belly hurt, but the pain assured me that my baby was alive and strong.

The clock said 3:15 a.m. It was September 5, and my baby wasn't due until the 26th. I was awakened by a distinctive sensation. No pain or cramping. It felt like sharp little fingernails pinching me from the inside. I was amused.

They wouldn't be consecutive, but I might still be able to get a full eight hours of sleep after this trip to the bathroom. I raised my head to get out of bed and felt a warm gush.

This can't be happening to me. Women talk about losing bladder control, but older—much older women. Is this how it starts? You'd think there would be some warning. I won't be twenty-nine years old for another three weeks. This is unfair!

I threw back the covers, got out of bed, and turned on the light. When I looked back at the sheets to assess the damage, I didn't like what I saw.

"Jan! Get in here! My water broke, and it's green!"

From the bedroom around the corner came my sister's response: "Huh?"

"Look at it. Is that green?"

She stumbled in and stared for a moment. "Maybe it's something you ate?"

"No. They call it meconium stain. It means my baby is in distress. I need to get to the hospital."

Another contraction. This one I would not have been able to sleep through.

"Go wake up Mom and Dad."

They were already on their way downstairs. Mom was tying her robe. Now that I had raised the level of excitement to just below panic, it was time to be calm.

The four of us developed a plan. Mom, Dad, and I would get dressed and drive to the hospital. Jan would stay home with Robbie and Paula, who were still sleeping. And then another contraction. My dear sister, the same one who years earlier had told me I was adopted, helped me out of my pajamas and into clothes suitable for travel to the maternity ward. She watched from the picture window as we drove away.

Ordinarily, Dad would not have been allowed to leave the house with his hair uncombed and a partially tucked, unevenly buttoned shirt, but Mom didn't notice until we saw the flashing lights of a police car. In spite of her urging, Dad drove another block or two before pulling to the side of the road.

"Howard, just stay put. He'll come to you."

Dad wasn't going to wait for the police officer to call in his information. He bolted from behind the steering wheel and walked faster than usual toward the police car. The officer stepped out of his vehicle, hand near his hip, ready to serve and protect himself.

Mom noted it was about closing time for the taverns and men's clubs along that stretch of the road.

"Tuck in your shirt." She mumbled as though he would hear telepathically and obey.

She turned to face me. "He looks like a nightly customer. We sure don't need this. He is going to get himself hauled off to jail, and your baby will be born in the back seat of my car."

The conversation between Dad and the officer ended with a friendly wave, but Mom didn't let that stop her from telling Dad about what could have happened. The police officer followed us until we crossed a bridge, out of his jurisdiction, where another attentive police vehicle followed us to the emergency room.

My labor progressed fast. I was ready to move to the delivery room after a couple of hours. Dad mentioned to the nurse that he had not been able to see any of his own children born.

"Is it all right if he comes in with you?" the nurse asked me. "All moms need someone to hold their hand, and we can maintain your modesty."

It was more than "all right." I didn't want to be alone, and I thought about how special it would be for Dad. The nurse handed him some surgical scrubs, with directions to a changing room and the delivery room where he would join us. They wheeled me away.

"A couple of good pushes, and we'll be done here. You're doing great," the doctor said.

A nurse reminded everyone in the room, "This is a meconium baby."

Meconium is the term used for a baby's first bowel movement. When it happens before birth, it indicates that a baby is under stress. Because it can cause a serious lung infection, every precaution is taken not to allow the newborn to take a first breath until the meconium is suctioned from the baby's airway.

With the next contraction came the kind of pressure that would have caused my baby to be born—except the doctor pushed back before the contraction ended.

"Don't push. We need to suction before your baby takes a breath. Hang on."

Everyone in the room (I quit counting after six) moved to the foot of the delivery table. The obstetrician worked quickly, but twenty seconds felt like ten minutes. As soon as he quit holding pressure, my baby girl was fully born.

She was carried to the other side of the room, where specialists were prepared to work on a baby with a dangerous goiter. One of the doctors had been in my room earlier, offering reassurance of their ability and readiness to resuscitate a baby with life-threatening airway issues. He was young and seemed arrogant. Or did he own the kind of confidence my baby would need?

I heard my baby cry and watched the same doctor lead the majority of people from the room. I sensed their disappointment in the loss of a teaching opportunity, which was great news for me. My baby must be breathing on her own.

My heart began to pound hard and fast. I pressed my hand into my chest as though I could restrain my heart from exploding through my rib cage. No pain, just a sensation of impending doom. All of the people who had sauntered out of the room a minute before, were rushing back in as I was losing consciousness.

When I woke up, the same group of bystanders was leaving the room again.

"Is she okay?" I asked.

"Your baby is fine. She's perfect. Ten fingers. Ten toes. No goiter. A nine Apgar score."

"Where is my dad?"

One of the nurses snickered. "We lost your dad. He never made it to the delivery room."

Mom told me later that Dad was in the restroom the entire time, under a little "stress" himself. He always did get a little weak in the knees if he saw one of us injured or bleeding, but this was a first.

My obstetrician finished with that thing obstetricians usually do after a delivery. Another doctor explained that I had experienced a thyroid "storm." My thyroid released a surge of hormone, causing my heart rate to speed up, but they had given me a drug to stop my heart and force it to do a reset.

"The drug did what it was supposed to do," he explained. "Your heart is now at a normal rate, and you should be fine. You know you'll be on some medication that your baby can't have. You know not to breast feed your baby?"

"I know."

They wheeled me back to my room, but kept her for testing and observation. I didn't get to hold her for at least an hour after her delivery. When the nurse finally brought her to me, I heard the same caution against breastfeeding. Over the next forty-eight hours, I would hear the rationale for bottle-feeding at least seven times. "This medication gets into mom's milk and it's not safe for baby."

The baby was more sleepy than hungry, but the nurse handed me a bottle of formula and waited for me to start the feedings. She took to the bottle, almost against her will, as she gazed into my face. I thought her eyes looked like Jack's, and I didn't want them to close.

"My baby smiled at me."

The nurse didn't believe me, "Probably just gas."

"Look, she did it again."

"Babies do that," she said. "They make a million adorable faces and gestures until you get your camera focused or someone else walks in the room. Get used to it, honey. She'll be trying to make a fool of you for the next eighteen years."

My roommate, who had delivered her little boy the night before, asked if she could take a closer look at my baby. "She's beautiful. What's her name?"

"I don't know yet."

"I heard that you couldn't nurse. Is there something wrong?"

I explained about my thyroid and the medication I had to take while I was pregnant, the medication they gave me in the delivery room, and the medication I would need when I went home. My roommate was the first to hear me tell the whole story behind the pregnancy, from the vasectomy to Paula's prayer and Jack's death. The dress rehearsal didn't go well. She interrupted every few sentences with a question or sympathetic comment and closed with an apology for causing tears on what was supposed to one of the happiest days of my life.

I appreciated the kindness in her listening. Her considerate questions seemed to come from a place of concern rather than an opportunity for gossip. I knew people would talk and the truth would get twisted. The truth mattered to me. I trusted her to treat me fairly in any of her future conversations. The experience of telling my story to my hospital roommate helped me know that, for the average listener, less of my story was better.

The minute my roommate returned to her side of the room and her newly born, baby boy, I sat upright, and laid my baby on my lap. The receiving blanket and the little undershirt came off. I checked her over, counting everything that could be counted, feeling for any abnormal lumps or bumps. I checked both her tiny feet for reflexes, and made sure the creases in her arms and legs were symmetrical. Then I counted everything again. I opened her diaper. "Yep," I told her. "You're a girl."

If anyone had made that official announcement in the delivery room, I didn't remember.

Mom and Dad brought Robbie and Paula to see their new sister.

Robbie was every bit as excited as Paula, engaging each and every staff person who entered the room with questions. Before he left, he knew the purpose of every piece of equipment in the room. Paula just wanted to touch and stroke her real baby's hair. It was fine and blonde.

"Look Mommy, she smiled at me!"

"Oh, that's just gas," my mom said, but Paula and I knew better.

"What should we name her? We need to decide today."

My question was directed toward Paula. Jack and I had decided to give Paula's choice of names extra consideration, but beyond that, there had been no talk of names.

"Can we name her Amy?" Paula asked.

"Oh, I don't know. I haven't decided yet. I was thinking about Joy, since she came early in the morning."

Mom cleared her throat. "I saw that name in a book, spelled A-i-m-e-e. It's French. I think it's cute. It means beloved."

Apparently, she and Paula had been talking. Between the two of them there were several suggested middle names. Some of them already in use by Paula's dolls.

"All right. Let's name her Aimee Jo. I like it. Short and sweet. It suits her. We can tell Uncle Joe we named her after him, but we had to leave off the 'e' because they charge by the letter for a birth certificate."

Aimee Jo was perfectly healthy. I cried tears of joy at the saying of her name. Hormones can cause a temporary euphoria that lasts for a few hours, but this was joy. Aimee brought joy.

I thought of the verse, "Weeping may endure for a night, but joy comes in the morning" (Psalm 30:5b). Later, when the nurse brought in the birth certificate form, I almost added the letter y to the end of her middle name, but we already loved her as Aimee Jo.

The day Aimee was born was the day I decided to never stop dreaming. A fairytale happily-ever-after was not to be, but Jack's death didn't take away my dream of watching our kids play, grow, accomplish good things, and experience great love.

I've noticed how the best fairytales balance struggle with hope.

The struggle must be difficult enough for hope to be nearly invisible, and the ending needs to be appealing enough to attract even the most hopeless. That's where I found myself on the day Aimee was born—balancing the greatest struggle of my life with hope for the happiest ever after possible. Goliath would be relentless, but I knew, deep down, that God is faithful. My life was so much better than a fairytale.

26

ISN'T ONE GIANT ENOUGH?

The hospital offered new parents a candlelight dinner on the evening before taking their newborn home. They presented a lovely meal, complete with crisp white linens, fine china, and a small vase with either a pink or blue carnation. The food smelled amazing as they wheeled the table past me to the couple on the other side of the curtain.

I was already crying hard enough that my roommate and her husband must have heard me stifling sobs. The more I thought of reasons to be grateful, the harder it was to control the tears.

I tried apologizing through the short curtain dividing our room. "I'm sorry. Enjoy your dinner. I'm having a hard time dealing with all my emotions, but I'm all right. Please enjoy your dinner. It smells amazing." My apology went unanswered.

A nurse outside my door was stopping someone. "This visiting hour is for fathers only."

Jan was in the hallway, about to enter our room. Compassion prevailed after Jan explained why I was crying. She sat with me and Aimee during father's hour. I picked at the food on my hospital tray, Jan held her new little niece for the first time, and Aimee Jo slept. Other than the sound of flatware scraping plates, my roommate and her husband ate their celebratory meal in absolute silence.

I knew enough single moms to know I'd be judged, and done some judging of my own, so I didn't remove my wedding rings. Innocent and ordinary comments by hospital staff about fathers were painful and plentiful. I understood, and thought no less of anyone for the awkward and pity-filled responses when people first learned I had recently been widowed.

I told myself it didn't matter what people thought, but it did. The most difficult question to answer was also the most common: "What happened?"

It wasn't only about shame or embarrassment. There was no brief answer. I tested every conceivable reply to that question. All of the short answer options said suicide, even if the word wasn't used. I saw judgment on the questioner whether it was present or not. Judgment on Jack, and judgment on me. My own attitudes didn't hurt me much until Jack died. Then, they began to sting.

There was also something about the timing in having someone ask me what happened. When "What happened?" was the first thing out of a person's mouth after hearing I was widowed, I believed they cared more about the scoop of my story than about me.

By the time we left the hospital I had memorized a brief response to the question I heard most often: "It's too painful to talk about right now. Do you mind?"

The majority found a gracious way to verbalize a brief condolence after that request and move on, to a different topic or a different room. More than a few (people who should have known better) thought their own need to know outweighed my request and continued with their investigation into my private grief.

In the crowded waiting room of my doctor's office, there were only three empty seats. I took the middle one and used the diaper bag as a barrier between me and the person to my right, and my purse to hold the seat to my left. Aimee, the only newborn in the room, caught the attention of the other patients.

A friendly young lady, with a large birth defect on her face, offered a typical compliment given to the mother of any baby. Then she followed with a comment and a question typically offered to me.

"Her hair is so blonde. Did she get that from her daddy?"

"Could have."

My one and two word answers weren't discouraging her small

talk. The young lady couldn't have known I also had a defect, a hidden scar that I wanted to keep hiding. She continued until one of her questions led to, "My husband passed away."

The phrase came out so easily, considering it was the first time I had used it, but then I felt guilty for telling a lie. No part of Jack's death was passive.

"What happened?"

I gave my rote answer, "It's too painful to talk about. Do you mind?"

She didn't give me an awkward look or search for her next word. I saw no pity. Her hand reached out to touch me, but she landed it on the diaper bag as though she'd been the object of a stranger wanting to touch, and had learned the importance of boundaries.

"I'm sorry to hear about your husband. I expect you get a lot of questions from complete strangers?" She took a breath. "You know, I get questions about my birthmark. People need to know how it got there. It was hardest when I was a teenager, but I'm used to it now. One time I told a cashier it was contagious and rubbed my money on my face before I handed it to her. That was way overboard, but it sure felt good. A schoolteacher once asked me why I didn't have surgery. He told me he thought I'd be pretty. I knew I wasn't pretty. He didn't need to remind me. I have to let comments and questions like that bounce right off, otherwise I'd get mad every day. People don't know what to say, but they have to say something."

The nurse called the young lady toward the back hallway and the exam rooms. I sensed that God had sent an angel to tell me I wasn't alone, and to talk to everyone present about careless conversation and curious questions.

Family and friends were sensitive to my emotional state. They gave us a baby shower and included Robbie and Paula in the gift-giving. One of the most difficult things for them was to talk about Jack. They didn't do it often, but sometimes his name would slip out. Some of the things they said, I needed to hear. Yes, Aimee Jo did look a lot like her father, and yes, he would have been proud.

Tears came any time Jack's name was mentioned, and often when it wasn't. If someone felt awkward around me, afraid to say the wrong thing, I sensed it, and the tears would come. When a conversation hushed the moment I entered a room, I assumed why, and the tears would come.

When I was six years old, and Dad warned me about the "goliaths out there," I prayed whenever I passed through big shadows and dark alleys. Now, I was twenty-nine years old, and still afraid of giants, some real and some imaginary. I questioned whether my prayers would be effective, but I prayed anyway.

Thyroid surgery was scheduled for the November after Aimee was born. It wasn't that surgery compared to the goliath I met on the night Jack died. I dreaded the pain, but I knew it was manageable. I trusted my doctors, and was ready to be done with it, whatever "it" was. The giant that scared me now was cancer.

Wasn't one goliath enough? You have to let all these other giants beat up on me? Those weren't my exact words, but that was my attitude and my prayer.

I woke up in the recovery room with excruciating pain, and couldn't speak. My throat felt as though it had been stuffed with sandpaper, and it hurt to move my head in any direction or move my tongue to moisten my dry lips. I knew what that meant, or at least I thought I did.

My arms and legs were restrained. I was alive, but I wondered for how long and if they had "gotten it all." I'd spent enough time in hospitals, both as a patient and as a student, to know how to get the attention of nursing staff. I fought the restraints enough to make the gurney dance. In return, I got some medication in my IV and a nurse's promise that the restraints would be removed if I would lie still.

The pain subsided, and the restraints were relaxed. I kept my part of our deal by calmly bringing my hand toward my throat, to find—no bandage?

The nurse answered my puzzled gaze.

"The anesthesiologist was unable to insert the breathing tube needed to perform the surgery because the nodules on your thyroid were large enough to deviate your trachea. He tried several times, which is why your throat hurts. Your surgery has to be postponed until your throat recovers from the trauma, and a specialist is available to use a scope-type instrument for inserting the breathing tube."

Two weeks later, my throat was sprayed with some awful stuff that smelled and tasted vaguely of banana. It numbed my throat, for which I was grateful. I would need to be wide awake and cooperative when they inserted the breathing tube.

The specialist, a pulmonologist, coached me, "Let's do this in one attempt. No matter how much you want to take a breath, you need to hold it."

"Okay."

"Take in as much breath as possible and hold it. Two practice breaths. We'll go on three."

After the first breath, I apologized. "That wasn't very good. I can do better."

My second breath wasn't as good as the first, but it didn't matter. The scope was blocking my airway.

Someone said, "You're doing great."

I wasn't.

"Swallow."

Or did he tell me not to swallow? My brain sent signals that rebounded and went nowhere. I tried, but I couldn't swallow. Or was I swallowing and couldn't tell because my throat was numb?

My left arm had an IV and was taped to a side board. The nurse tasked with preventing my right hand from grabbing the tube must have been an athlete. I'd been instructed, and I'd understood this would be "uncomfortable," but I was suffocating.

"Five more seconds. Hold it. Hold it."

My mouth and lips were dry, but I heard myself gurgling on a gel lubricant that turned to liquid in the warmth of my throat. The confidence with which I had signed the form giving the doctors and hospital permission to take me to the brink of suffocation was gone. *This must be what it feels like to drown.*

I prayed, "*Lord, help me.*"

His answer came in the form of a cool fluid traveling from a vein in my elbow to my head. I didn't have time to count backwards from ten to eight before I was feeling the influence of anesthesia.

It would be a couple of months before I was ready to offer a prayer of praise and gratitude for skilled, compassionate physicians and that strong-armed nurse, but I woke up peaceably. Two-thirds from the left side and one-half of the right side of my thyroid were removed, but no cancer.

This time, a large bandage covered an incision. It hurt to raise my head or shoulders, and my throat hurt, but I didn't need to shake the gurney to get pain medication.

The last day of our medical insurance coverage through Jack's employer was thirty days after his death. The same attorney who was handling Jack's worker's compensation claim wrote a letter, using the term pre-existing. He requested the company extend coverage for both the pregnancy and the thyroid conditions. According to the policy, they had no legal obligation, but it was worth a try.

"No charge. It's just a letter," he said.

When the thirty days had passed and the insurance company hadn't answered, I was forced to either buy an individual policy (pricey!) or accept an unknown amount of medical debt (risky!). Jack's worker's compensation claim was settled within days of that phone call from the attorney, and the check arrived before my first premium was due. Using the bulk of that money to buy insurance was almost as painful as the childbirth and thyroid surgery would be.

A written response from either Jack's company or their insurance carrier was never produced, but from a confounding telephone explanation, I gathered that newborn delivery would be covered because fifty percent of the pregnancy was Jack's responsibility and Jack was the employee. Newborn care, and any procedures involving my thyroid, would not be covered.

The receptionist who made the call, turned out to be a woman of her word, and the delivery was not included on my part of that hospital bill. Newborn care was, which gave me one more reason to be thankful for my beautiful and healthy baby girl.

Mom prepared, per usual, a huge turkey dinner for Thanksgiving Day. I was struggling with being thankful when my heart was still breaking over Jack. I could smell the turkey and all the fixings, but something had happened to my taste buds during surgery, and I couldn't taste anything salty, sweet, sour, bitter—nothing. Just one more reason I didn't want to celebrate Thanksgiving Day.

In his blessing over our meal, Dad found a way to pray what we all were feeling. We hadn't expected our typical Thanksgiving holiday, and knew tears would happen. Dad's prayer got them started. Some families sit around the table and list reasons for being thankful *before* the first bite. Not us. Mom worked hard to serve hot meals and would have been insulted if we let her effort get cold. We ate while it was hot and counted blessings between bites and through some tears.

I think I was the last at the table to voice thanks. "I'm thankful that God answered Paula's prayer with a baby girl instead of a baby boy."

"Why is that?" someone asked.

"If he had given us a boy, I would have to pay for a circumcision, because that comes under "newborn care."

I regretted use of the word "circumcision" at the dinner table. It gave Robbie incentive to create questions and be an obnoxious eight-year old boy, but it was good to laugh around Mom's dinner table again.

As it turned out, the total of all the hospital bills was within a hundred dollars of what I paid in insurance premiums.

Some financial planning would be necessary if I wanted to enroll in winter classes, and delaying my entry into the workforce by one more semester was not an option. I called the offices of two of my doctors.

"I'm calling to find out how much I owe for doctor's visits. It's been eight weeks, and I haven't received a bill."

Both receptionists responded as though I was crazy. Both came back with the same answer. "Your balance is zero."

"No. It can't be."

"Yes, it says you have a zero balance. The doctor wrote off your office and hospital visits as professional courtesy."

"Professional courtesy?" I knew the term, but didn't expect it would be applied to me.

"But I'm not a doctor. I'm just a nursing student."

"That's what is says on the balance sheet, ma'am."

I was ready to be thankful for my skilled, compassionate physicians and that strong-armed nurse. What a feeling. That's the way my God slings stones at giants.

We gradually began our move back to Bellaire Street. Mom and Dad never complained about our intrusion into their home, but I was well aware the four of us had taken over controlling interest in their home and lives. They let us decide when, but once I recovered from my surgery, it was easier to stay home than it was to go back and forth, especially with a baby and all the baby paraphernalia. I think it was the need of space for all the Christmas toys that prompted our move home.

Grandma's house would always be a second home for Robbie, Paula, and Aimee. The same recipe tasted better when served at her table. Grandpa spoiled them with praise. My kids weren't perfect, but Grandpa saw only their good. They did everything possible to keep from disappointing my parents.

Moving back into our house on Bellaire wasn't easy, but financially, it was our best option. The kids had already lost enough. It would be too much to ask them to give up their neighborhood. Just writing the words "our best option" takes me back. Without Jack as a confidant and partner in decision making, my children were involved in every one of my major decisions, and most of the minor ones.

The easiest decisions were those involving money. The answer was too often, "No." So, when Robbie and Paula asked to go to Florida for a theme park and beach vacation, they were awe struck when I said, "Yes." My mom used her vacation time to watch Aimee while Robbie, Paula, and I flew south for a spring break. That was a good decision.

During the early months after Jack's death, I dreaded stepping over the threshold of our home without him, just me and three kids. I think that's when I started to develop a reputation for being the last to leave a party. It was easier to stay and help someone else clean up their mess than it was to go home and face my own.

Seeing happy couples holding hands or a man sitting with one arm around his wife could bring on my tears. Watching my happily married friends and neighbors sometimes swept me into a depression. If those images bothered me, then images of fathers with their children must have been hard for my children to see.

As difficult as it was to observe what I thought was the ideal family, I wanted Rob, Paula, and Aimee to know what it looked like and to strive for it. I prayed for them to have excellent dreams and expectations. I prayed for their future spouses.

We were in church every Sunday. The kids were used to attending children's church, but now they preferred to sit in the sanctuary with me. I hoped the change was because they wanted to stay close to me and not because they wanted to avoid negative looks, comments, or questions from teachers or other children. I knew they were loved by their teachers, but I liked being able to watch over them.

God used music. The songs Jack and I played on the stereo, or that his father sang in church, didn't bring a tear or two; they caused tears to flow. But there was healing in some of those tears.

Every song printed in one Sunday's bulletin had something to do with heaven. The mix of old hymns and new choruses prepared our mood for a sermon about life after death. I'd been able, with discretion, to wipe away tears as I exited the choir loft to take a seat in the congregation with Robbie and Paula. They too had been discrete. We listened through the sermon with dry eyes. Then the music started again, and so did my tears.

My thoughts were on Jack. He had no more pain or suffering. He would have cried, and Jesus would have wiped away his tears. I would see him again, and he would be more perfect than in any of my memories.

They were happy tears—tears of relief—but I wanted to be alone, and I didn't want to involve Robbie and Paula in a public weeping session, so I slipped out of the auditorium. Other than a little smeared mascara, I had composed myself by the time the rest of the congregation was dismissed. The three of us usually went as a crew to pick up our precious Aimee from the church nursery, so I waited for Robbie and Paula in the church foyer.

I noticed arms reaching and a hug heading my way, so I intervened by offering my right hand to a fellow worshiper. She assaulted me anyway—with a full chest hug.

"Rita, I know how you must feel," she said. "You may not see Jack again, but you'll be reunited with so many other family and friends when you get to heaven."

I pushed to be released. She squeezed harder. I patted her back, signifying an end to the hugging. Now, I was aware that several pairs of eyes and ears were focused on us, Robbie's and Paula's included. Was she ignorant of what the Bible teaches and doesn't teach, or was she just plain mean? Against my will, the rest of my mascara was smeared onto her pastel blouse. My verbal arsenal was stocked and ready, but I stopped short of slinging stones. Our friendship would not have survived the onslaught. I would have gone for a knockout, but this lady was not a goliath. She wasn't even a giant.

27

FIRSTS AND LASTS

Firsts were hard.

Aimee was less than four months old on New Year's Eve of 1984. I had no plans to party or celebrate. Even so, it felt like a punch in the gut when someone invited me to be the volunteer babysitter rather than join the party.

We played games. I had more than enough salty and sugary snacks prepared with bottles of soda to wash them down. The kids had a blast, all seven of them, and I must admit, I played too. We must have played too hard, because the kids fell asleep by 10 p.m.

When the ball dropped at midnight, I jumped off the sofa to press tears from my eyes with a cool washcloth. Parents would start knocking on my door to claim their sleeping kids within minutes, and bitterness is no way to start a new year, or a new life.

Rob, Paula, and Aimee managed, on a regular basis, to remind me of the joy in my life. They forced me to see that joy, tainted with sorrow, is still joy.

The one-year rule (you know, the rule about moving on after a lover is gone) made sense for me logically and emotionally, but I never did see a magic difference between day 365 and day 366. Life continued to throw firsts and lasts our way. That was neither a good nor a bad thing. As far as I cared, it could have been a five-year rule.

The first song Paula played on her child-sized violin was "Mississippi River." Jack's little girl could spell it fast and play it well.

She practiced in front of a mirror. Paula loved mirrors, and mirrors loved her back. I took a picture of her with her first official backpack on her first day of school. No drama. It was a day for new friends. She loved everyone and everything about kindergarten.

Robbie got into his first real fight that winter. No fists were involved. When a boy, a year older and a head taller than him, threatened Paula on the way to school, Robbie grabbed the back side of the bully's coat and proceeded to slam his face into a pile of hard-crusted snow. A neighborhood mother witnessed the incident and praised Robbie for standing up to the long-time neighborhood bully.

Paula had her first and last violin recital that year, and I never heard any more of Robbie fighting. It was Aimee and her firsts that we celebrated most. Her first word was "Dada," and, yes, I heard it with a capital D. She met every infant milestone on time, if not early.

Other than her middle-of-the-night feedings, Aimee was an easy baby. She saved most of her fussiness for between 11 p.m. and the wee hours of the morning. The rocking chair soothed us while we grieved.

Paula requested something other than drive-thru food for her seventh birthday meal. We went to a burger joint where hamburgers and fries were served on breakable plates and soft drinks came in heavy-duty glasses. We could eat inside a restaurant, and I would still be able to pass out lunch money the next day. My goal was no spills, no fights, and not a wasted bite. We were well on our way to meeting it and waiting for the check.

Ten-year-old Robbie had been manipulating us with kindness, and we were loving it. I planned to understand his motive later. He also thanked the server each time she came to our table. He suggested, with her in close proximity, and using a most grown-up voice, "We should do this more often."

Did I mention that ours was the cutest and curviest server in the place?

Two-year-old Aimee was traveling for the first time without a diaper bag. Paula made her restroom request, every bit as urgent, right after Aimee's. I translated Robbie's grown-up behavior as a sign he could handle a bit more responsibility. It was Paula's birthday, but he was the one who seemed older.

"Robbie, all the tables are full. We need to make room for more customers. Go to the counter and pay the tab while I take your sisters to the restroom. Then go back to the table and use the change for a little tip."

"Okay."

Minutes after we buckled up and I drove away, I requested my change.

"What change?"

"The change from the money I gave you."

"I used it for the tip, just like you said."

That young lady, who would become our favorite server, must have been thrilled to get a $19 tip for our $21 tab. A quiet voice told me not to spoil Paula's birthday or our memorable evening. Then another voice came from the back seat.

"Mom, doesn't God love a cheerful tipper?"

Later that week we discussed, as a family, the practice of tipping. We talked about how both Jack and John appreciated good service, and they tended to over-tip. The cutest and curviest servers knew the way to their tables. A talk about manipulating females with kindness and pretentious words should probably have happened, but I didn't have a lecture plan that wouldn't critically warp a skill that Robbie might depend on one day.

The fifth chapter of 1 Timothy encourages younger widows to marry, supposing the temptation to enter into an ungodly relationship is great, but neither the one-year-rule nor biblical teachings had anything to do with my choice to avoid men.

I was still angry with Jack much of the time. I was afraid of being hurt or rejected. I was afraid to let a man get close to my children. Boyfriend and stepfather stories were never far from my thoughts of having a relationship. On those rare occasions when I wondered what it would be like to date, my self-esteem was at an all-time low. What man is looking for a woman with two school-aged children, a baby, and braces on her teeth?

Any man who expressed interest was turned away. The first few men who approached me looking for female companionship validated my feeling that there would never be another man in my life. It didn't matter whether it was anger, fear, or lack of self-esteem. I wasn't interested, or planning to ever be interested.

Men, who never before had reason to place a hand on me, seemed to feel liberty in offering comfort with a physical touch. Unless they were old enough to be my grandfather, a close family member, or a long-time friend, any touch other than a firm handshake repulsed me. It embarrassed me. I wasn't comforted.

I received invitations from single male acquaintances to "talk" or "have a cup of coffee." They tried to seem nonchalant, casual, and caring, but they were farther along (or pretended to be) on their singleness journey than me. I might have said yes to an impromptu invitation from a single male *friend,* but I didn't have any single male friends.

Jack wasn't one to have a long "to do" list. We had recently had some new carpet installed and he needed to replace the wooden floor trim. That was everything on his list. Two broken windows in the garage were added to the list.

The first one was broken by a fireman on the night Jack died. I'm not sure how or why, because the overhead door was unlocked. Robbie cracked the other window within a few weeks of the first. Never mind how that happened. Ten months later, the openings were still covered with cardboard and duct tape.

When a neighbor offered to do the repairs, I didn't resist. He completed the jobs as though it were his own home, or better. He carried his toolbox from the hallway to the kitchen where I was sitting at the kitchen table, paying bills.

I looked up. "Are you sure you won't let me pay you for more than the price of the glass?"

"No. No. You don't need to pay me for the glass."

I'd already pulled cash from my wallet—I'd promised to buy the glass since he offered to do the repairs. I held it out, but he hesitated.

I stifled an aggravated sigh and forced a smile. "I really appreciate this. Jack was talking about buying a saw to do the trim work. I think that's why he kept putting off doing the job. You saved me a lot of money."

I waved the money.

"He could have borrowed my saw."

"I doubt he would have. Jack didn't like asking for help."

"I still can't believe what happened." Condolences, like this one, were still common.

"I know. Me too."

"You look great," he added.

"Thanks, but I'm pretty run-down." The conversation was heading nowhere, but I wasn't sure how to close it. "The trim looks good."

"It was easy."

"With that saw, you can really make woodwork look professionally done."

He looked around. "Do you have more to do?"

"No. That was it. And the windows you did yesterday—they look like new."

He accepted half of the cash I was holding. I had been working him toward the door, but he stalled in front of the kitchen sink, where he asked for a glass of water. I went for the cupboard. He stopped me. "That's okay. I can get it myself."

Then he opened the wrong cupboard. I stepped in to get him a glass. We were alone in the house, and the little dance to avoid bumping our heads against the open cabinet doors made me uncomfortable.

"I don't mind mowing or doing any heavy work that you need. Moving furniture. You know . . . I'd offer to take care of your car, but that would be dangerous."

Maybe I was misreading our uneasy encounter. He and his wife had been good neighbors. We had spent lots of evenings standing around talking and laughing about our kids and other things. He hadn't said anything he wouldn't have said in front of his wife or Jack.

Then he said, "It's good you got your figure back."

"Not really. I have about fifteen pounds yet to lose."

"I don't know how you do it." He leaned in with outstretched arms, making me think this would bring closure to our interaction. The hug was longer and tighter than I expected. I pretended to hear a child calling, pushed him away, and stepped out the kitchen door. His wife had just stepped out onto their driveway and was calling his name. I wondered how long she had been looking for him, and from the look on his face, he wondered too.

When he didn't come around for several weeks, I thought I might have hurt his feelings or misinterpreted his intentions. He went back to being a good neighbor, and I no longer needed to ask advice or borrow tools. Jack's "to do" list was done.

I remember the time when an acquaintance stepped between myself and her husband. He had told me a joke, or said something causing me laugh. She made her disdain clear, and without knowing it, helped me to see how easily my own motives could be misinterpreted.

It's hard to read intention. I believe I got it right most of the time, and after talking with other newly single women over the years, I know my sense of vulnerability was a gift. The few men who crossed the boundary between awkward and inappropriate, I remember. The men who cared but were clumsy expressers of emotion made me feel uncomfortable for a moment, but those encounters have long since been forgotten with nothing to forgive.

My marital status changed the night Jack died, but emotionally, I was still a married woman, and responding to men like one. It was my mother who noticed, three years after Jack died, that I was still letting the diamond in my wedding rings capture the sunlight and my mood. Happy occasions turned melancholy when the diamond reminded me Jack was gone. It was time to accept my single mom status.

The rings came off. Mom gifted me with some cash, and a suggestion to have a local jeweler use the diamond to create a necklace. I tucked away the sapphire necklace Jack had given me and wore my beautiful diamond necklace day and night.

I returned to school in the fall of 1985, but nursing was more than a part-time interest now. I needed a career, so I transferred from a junior college to a university in order to earn a bachelor's degree.

During my first two semesters of nursing at the junior college, I had been in the hospital giving bed baths, medications (including injections), placing catheters, changing dressings, and observing surgeries, while the four year university students had been taking general education hours. The change in curriculum required I repeat all of the courses specific to nursing, including the clinical hours. I joined the juniors who were stepping into the hospital for the first time. It wasn't such a bad thing—repeating my clinical hours.

If they had asked me to repeat history or math, there would have been an argument, but I wanted to be a nurse, and I wanted to be a good one, so I didn't mind the repetition. It surprised me how much my pregnancy and Jack's illness had distracted from my learning. Tests were easier the second time, and I mastered the required nursing skills with much less anxiety than my new classmates.

The busyness was almost as helpful as the repetition. I had no room or time in my life to worry about men. Convincing myself that male affection was unnecessary and hazardous was easy, yet my eyes were adept at identifying a single man in a crowd.

When I needed a break from studying, I read books about strong, independent, unmarried women. I took pride in managing both the male and female roles for our household. When I couldn't pull off the role of Superwoman, my backup was reliable. Dad helped out by diagnosing car, heating, air-conditioning, and plumbing problems. There were few things he couldn't fix.

A few of my male friends were taking college courses to advance their careers. They complained about having to make time for study, but they had wives who prepared meals, cleaned house, did their laundry, and spent time with their kids. They had wives who mowed their lawns, called repairmen and typed their papers.

My brother, Kevin, pitched in to babysit for Aimee while I took classes. According to him, he wasn't the babysitting type, but Aimee was comfortable in his care because we had spent so much time around him. There were days when I would reach for her after coming home, and she would turn her face from me to bury it in his neck.

Jack's brother Joe and his wife, Debbie, opened their home whenever I needed a babysitter. Paula and Aimee enjoyed playing with their cousins, and Robbie liked having two more girls to tease and torment. Debbie ended up being the primary babysitter for Aimee during her preschool years. We shared a lot of firsts and lasts with Aunt Debbie and Uncle Joe.

I never sat with my little girl to tell her the complete story, but before Aimee was three years old she knew she was an answer to her sister's prayer and a miracle baby. She knew her daddy had died while she was still in my tummy, and she knew there were an awful lot of people who loved her.

One day, while waiting in line at the grocery store, a stranger started something.

"You sure have pretty blonde hair. Did you get that from your daddy?"

"My daddy died while I was still in mommy's tummy."

It was the stranger who deserved pity in this situation. Trapped with us in the checkout lane, she grabbed a handful of candy and a toy as if to apologize for her question.

"Here. Let me get these for you."

Aimee reached out her hands and accepted, of course.

"You don't need to do that," I said.

She insisted. It was awkward for me, waiting while a stranger paid for what felt like a handout.

"Aimee," I prodded. "What do you say?"

The stranger got her thank-you, and we got out of the store as fast as a woman with a cart full of groceries and a toddler could.

We waited in another line the next week with a different stranger who commented on what a "good little girl" she had been.

Aimee replied, "My daddy died."

The kind lady didn't hesitate to reach for candy and place it on the conveyor belt.

This time, I was ready with my response. "Please, no candy."

She ignored my soft request, and with a nod, instructed the cashier.

Week three: Aimee was a fast learner. I was so busy moving groceries from the cart, arranging and separating fragile items from the clumsy, crushing larger items, that I didn't pay attention to her words—but I heard the sad smile in Aimee's voice. Another stranger was reaching for a treat to pacify the poor little orphan. My sweet little toddler had created a perfect scam.

Once again I tried to stop it. "Ma'am, thank you, but I'm trying to teach her not to accept candy from strangers."

This determined lady stepped over to the next register, paid for the candy, and had the cashier put it in our basket. To top it off, both cashiers gave Aimee a lollipop.

When we got home, Aimee heard a lesson about how it was fine to tell people about Daddy if she wanted to, but she was never again to use that story to gain special favors or sympathy. To make sure she got the message, I made her share the candy with Robbie and Paula. I don't remember what words I used in my lecture, but I was cautious not to tarnish her innocence or bring her shame because of her fatherless situation.

I can't guarantee Aimee hasn't used the sympathy card since she was a toddler, but that was the last time it happened with me around.

I prayed she would come to me, and no one else, when she first questioned how her daddy died, and I prayed for the right words when that day came. Aimee's candy scam days had been over for a week, or two, when God answered that prayer.

Firsts got easier. Lasts became fewer and less painful.

28

UNDER CONSTRUCTION

The first year after Jack's death was about maintaining and guarding against opportunistic goliaths. The next few years were about rebuilding. A cute little song, "Kids Under Construction," reminded me that God wasn't finished with us. Survival was not in question or on my lips anymore as I prayed. We would survive. It was about trusting the Lord with our new kind of life.

Once again, we laughed. Not every day, but we laughed. We trusted. God proved himself to be our faithful friend. We worked and waited. In Mark 10:14–16, Jesus challenged the disciples (and me) to have faith like a child. Technically, those words were intended as less of a challenge and more like precise instruction. No adult could show me what faith was supposed to look like better than my toddler, my second-grader, and my fifth-grader.

I memorized Philippians 1:6 this way: "He who has begun a good work in *us* will complete it until the day of Jesus Christ." My children had their mean and ornery streaks on a regular basis. Come to think of it, I did too. But God was faithful.

Paula was a good big sister. She enjoyed holding Aimee's bottle. She folded laundry and arranged Aimee's clothes according to style and color. She lined up baby food jars, making meat, vegetables, and fruit easy to grab. She kept her covenant by sharing her room and toys. She loved reading to Aimee, and Aimee listened to her every word. If I had let her, Paula would have changed diapers. Potty-training Aimee was made easier with Paula's help.

She was the go-to person whenever anyone needed to know how to take care of her little sister. The pink sweater came out of her bottom drawer every few months for a fitting, and she was the one most proud when Aimee's arms were long enough (with the sleeves rolled) to wear her 3T hand-me-down.

Paula was a lovable girl, unless you were a stranger. She'd memorized every safety lesson from school, church, television commercials, and posters. Woe to the stranger who complimented her on her looks or attempted an innocent touch, particularly if the stranger was a man.

One old guy was sitting in a booth with his wife and another couple eating fried chicken. The place is a donut shop now, or I would seriously go there today for a mom and pop style meal. Paula was twirling around in her frilly Sunday dress, taking advantage of slippery shoes on a hard-waxed floor, while we waited for a table to be cleared. She loved that dress. The man noticed her. As we walked by their table, he held a hand out toward Paula and asked her to "do that again" for his wife and their dining companions.

"I don't talk to strangers!"

She might have adopted my anger toward and fear of being hurt by men. She had also taken on my irrational fear of dogs, even the small, family pet kind. I began to pay closer attention to my reactions and casual combination of verbal messages about men and dogs. If that poor old guy is still alive, and would come forward, I'd buy him another chicken dinner to replace the one we ruined.

Robbie, like a lot of boys his age, was embarrassed to hug his mom, and Aimee was just a baby. Paula still liked to sit on my lap and be rocked to sleep. There were many evenings when I had Aimee on one shoulder and Paula on the other, but I didn't mind. Paula was my everyday hug. Weeks or months would go by, and Paula would be the only person with whom I had shared a genuine hug.

After Jack's death, we gradually began to call Robbie "Rob." He fought doing his homework and struggled with getting passing grades for a couple of years. He saw a counselor at school for a while and then one day announced, "If I didn't leave class to spend time with the counselor, I might get better grades."

I'm not sure if grades were his true motive or if he was tired of being set apart from his classmates. Either way, he wanted me to be sure to let the counselor know he liked her and the decision to stop her services was not a personal one. It was still a struggle to get him to do his homework, but his grades did improve. He was promoted to the fourth and then the fifth grade.

The physical fatigue and weight of single motherhood overwhelmed me one day, and a break was not in sight. Rob felt a burst of compassion and forgot to be embarrassed. He hugged my neck. "We're doing so much better than some of my friends," he told me. "Their dads divorced them to live across town with another woman. The other kids get more toys than my friends do, and the other kids got to go on vacation in Florida."

When Rob was in the fifth grade, he brought home his report card with a checked box, indicating a parent-teacher conference was desired. I was puzzled by the request, but called the school and made the appointment.

The teacher had been good for Rob's self-esteem. He must have loved history, because Rob had begun to read more and ask questions whenever history was concerned. When it was time to prepare for the required fifth-grade test on the U.S. Constitution, he spent his free time reading and then repeating everything he had learned to anyone who would listen. He got a perfect "100%" on that test.

"Come on in and have a seat." Rob's teacher motioned for me to sit at a student desk and then adjusted another desk so he could sit facing me. I thanked him for accommodating my schedule and staying later than usual.

"You're my only parent conference, so it's not a problem. What are your concerns?"

For the first time in a long time, I had no concerns to offer Rob's teacher, but I mentioned some things that had been issues in past years. The teacher assured me that, except for some class clown type behaviors, typical among fifth-grade boys, Rob was doing better. He reported good things. Things I hadn't heard about Rob since before Jack died.

But what he was saying didn't add up. "I'm curious. If Rob is doing so much better academically, what did you need to discuss at this conference?"

The teacher looked confused. "I didn't request this conference."

"The box was checked on his report card, so I made the appointment."

"I didn't request any parent conferences this grading period."

We stared at each other as we came to the same conclusion. Rob had checked the box because he wanted us to meet.

When a forced confession took place over dinner that evening, I didn't scold. Rob wasn't the only fifth-grader to consider a scheme to unite their attractive male teacher with a single mother, but he was the only one bold enough to check the box.

The kids were excited to arrive at The Heart of Illinois Fair. It must have been in 1988, because that was Aimee's first fair experience, and I remember being able to promise the kids an all-inclusive, no worry about expense experience. I was working as a registered nurse by then. As I watched for an open parking spot, Paula explained (for Aimee's benefit) how it's possible to be cautious but polite and kind to strangers.

Then: "Whatever you do, always hold hands. That goes for you too, Paula."

It was Rob, and not me, instructing his sisters. I glanced through the rearview mirror and saw Paula and Aimee take each other's hands—respecting the wisdom of their preteen father figure.

Our lives had undergone the messiest part of the remodel. We had a new kind of life. We still lived on Goliath's Mountain, but once you know a goliath can't keep you down, other giants lose their power.

29

SLEEPING SINGLE IN A KING-SIZED BED

How often does a Midwestern, college student, single mother of three get to spend a huge chunk of her summer in Europe?

Some of my classmates were buzzing about an opportunity to earn a semester of college credits while traveling in Europe. The posters and flyers were enticing. It would be a once-in-a-lifetime, unforgettable experience, and the cost of a summer semester abroad would be about the same as a semester on campus.

Summer school was necessary in order for me to graduate with the traditional nursing students. I could spread the twelve hours of general education classes over two summers, or I could go to Europe. I read the fine print on the brochure over and over, looking for a reason not to experience Europe. I couldn't find one.

Being in Germany on the third anniversary of Jack's death would rekindle both good and bad memories, but three children would be my main consideration.

After a brief discussion with Mom and Dad, we determined the kids would be fine spending evenings and weekends with them. Monday through Friday would require a babysitter during the day. Most events in my life either involved the kids, or else they would tag along and find a quiet corner to entertain themselves while I did what I had to do. Babysitters were called upon only in desperation.

Rob and Paula celebrated when a friend, who happened to be the mother of two of their friends, agreed to watch them while I was gone. Problem solved, before any desperation.

Instead of sitting in classrooms the summer of 1987, I was going to study English literature in London, European history in Germany and Belgium, then learn a greater appreciation for music in the Austrian Alps near Salzburg. The final three credits for a course titled Western Civilization were earned upon turning in a postcard diary with descriptions of the significant architectural structures we visited throughout our travels.

London was just plain fun. There's no other way to describe it. All the required reading was to be done before we traveled. Our time in the city was meant to supplement and reinforce the impressions communicated in the literature. I finished the last chapter on the plane. Some students opened their first novel after checking in at the airport.

Every day, as advertised, was a once-in-a-lifetime experience. We walked where Charles Dickens walked. We discussed the writings of Virginia Woolf from inside the massive marble walls of museums and while relaxing in famous parks. We saw members of the royal family from a ten-person-thick parade route.

No matter how many times you circle Trafalgar Square, you can't see Big Ben from a seat on the wrong side of the bus. That wasn't in the syllabus outline, but I learned that important fact.

The trip meant more than education and new sights. In a way, it marked a re-opening of the warped doors leading to my heart, to my self-image, and to my beliefs about how a life without Jack could be.

I met a handsome physician from South Africa on our first day in Germany. He was dreading being alone for his last free afternoon at a conference being held in our hotel. When he heard we were from Illinois, he blended into our tour group. He had family in Chicago and hoped to join them after completing a fellowship program in pediatric oncology. I was singled out for some unknown reason, and he spent the afternoon walking with me through one of the castles on my list of assignments.

In the course of about four hours he heard my life story, and I heard his. His parents were conservative Baptists, like mine. He laughed at stories about my children and said he envied me for them. He and his wife had delayed adding to their family until they were settled in Chicago, and now he was both childless and widowed.

Midway through our afternoon, it occurred to me this handsome "doctor" might be creating his past to match the person he thought easiest to take advantage of. My first clue came when he expressed a desire not to "talk shop." Ah-ha! I'd caught him avoiding a conversation that would expose him for the fraud he was. But I honored his request and continued to enjoy his company.

It wasn't like a date, yet he insisted I join him in the hotel restaurant that evening. We ordered the same meal being served to my group from the university. He paid for my dinner and my company when both would have been free. It was a quiet booth, with a view and ambiance, as opposed to cafeteria seating in a large conference room. He drank a cola with his dinner. *Maybe he really is a doctor and a Baptist?*

We were running out of interesting conversation topics when he mentioned the advantages for healthcare providers working in the U.S. Since he was the one who turned the topic, I didn't mind adding my own comments and tossing him a few questions. He didn't realize he was being quizzed, but he passed my test. If he was a fraud, he was sophisticated enough to fool a nursing student, and had the forethought to print business cards.

He pulled one from his wallet. As I was examining it, looking for clues Sherlock Holmes style, he grabbed the card from my hand.

"Let me give you my home address and number."

He gave me the card after scribbling some weird looking letters and numbers on the back. Then he took out another card, and handed it to me. I used large block print, and included my middle name. I had just shared my address and phone number with a complete stranger—a first for me.

We shook hands. He touched my shoulder, and we said, "Goodbye."

I used one of my free days for a train ride and an emotional reunion with old friends. Reminiscing with Gene and Paula was sweet and fun, like I knew it would be. They were still doing the army life and had returned to Germany for another tour of duty. Gene was using his German language skills to advance his career, and they were a family of four by now.

Paula and I had let a few years pass without a phone conversation. It was easy to do. Anytime we picked up the phone to dial the other, we knew to allow at least an hour, and both of us had few uninterrupted hours to spare. This face-to-face meeting—a big factor in my decision to do the semester abroad—was a highlight of my summer.

It was good to be reminded of army life in Germany. It was good to laugh, instead of cry, during a conversation where Jack's name was used. The afternoon was too short. I fought tears on the way back to the train station. Soon after the conductor collected my ticket, the tears won.

The manager of our hotel, just outside Salzburg, was from Sri Lanka. Every morning he would bring a menu to the lead professor for approval. I was going over an assignment with the professor when the manager approached. He apologized for the "brief interruption." The professor approved the day's menu and then returned his attention to me.

"Have you ever had trout—fresh from a mountain stream?"

"I can't say that I have. I love catfish. Does it taste like catfish?"

"Just wait. You're in for a real treat. This will, I promise, be your best meal this summer."

I carried my books to a patio, where in order to study, I had to fight off daydreams brought on by the view of mountain peaks, winding streams, and wildflowers.

A group of hikers walked single file along a trail. They were about a half-day's hike away, and close to the top. My eyes were too weak to see which of them were male and which were female, but their laughter traveled with such clarity I could hear the difference. One of them started to yodel, and my impulse was to confuse them with a yodel of my own. I had yodeled, in the shower once, and if I yodeled now, the sound couldn't reach my family and friends back home, but word of it most certainly would. The thought that those faraway hikers probably had better vision than me was another constraint to my impulse.

Some of those wildflowers had been transplanted into small gardens around the hotel, where nothing about them was wild. Gardeners looked up from their pruning, weeding, and sweeping to wave at the hotel manager, who was approaching me. His name was Ravith, and he had noticed me and my textbook.

"If you need to study, you must return to your room. With all this beauty around, who can concentrate on study?"

I gave him a smile, then took it back. I was okay with him noticing me, but not with him seeing that I noticed him.

"I love the clean fresh air and the noises of nature." True, but so unlike anything I would say.

"We have nothing this beautiful in Sri Lanka."

"You're from Sri Lanka, and there's nothing this beautiful there. Really?"

"Really."

He leaned on a beam supporting the patio roof and enjoyed a couple deep breaths of mountain air. I re-opened the book to where my fingers had marked the page, and attempted to prove myself studious. It wouldn't be the beauty of nature that distracted me now. It would be his glances and his cologne.

He offered to bring me a beer.

"No, thank you."

"Americans want their beer cold. I forgot."

"No. I don't drink alcohol."

Ravith returned with a beer in one hand and a cola (warm) in the other. I thanked him for the cola and turned a page. He pulled a chair close to my chaise lounge.

"Do you have a boyfriend?"

"No."

"What? A pretty woman like you without a man?"

I smiled and gave him a slanted nod, letting him know I recognized his line. I'd heard it only one other time, but I'd seen his type in movies and on television.

He changed his approach, "You like trout?"

"I'm sure I will. The professor said our dinner was caught this morning from one of these mountain streams."

"I should give the professor the biggest one, but tonight I will set it aside for you."

"That's nice, but no need. I don't have a big appetite."

"I have never kissed a woman with metal straighteners on her teeth. May I kiss you?"

"No."

He jumped from his chair, dropped to one knee, grabbed both of my hands in his, and began to apologize. Sincere as he sounded, I thought he was overcompensating in order to avoid being reported to the professor, who might decide to take his next group of students elsewhere. I accepted his apology. His exotic accent, and the way he looked me in the eyes, gave me no other choice.

Ravith was not far from my thoughts the rest of the day.

Ann, another nontraditional nursing student, was my roommate for the semester. Other than the professors, we were the only ones on this trip over the age of twenty-one. We joined our classmates in the dining room when the aroma from a dessert tray passed through the lobby and under our noses. Pristine white linens, candles in crystal globes, and a bouquet of fresh flowers on each table caused us to stop and check that we were in the correct room. We had been given a dress code for the evening and expected a special meal, but this dinner looked to be above a student's budget and beyond most of our experience.

"The only thing missing is music." Ann's wish was granted inside a few minutes. As one server began to light candles, another brought in chairs. Musicians carrying stringed instruments followed.

By this time in our travels, Ann and I had regular mealtime companions in two academic, sober-minded, sophomore boys who hadn't managed to match up with any of the age-appropriate female students. The two of them had become comfortable with both Ann and me advising as to which girls to avoid, and which ones might be suitable for a date—a study date.

The boys were grateful (or at least they said so) to learn the proper use of eating utensils. A server brought wine, white towel over his forearm. Ravith came alongside him and placed a chilled cola in front of me.

"For you, Miss."

"You can call me Rita."

"Reetah," (elongating both short syllables), "enjoy your dinner."

According to the open-mouthed stares from my table partners, I had some explaining to do.

"What?" I asked. "He offered me a beer earlier and I told him I don't drink."

Ravith went on to check the head table. He had perfected the art of balancing service with socialization. He stepped back to let the servers do their job, and made it his pleasure to see that diners were content.

The next course was served whenever the lead professor placed his eating utensil on top of whatever plate was before him, and each course left us feeling anticipation for the next.

Ravith returned to our table.

"Is the music pleasing you?"

"It's beautiful, a very nice touch."

"Would you have a request?"

"Hmmm? I'd like to hear any of the songs from *The Sound of Music*. We toured the area where the movie was filmed this afternoon."

My request was relayed. There were only five musicians, but every harmony was covered. They were directed, not by the waving of a wand or a leader working rarely used facial muscles to pull music from them, but by some sort of intoxicating connection to notes on nonexistent pages.

Anyone making noise with their lips, crunching greens and raw vegetables, or dragging silver utensils across a plate was silenced and shamed for disturbing the passion between horse-haired bows and their polished, hourglass-shaped mistresses.

Having the entrée carried in on large trays held high in the air released us from our reticence, and the chatter of hungry college students soon equaled the sound of the music. The four of us were waiting patiently when Ravith relieved one of the servers of the final tray and placed it on a wooden stand near our table. He served Ann, then the two boys.

"This one is for you, Reetah." Again, with that accent.

My "thank you" was reminiscent of the shy girl who sat in the back of my junior high social studies classroom during roll call. Was it Ravith? Or was the queasy feeling because of the platter he had placed in front of me? I was stunned to see, not a trout filet, or the body of a fish, but a *trout*—head and all, with one eye looking my way. The tail extended over the end of the oblong platter farther than any of the others. This small-town girl had never looked into the eye of the fish she was about to eat.

"Bon appétit." Ravith walked away smiling and humming along with the instruments.

"One fish is enough for two of us. Rita's is enough for three."

The boys got busy using their utensils to slice away and enjoy their meaty fish. I blindfolded my poor dinner with my napkin.

Ann, by this time, had excellent nursing assessment skills. "Rita, you don't look so good. Are you alright?"

I was afraid to open my mouth and answer. A server jumped out of my way as I raced toward the exit.

Ravith was knocking on the door to my room before I finished washing my face. He had warm ginger ale and a small assortment of over-the-counter medications to offer. I was already feeling better, but I took the ginger ale.

"I'm sorry I had to leave before trying the fish. I hate to see it wasted."

"It won't be wasted. Your friends are sharing it."

I denied Ravith entrance into the room. His insisted that he only wanted to talk, so we compromised, and I carried my drink to the patio. The sun was beginning to make its way behind the mountain. If the hikers were still out there, they had about an hour to either find their way back or set up camp for the night. A pathway around the hotel was already lit with hanging lanterns.

Since Jack, this was as alone as I had been with a man.

"Are the sunsets here always so beautiful?" I asked.

"Rita. You are more beautiful than a sunset."

"Is that a line from an English movie? I haven't heard it."

"You made me think of it. It isn't from a movie."

"I wish you wouldn't try to manipulate me with over-the-top flattery. It will get you nowhere."

We sat, without speaking, for several minutes while I sipped my ginger ale. A warm breeze carried music to us from the dining room. It was a party of crickets that restarted our conversation.

I followed Ravith's poetic lead. "Have you noticed how the crickets are silent as long as the music plays, but when a song ends, they join together and cry out for an encore?"

"What is 'to manipulate'?"

I smiled. "I'm sorry, Ravith, if I misjudged you. You do think like a romantic, and I'm not used to that. I've only been with one man—my husband."

"You are married?"

"I was."

Knowing I had such a short time in Austria made it easy to answer and ask questions about personal life experiences with a man I didn't know and shouldn't trust. I'd seen him work in the dining room and knew he was working me. He must have weighed the odds between me and one of the younger college girls and seen me as an easier target.

Did he think I was wealthy? He had mentioned wanting to come to the States after finishing his hotel management courses. I wondered if he could be looking for a sponsor. A description of my lifestyle dispelled his assumption, or at least I hoped it did.

We talked about our childhoods and what had brought us to this place. We also talked of our goals, which were similarly simple. Our pasts were hugely different. He had been in several relationships, the most recent one ending when he had to choose between sending money home to his family and buying his girlfriend all the things she wanted.

What he told me sounded true enough. Was the skeptic in me causing me to feel this way, or was the eye of that poor bass still messing with my stomach?

"How many other women have you had this conversation with?"

"Only you, Rita. I don't enjoy talking with a woman. I do with you."

"Sure."

"Other women let me kiss them when I ask. You would kiss me too, except your friends might see." He was partially right.

"You only want to kiss me so you can say you've kissed a woman with metal in her mouth."

"No. I want to kiss you for the reason a man wants to kiss a woman. I want to manipulate you."

Ann was asleep when I turned out the light and crawled into my bed. I was restless for at least an hour, not concerned for the final exam in music appreciation that would occur in two short days, but regretting a missed kiss, and contemplating how I might arrange a second chance. Then there was guilt, over letting Ravith misuse the word manipulate. I would explain first thing in the morning.

The summer semester was coming to an end, and we were offered a few options: stay in Salzburg to study for the last day, spend the day skiing on a glacier, or take a bus trip to Venice. I chose Venice.

Ravith didn't like the idea. "Stay and spend the day with me. We could take a picnic on the mountain. I want a chance to know more of you."

"You mean you want to manipulate me."

"Yes."

Ravith heard my explanation of manipulate as I boarded the bus for Venice.

One day was not close to being enough, but I did enjoy St. Mark's Basilica, some shopping, a gondola ride, and the ambiance of the ancient city. Real Italian cooking served during an early evening cruise was meant to be the highlight of the trip, but it was hard to choose one thing as the best part of my day. It was well after midnight when I dropped into bed. Venice had been a good decision.

With the exam over (I did well), it was time to re-pack for the final time. I carried a box filled with souvenirs for the kids to the lobby, prepared for shipping. Lunch was being served, but I wasn't hungry. I decided to take one last stroll through town.

My thoughts of returning to enjoy these mountains with Rob, Paula, and Aimee were interrupted by a tap on my shoulder.

It was Ravith. We took our time walking back to the hotel while he shared more of his disappointments and dreams. He told me how even though he had been in Salzburg for nearly a year, he had seen a small portion of what I had seen in just ten days. He had never been to Venice. He wanted to bring his parents to Salzburg when he completed his schooling. They had never been more than one hundred miles from where they were born.

"Thank you for being friendly with me. Most of the American students talk with me only when they want something."

"You don't need to thank me. I enjoy talking with you."

He took me into the kitchen to introduce me to the staff, and asked the cook to bring us lunch. Except for the servers who were preparing tables for the evening meal, we were alone in the dining room. A second attempt to kiss me might have succeeded, but he asked permission first, and I wasn't sure how to respond. I couldn't admit, *Yes, I'd love to be kissed, but I'm not sure I want to be kissed by you.* The tilted shake of my head was intended to encourage without giving permission, and Ravith was a gentleman.

Our late lunch ruined my appetite for dinner, so I nibbled and relaxed with our party of four, listening to how everyone had spent their last full day in Europe. Ann and the boys turned to me. They had seen me with Ravith and expected more of a story than the truth had to offer. At first I was chided for not allowing him a kiss, but the teasing paused after I explained his request suggested more than a kiss. They acknowledged I had made a wise decision, then rummaged through every cliché and junior high-school joke until they had teased every strand of humor out of my situation.

One of the boys took a final comedic jab at my lack of a love life, then must have felt the pinch of irony in his teasing me, and a need for penance. He stood for minute of self-degradation, and without invitation or request, started singing the tune "Sleeping Single in a Double Bed." His classically inclined voice drew the attention of everyone in the room. What a relief when he couldn't remember all the words. And what a relief, when one of the junior girls had no idea he was satirizing a country music favorite, and took his focus off me by complimenting his singing.

She reminded me of a younger me when she encouraged him, "Why aren't you in choir? You should audition for fall semester."

He reminded me of Jack when he answered with a question, "There is a choir?"

Ann and I were startled by a soft knock on the door about an hour after settling in. We were hoping for at least six hours of sleep before our morning wakeup call. Ravith invited me to join him on the patio.

"Just a few breaths of night air. I promise to have you back in less than an hour. You can sleep on the plane. Come sit with me?"

A tray of cheese, crackers, and fruit was waiting for us on the patio. It occurred to me that, years ago, I had been wooed by a few teenaged boys, but never a man. I wished it could be Jack doing the wooing, but didn't let that stop me from savoring the attention.

Ravith had no idea the affect he had on my stomach. "I can get you something else if you like."

"No. I wasn't expecting this." I took a bite of cheese.

He asked me to "write" and send him "pictures."

"I don't have any good pictures. Maybe when my braces come off."

"No. No. I will take a picture of you tonight. You look beautiful in moonlight."

"But not more beautiful than the moon?"

"I wouldn't use words to manipulate you."

He took my hand and led me onto one of the paths away from the hotel.

"Where are we going?"

"To my apartment. To get my camera."

I pulled back.

"I'll wait here."

He was gone long enough for me to consider several scenarios for what might have happened if I had gone with him and stepped inside his apartment. I worried as much about what this man was thinking of me as I did for my virtue. I wasn't sure how I felt about Ravith, but even if he could be trusted, I was certain, he wasn't Jack. The conflict made me feel guilty.

He took a few pictures—most of me alone, but then he placed the camera on a ledge where he could activate a timer and dash into the frame with me before the flash. I agreed to write back if he wrote and sent copies of the pictures, but he didn't ask for my address, and I didn't offer.

He put his arms around me as we were saying our good-byes. It was a hug from a friend, but then we didn't separate. I expected a request, and I had three, four, maybe five seconds to decide how to answer when Ravith asked me for a kiss, but this time he didn't ask. He kissed me on the cheek, close to my lips, and then whispered in my ear, "I will miss you."

In less than twenty-four hours I would be home, having hugged and kissed the three most important people in my life. This Midwestern, college student, single mother of three was ready to curl up and sleep single in her king-sized bed.

Within a week of arriving home, I received a lovely letter that made me smile. Ravith had copied my address before letting the mailman take my package.

Another letter, from South Africa, was in my stack of mail when I arrived home. I corresponded with the physician for about a year. And I mean "corresponded" in a business or professional sense. It seemed we mailed monthly newsletters. Still, I enjoyed reading about his studies, interesting cases, and of course, his plans to move to Chicago. He always commented on the reports of my children. I sent him pictures.

If I mentioned a test or college course that presented a challenge, he would enclose an article or scribble out some notes of his own.

For such an intelligent man, didn't he realize that by the time his study aids arrived, my test score had been posted? As he stuffed the envelope, he might have been thinking, for such a smart girl, I should have started reading on these topics weeks ago.

I don't remember which of us sent the final newsletter, and I don't know if my former pen pal ever came to Chicago.

Ravith's letters stopped within a few months, with no hint of a reason. He caused me to realize that with every decision, a memory is made. Bad memories generally come from bad choices, and I believe that our fondest memories were made possible because of a good decision, whether it's ours or someone else's. I hoped that Ravith would consider me a fond memory, and that he would remember me for as long as I would remember him, but I expected he was already writing to another traveling female.

I am blessed with memories of that summer semester in Europe. My thoughts go back to London whenever I pick up a Charles Dickens classic. Castles and cathedrals, even in pictures, remind me of times in Germany. Some songs will always deliver an Austrian mountain view as clear and perfect as a postcard.

Once or twice a year, I pick up a garment or a fabric household item and notice a tag indicating it was made in Sri Lanka. I'm grateful for the privileges that come with being born in America each and every time I see that. What a relief it is to see one of those tags and not be reminded of how foolish I'd been to let a strange man take advantage of me. Instead, I smile and remember the man who wanted to kiss the lips of a woman with metal straighteners on her teeth.

30

FOR THE LOVE OF NURSING

From the moment the female patient was admitted, loud crying, alternating with random groaning noises had traveled through the door and walls of room 714. Her diagnosis was expressive aphasia. To lose one's ability to communicate through speech (expressive aphasia), without having had a stroke, was not so interesting a problem that any of my coworkers begged to be assigned to room 714.

I was fascinated, and would hear her noise whether she was my patient or not. I wrote "chest pain and traumatic expressive aphasia" next to her name and room number on my list of patients for the day.

It was chest pain that landed her on our cardiac unit. Our community hospital didn't have a psych unit. In giving report, the night nurse mimicked "714" by throwing her head back, pounding her chest, and otherwise adding a dramatization to the reporting of her "rough night." Liberal doses of pain medication hadn't helped, and no objective reason for the patient's behavior was included on her medical chart.

I walked into the private room, the one usually reserved for VIPs. Starting with the sickest patient had become routine, so I would have seen the patient with a low hemoglobin and worsening back pain over the past two hours, but he was already in the hallway, headed for the CT scanner.

I greeted 714 with, "I hear you didn't sleep well last night."

Like the night nurse, I interpreted her chest pounding and wailing gestures as attention seeking. As I straightened the bedside table and picked up tissues that had missed the trash can, I scrolled through my mental list of available mood-altering pills, then began to explain "our" plan for the day.

A burst of sobbing convulsed from deep inside her, interrupting the stating of my agenda. I recognized the pain in her eyes and felt the twinge of a familiar heartache.

"Is there something else going on? Something other than chest pain?"

She nodded with a look of relief. I handed her my clipboard and my pen.

Her hand trembled, but her penmanship was quite legible.

I just heard the news. My son committed suicide.

My inadequate, but automatic response: "I'm so sorry."

Five years after his death, the thought of Jack could still uncork a reservoir of tears. That day, it helped to remind myself that a license made me a registered *professional* nurse. Smeared mascara, a runny nose, and blubbering speech were not professional. Neither was providing anything less than my best nursing care to this patient.

I sat on the side of her bed, and in the time required for a deep breath and a sigh, I visualized an outline. The headers were:

I. This is an awful circumstance.
II. God knows, understands your loss, and cares.
III. God is able.
IV. I've been there, I'm proof, and I'm listening.

I shared just enough of my story to support the outline. She took my hand in hers—to comfort me. As had happened many times before, the conversation did an about-face the moment someone learned my husband had taken his own life, leaving me with an eight-year-old, a five-year-old, and a seven-month baby in the womb.

She was the patient. I had no cure or medication to cover her pain. All I had were words. It had been less than twenty-four hours since she had received horrible, life-changing news. I could think of nothing other than clichéd comments that, five years earlier, had landed on my personal scale somewhere between annoying and infuriating.

So I said, "Would you be able to describe the kind of pain you are experiencing?"

She wrote about the heavy feeling, starting in her heart and going into her neck. She wrote the words *constant*, *deep*, and *ache*.

"It's been a while, but I remember having similar symptoms when my husband died. You might have what is called Broken Heart Syndrome. I'll make sure the doctor knows everything that's going on and see what he thinks. I'm just an RN."

"So I can live with a broken heart?" she wrote.

"You can live with a broken heart."

We wiped our tears. This emotional and needy patient, with whom I had dreaded a mandatory encounter, was now the patient who drew me. Room 714 was where my skills and experience were needed most that day.

I had taped photos of Rob, Paula, and Aimee on my clipboard so their images would be with me at work. They provided the start of many casual conversations. Their happy faces opened my second encounter with the patient in room 714. She pointed to my clipboard.

I handed her my pen again. She wrote, "How did you do it?"

I gave her my answer, giving credit to my family, friends, and faith in Jesus Christ. "Tell me. At any point in your son's life, did he hear that Jesus loved him?"

God knew where I was going with this question, but I didn't. I practiced my praying without ceasing, and reminded God of his promise to be with me "always."

"He went to church and Bible school on a bus when he was young."

She continued to write, telling me that she didn't think he'd read it lately, but he had been given a Bible for memorizing verses at Vacation Bible School. She also wrote of her son's most recent struggles. The page was nearly full. Her last sentence was, "He used to love Jesus."

I noticed a Gideon hardback on her bedside table that wasn't there earlier. I assumed she had been the one to remove it from the drawer. There was something I wanted my patient to hear.

I opened the Bible and read, "For I am persuaded that neither death nor life, nor angels nor principalities nor powers, nor things present nor things to come, nor height nor depth, nor any other created thing, shall be able to separate us from the love of God, which is in Christ Jesus our Lord" (Romans 8:38–39).

I closed the Bible and put it back on the table.

"It comforts me to know my husband decided to trust Jesus when he was a child," I said. "If your son confessed he was a sinner and needed a savior, if he trusted Jesus as that Savior and asked for relationship with him, then your son is with Jesus right now."

We cried, we hugged, and she allowed me to pray with her. Did those verses in Romans mean anything less because her son and Jack had died from complications of a mental illness as opposed to an accident, cancer, or any other disease?

Did her sobbing and groaning stop? No, but she quieted, and because she was tired after a restless night (or maybe it was the medication) she napped during most of my shift.

My patient returned to the unit with her husband a week after being discharged. They brought me a box of chocolates and a photo of a handsome young man. She wanted me to see the son she would remember. Her husband hugged my neck and kissed my cheek. She told me, without needing paper or pen, how much she appreciated my care.

Sometimes, when the words in my brain can't quite make it out of my mouth, I think of my patient with expressive aphasia, and I pray for her. I also wonder how she's doing and if she remembers the nurse assigned to room 714.

Another patient made quite an imprint in my memory.

He had suffered a severe heart attack, been resuscitated by paramedics, and would have gone straight to surgery, but his kidneys had failed, and multiple medical problems complicated his already poor prognosis. Each of his doctors, during their discussions of prognosis and risk, offered an opportunity for him to decline the procedure.

I was his dialysis nurse while he was in the intensive care unit, which meant we spent about four hours together every day. His treatments were challenging. I initiated a code blue twice during the week prior to his surgery.

On the morning of his surgery the hospital chaplain came into his hospital room.

"If I ever stepped foot inside a church, the roof would probably cave in," the patient told him.

The chaplain had no response, except to offer a prayer. My patient didn't agree to a prayer, but he didn't refuse, so the chaplain prayed, wished him well, shook his hand, and left. The patient was one of those people whose sense of humor would be "the last to go." He had a joke for everyone who entered his room, and few were re-runs, but the chaplain had nothing new to offer from one day to the next.

Each of the chaplain's visits opened the door for conversation during the dialysis treatment. We talked about church. He brought up some common excuses for not attending, most of them funny. He described hypocrites (calling a few by name), worshiping on the golf course or under the covers, and the fact that Christians can't decide which denomination is right. I was able, a couple of times, to mention Jesus and relationship as opposed to religion, but my patient was a jokester.

The nature of my job placed me in hospital rooms in the middle of what would otherwise be private family conversations. I was used to tuning out voices and conversations that didn't involve me, but I overheard the chaplain being ridiculed for his memorized prayer.

"If that chaplain's prayer works and I make it through this surgery, I'm going to quit smoking, and we should go to church."

His wife laughed.

I was already exposed as a Christ follower, and assumed that when I left the room, my patient and his wife would enjoy a word or two about the Jesus freak of a dialysis nurse. I thought I may as well give them something to talk about.

"I heard that, and I'm going to hold you to it."

With that said, I wondered how he could make it through open-heart surgery when he barely made it through his dialysis treatments. Since that uninvited comment didn't get me thrown out of the room, I took another risk.

"In case the chaplain's prayer wasn't enough, do you mind if I pray with you too?"

He acquiesced, in the same way he had with the chaplain. I wasn't encouraged, but I had committed, so I prayed. Nothing flowery or particularly spiritual, as I recall. Perhaps even clumsy.

He was still attached to the breathing machine from surgery two days later, unable to speak and on strong sedatives. There was talk he wouldn't make it out of the hospital. His wife sat at his bedside, except for occasional breaks. We were both in the room one day when the same chaplain came in to recite his prayer.

After he left, the chaplain was once again the topic of a conversation. This time, it wasn't ridicule.

My patient's wife asked me. "Have you noticed he says the same prayer every day?"

"Yes."

"He lays a hand on the person's arm and prays with one eye closed and the other on the TV screen."

I had to agree. He did seem insincere, and unprofessional. We had a brief discussion about prayer. Okay. I did most of the talking, but she contributed enough to the conversation for me to know she was interested.

"I definitely believe in prayer," I told her. "I've got three kids because kid number two asked for a baby sister. I'm reminded that God answers prayer every time I write a check for school clothes and dance lessons."

She told me about some friends who claimed to have had prayers answered, ". . . but I can't say that God has answered any of my prayers."

She admitted to worrying about things like whether or not there was a hell, and how uncomfortable she felt when her husband joked about going there, but they had "built a good life without God's help, so why pray now?"

Lady, I thought, *your husband is laying there unresponsive. These may be his last days, and you wonder why you should pray now?*

I knew I might lose my job if I spoke my first thought, so I busied myself by charting my patient's vital signs and rearranging supplies. What made me think I was qualified for this conversation or to address this family's spiritual needs? Where were all the brilliant comments bolded and highlighted in the margins of all those Bible study workbooks when I needed them?

I wheeled the dialysis machine out of the room.

"See you tomorrow."

That's the best I can come up with? See you tomorrow! What if this woman's husband doesn't have a tomorrow? I had messed up. *Probably too late to pray.* But I did.

Instead of me taking my dialysis machine to his room, two days later, my patient was doing well enough to be wheeled downstairs where we could have up to six patients on dialysis machines at one time. He was all smiles and humming a pleasant tune. Midway through his treatment, another nurse asked him what he was humming.

"I have no idea, but it's been going through my head since I woke up from the anesthesia, and it won't go away."

My jaw dropped, opening my mouth too wide for words. My eyes locked into a questioning stare. He was humming the tune to "All Hail the Power of Jesus' Name." I imagined my reaction unbecoming, and before speaking, I recovered the demeanor of a professional nurse.

"I know that song."

"You do? What is it?"

I sang the first verse softly. "Is that the song you were humming?"

"It is."

There were a hundred things I wanted to say and ask—starting with how that particular song got into his head. It wouldn't have been played on his favorite country radio station.

His treatment was complete. Duty calls, and schedules rule

sometimes. I disconnected his tubes with my usual speed and readied the machine for my next patient.

The hospital transporter was slow in bringing a wheelchair to take him back to his room. Ordinarily I'd have been calling the transport dispatcher to speed things along, but I tried patience this time.

"Sing the words to that song again."

I sang another verse as I threaded new tubing on the machine for my next patient.

"I can't get that tune out of my head," he said. "Maybe God is trying to tell me something?"

This had turned into an amazing day. First, an opportunity for my alto voice to sing the melody, and now, a front row seat to watch God work!

"Do you remember what you said right before being wheeled away for his surgery?" I asked.

He remembered. "Do you think I should call the preacher, and make sure their insurance covers roof cave-ins?"

The next day he asked if I would write down the words to the tune. I went to my purse and brought out a photocopied page from a church hymnal. The name, address, and phone number of a familiar church (near his home) was written on the back.

"Just in case you want to call first, and check on that insurance thing."

Falling in love with nursing was easy. It happened within the first few months of graduating. Patients, like these two, confirmed that a commitment to my profession was worthwhile. Nursing has never let me down. People and organizations have forgotten and broken promises, but the profession of nursing has been faithful.

Nursing became my best friend. But as a best friend, it's never been enough.

With Jack's death, I lost my best friend on earth. Three kids, church responsibilities, nursing school, and then a career, left little to no time for finding a new one. All the good ones, the traditional human kind, were taken.

About five years after the suicide, my need for friendship turned to a craving. For Jack's absence as a provider, and a handyman, there was a substitute. My parents supported my single parenting, and I had accepted the empty side of my bed, but I still longed for my best friend.

I began to actively consider and mentally interview potential new best friends. The process felt a little like moving on. If I had put an ad in the paper, it would have read something like this: *Wanted: Best friend. Must be available all hours of the day and night. Must be a good listener, financially independent, emotionally stable, and love supreme pizza. Ideal candidate will have reliable transportation and excellent credit rating. Applicants with past failures and/or well-behaved, potty-trained children will be considered. Willing to train. Liars and whiners need not apply.*

31

SILVER SMILES

More than one of the nurses and staff on my unit had noticed the recent interactions between me and a not so popular doctor. One of them was delighted to announce, "There's a chemistry between you. Everyone sees it."

"What? He's married."

"Go for it. He can either like you or make you miserable," one of the nursing assistants said. "I've seen his wife. He likes you."

Not knowing how to defend what I thought was my pristine reputation, I hurried into the restroom, claiming my lunch had not agreed with me. I'd seen how this doctor's sarcasm and arrogance put dread into the hearts of other nurses, but he had always been professional and pleasant with me. It fluffed my nursing ego to think I knew how to handle his unpredictable personality and had never been the target of his demeaning tirades.

My internal radar had ignored signals when our conversations turned personal, even after the classic hint of an unsatisfactory relationship with his wife.

I returned to my friends at the nurses' desk with a freshened face and an announcement.

"There is no chemistry between us."

Why this man would choose me was a mystery. I had another year before the wires and brackets on my teeth could be traded in for a less noticeable retainer. The heavy metal caused the inside of my mouth to bleed, made it difficult to manage my saliva, and ruled out eating many of my favorite foods in public.

I had considered my orthodontist a double blessing. He was correcting my overbite, while providing a great deterrent to romantic thoughts initiated by me or headed in my direction. My orthodontist wasn't foolproof, and neither was I.

A renewed professional demeanor, on my part, worked to prevent disaster. I also prayed, then thanked God when I still had my job a month later, but the strangest thing still troubled me.

I missed the attention, and felt a little jealous when a married nurse, from another unit, accepted to his advances. Nothing about the doctor attracted me in a physical way. He wasn't particularly handsome. Not nearly as handsome as Jack. So why did I feel guilty? I hadn't lusted after another woman's husband. But, I had remembered what it felt like to have a man lust after me. That's what troubled me.

Other men seemed able to bring out my silver smile. They were the goodhearted ones who looked beyond the tired woman with three kids, student loans, and a house in need of repair, but they were single for good reason, and lonelier than me.

I was also an occasional target. A few not-so-goodhearted men saw the braces and feigned interest when the conversation turned to kids, student loans, or the gutters that were starting to fall off the house. They saw me as the lonelier one—the vulnerable one. Two or three men were surprised to learn that lonely and vulnerable didn't add up to stupid.

At least once a week, a certain paramedic and his partner would wheel a patient into the hospital unit where I worked. I'd seen how other nurses left their regular duties to offer assistance in the room where he was picking up or dropping off patients. He had a handsome smile and confident personality, but his rotund physique made me wonder how he created such a competition among nurses.

I *may* have been one of the nurses to volunteer lifting help on the day he noticed I wasn't wearing a wedding ring. He invited me to meet him for a drink after work. I politely declined. "I don't drink."

"A cheap date. I like that."

Again, that feeling of being pursued caused me to blush, which can be construed as encouragement. "I'm flattered, but no," I said. "Saturday night is when I usually read my Sunday school lesson."

That, I thought, was the perfect line. I'd use it again, should the opportunity ever arise.

But he was a paramedic, trained in CPR and other things where one thinks long and hard before giving up. Now, I'd made him laugh. He thought I was playing along, and maybe I was.

Catching male attention didn't come easy for me. Intentional behaviors left me feeling goofy, awkward, and embarrassed. Accidents seemed to capture male attention, but the accuracy and effectiveness of Cupid's arrow suffers when you're falling down stairs or dragging a trail of toilet paper from a public restroom.

An older and wiser nurse called this paramedic a "Picasso-like flirt." I asked her to explain.

"Pablo Picasso is quoted as saying, 'Art is a lie that makes us realize the truth.' Your paramedic has mastered the art of flirting." She warned that I was a mere amateur.

The paramedic said something flattering every time he saw me. He used patients as excuses to call the unit and ask for me. His partner pulled me aside to plead his case. My coworkers began to shame me for not giving him a chance.

The break room majority voted, "Just one date."

I protested. He couldn't really be interested in me. I was five or six years older, with three kids and braces on my teeth. One more thought lingered, but I couldn't speak of it. *Would any man be interested in a woman after learning her former husband had committed suicide?*

"If he asks again. I'll go."

He asked again.

I bought a new dress—not too dressy, but less casual than jeans. Modest, but I thought flattering. I was nervously excited as I curled my hair and cut the tags off my latest purchase. Only then did I notice the label: DRY CLEAN ONLY. I didn't expect this date would be worth a dry cleaning bill. What was I thinking?

I was unsure what I was anticipating, but my stomach had been in knots all day. The lipstick I applied and wiped off for the fourth or fifth time left a natural pink glow. I used it to add some color to my cheeks. Then the clock and the bathroom mirror told me I had wasted enough time playing with thoughts of how to avoid an awkward good-night kiss. My silver smile turned upside down. I had nothing to worry about.

The time spent in front of my bathroom mirror wasn't a complete waste. I found myself reminiscing about soft, slow kisses that could melt my knees. Memories of Jack were becoming few and fleeting, but my imagination could feed on them and get carried away in front of that mirror. Then came the guilt—the moment I dared to consider another man might put his lips to mine.

When my date was ten minutes late, I threatened to put my jeans back on and take the kids to a movie.

"No, Mom. You probably got the time wrong."

I hadn't felt lonely on a Saturday night in quite some time, but when he never showed, I felt like a lonely fool.

"Mom! The phone! It's a man!" My kids had learned to hold their hands over the receiver before yelling, but embarrassing me brought them happiness. (I think, in that instance, it was Rob.)

It was nearly 10 p.m. The apology sounded rehearsed, and he didn't afford me the courtesy of a plausible explanation. I declined his request for a second chance. The next Monday morning, my coworker hit me with an, "I told you so," and without knowing it, a former high school classmate pounded those words in.

After not seeing each other for years, we happened to meet in the potato chip aisle of a grocery store. We chatted, and what a coincidence. She knew someone, who knew someone, who knew a certain paramedic.

It seems this paramedic had been talking to a nurse who was interested in him, but for some reason they had yet to go on a date. My old friend went on to say, "The nurse works at your hospital. I think on your unit."

Evidently, he had planned to take "the nurse" out to dinner, but his ex-girlfriend (a "sure thing") asked him to a party, and he couldn't resist.

"He ditched the nurse," she said. "What a cheapskate. Why buy an expensive meal, when our party was free and so was his ex?"

By now, I was thinking I knew the paramedic she was talking about, and was ready to confirm my suspicion by asking when her party was, but she continued with her story.

"You won't believe this, Rita! His ex was already getting chummy with another guy by the time he showed up at our house. He spent the rest of the night whining and getting drunk."

My former classmate hinted for the name of the nurse. Had she not even considered that it could be me? Did she think I wasn't pretty enough to have attracted the man, or did she assume I was too smart to fall for him? Either way, I saw no need to solve her little mystery. After excusing myself for rushing our reunion, and suggesting we "get together real soon," I flashed one of my silver smiles and moved on to the canned foods isle.

32

INVITING GIANTS

After being alone in a crowd for nearly six years, I agreed to my first-ever blind date. We liked each other instantly. The kids teased me as though I was a classmate, not their mother. They interrogated me, wanting to know everything about him, and didn't protest too much when they learned he was divorced and fifteen years older than me.

Rob was thirteen, barely responsible to babysit his sisters for a few hours at a time. Paula was ten. They preferred to stay at "Grandma's house" when I went on dates. Five-year-old Aimee liked to come along with me and my date on occasion, but Grandma always had food and games that made a date with Mom and her boyfriend boring by comparison.

In a different way than nursing, Rob, Paula, and Aimee had become my best friend in three. Rob could be counted on as an adviser. He got it right most of the time, and when he missed the mark, his comedic relief brought perspective to our problems. Household jobs requiring some muscle became his responsibility.

Paula was our defense attorney some days and our mama bear on others. Brave beyond her physical size, strong words and tenacity were but two of her strengths. When she rehearsed an argument at the dinner table, we all felt empowered.

Aimee liked to clean. She celebrated being able to stand at the sink (with a stool) and wash dishes. Giving her a mop and bucket, a spray bottle, or any sort of cleaner or polish, was almost as good as a trip to the toy store. Emotional messes brought out the best in her. Aimee was our encourager.

I found my boyfriend's attention intoxicating, and getting out of the house was a pleasant distraction from my homebody existence. We went to sporting events, out to eat, to movies, and (don't laugh) for long walks in the park. He listened. I trusted him. I could talk to him about anything, except the guilt I felt for the time I took from my children and gave to him.

I was still busy, raising three active kids, when he started building his retirement home. We lived separate lives. I didn't golf with him, and he didn't go to church with me. Neither of us was completely comfortable in each other's lives, but I loved him and was certain he loved me.

References to marriage were frequent, yet not specific. Against my better judgment, and with my eyes wide open to the inevitable, our relationship lasted five years before I gave him an ultimatum.

He declined.

I was heartbroken. Nothing like the syndrome, but angry and confused when he had a golf date with another woman inside a week, and married her within months.

Rob, my young but confident advisor, pointed out the necessity and wisdom of my ultimatum. Paula, my fearless defender, reminded me that I was fine before I met him and listed all the reasons I would be fine without him. Aimee, my domestic helper, joined me in some deep housecleaning therapy.

Word of my new single status spread. Social media in 1995 meant letting a few people, at every possible social gathering, know I was available. The string of one-time blind dates that ensued is proof that the old-fashioned grapevine method worked. That is of course, if quantity outweighs quality.

It took some time and awkward dinners before I figured out what was happening: matchmakers thought I would be good for the man, without considering if the man might be good for me. I developed a knack for making up my mind whether there would be a second date during the entree and letting men know this would be our one and only date before the server offered dessert. It didn't seem right to add expense to the tab (even if the chocolate looked luscious) for a one-date-stand.

Once, during my process of preparing a kind gentleman for his letdown, he beat me to the punch. "Rita, I've enjoyed our conversation, and it's hard to say this, but you're just not my type."

Ouch! He didn't offer dessert, and the chocolate did look luscious.

Failed attempts to find Mr. Right pushed me toward a resolve to appreciate the benefits of being single. Working overtime was a blessing in more ways than financially. The kids were older and their stuff did cost more, but they were busy with extracurricular activities, and some days I was little more than an ATM and a taxi. Any free time was spent sleeping, reading, or playing at the piano—which, to be sure, is not the same as playing the piano.

With no time to look, Mr. Right would have to find me.

But my work, my nonhuman best friend, had become stale. My life was stale. Even if Mr. Right came along, he wouldn't notice someone so uninspired and uninspiring as me. A change was required to either fill the void in my life or distract me from it.

I resigned my position at the hospital, and accepted a job working in a state prison. There was a gap between my last day at the hospital and the first day at the prison because of required background checks, drug testing, and the tons of paperwork. It would have been a perfect time for a vacation, but the kids were still in school. So, I took a notion to volunteer for a short-term mission opportunity, and was asked to go to an inner-city clinic in Baltimore.

The next day I booked a flight halfway across the country, and before the week was out, I was the only (albeit temporary) nurse in an inner-city health care clinic. Their one and only paid staff person, also a nurse, would be able to take a much-needed and well-deserved vacation. She hadn't seen her family in three years.

Part of me went to Baltimore hoping God would call me to a different life, but He knew all I needed was a different perspective and a break. Like a lot of people who go on short-term mission trips, I was blessed more than the patients I'd served.

I liked my new job, but I missed the nurses who had become

friends, the doctors with whom I shared a mutual respect, and the cardiac patients who trusted me. Now I greeted coworkers who, out of necessity, shared little of their personal lives; I seldom consulted with a physician; and my patients frequently challenged my decisions.

"Rita. Do you know how to tell when an inmate is lying?"

"No."

"His lips are moving."

It was part of my official orientation. I laughed. It was just a joke, wasn't it?

Sure enough. While passing out medication on my first day, an inmate purposefully dropped a pill and pretended not to be able to find it. He expected the new nurse would automatically hand over another narcotic.

"I may have been born in the dark," I told him, "but it wasn't yesterday. When you give me the tablet you threw under the chair, I'll replace it with a clean one."

Proud of myself for recognizing deceit, I thought I'd make a good correctional nurse.

Within my first thirty days on the job, an inmate complained of chest pain. I was summoned to his cell, where I assessed a genuine complaint. The prison physician didn't question my judgment when I paged. The officers called for an ambulance while I provided pre-hospital care for my patient. No lies. No threats. Just caution, protocols, and a thankful patient who happened to be incarcerated. I could love this new job, I decided.

Conversation between employees and inmates was limited. I understood the reasons for impersonal and brief dialogue, but impersonal and brief didn't need to be unpleasant and rude. When I smiled, the inmates smiled back.

One of my coworkers told me, "You aren't suited for this job. Your friendly ways will get you into trouble."

Another disagreed. "Inmates need a friendly smile and tone of voice, as long as it's professional. Most of them will get out of here. They won't always be inmates. Their kids might be going to school with your kids."

Observing some of the correctional officers helped me to see how both of my coworkers were right.

Some of the sicker inmates appreciated my skills and hospital experience. Policies and procedures related to security or safety required vigilance, but I was good at my job. One of the biggest deals was drawing blood specimens from HIV-infected inmates. Information about the virus was in the juvenile phase. I didn't let it bother me—much.

Walking through the yard among rapists, murderers, and thieves caused my heart rate to increase, but in the clinic or infirmary, one on one, they were my patients. Many of them were boys, not much older than my own son. Most of the inmates appeared as strong and healthy as their peers on the other side of the bars, but many of them had not seen a health care provider, of any kind, since early childhood.

It wasn't long before I realized what had put most of them behind bars in the first place. Fatherlessness was epidemic inside that tall, barbed wire fence. A majority of the inmates had left children of their own on the outside, perpetuating the disease. By the time our paths crossed, most of the men were hardened and emotionally cold, yet I've never seen so many grown men cry.

Where none of the officers or other inmates could hear them, they would express hopelessness and talk of how they had been condemned before they ever committed a crime.

I was lied to. Some told me they were innocent, when I had not asked. Some claimed to be guilty of crimes more glamorous than their reality, trying to scare or impress me. Early on, I decided to allow myself to be gullible. That came easy for me and helped to keep my focus on nursing and not on our gray, concrete, correctional environment. The quality of my nursing care or the amount of time I offered them would not be influenced by their status as prisoners. I was (nearly always) respected.

The incoming eighteen-year-olds disturbed my sleep. I considered Rob and his fatherless situation. What made him different? It was more than a churchgoing Christian mother. How many inmates had expressed regret for disappointing a good, hardworking mother? How long would it be before I would see some of these youngest of inmates return to the infirmary needing treatment for an "accidental" injury or a grossly infected, ill-gotten tattoo?

I grieved for their mothers. I whispered prayers for my own children and for godly father figures in their lives.

One inmate commented that he liked my car and recited my license plate number. Another questioned me about my former husband and my three children. I had only shared my family situation with my boss and a select few coworkers. I'd worn a wedding band since my first day on the job. They shouldn't have known my last name. I wondered what else they knew. Inappropriate remarks about my physique and the occasional "hey baby" were easily ignored, but the truly personal comments were troubling.

A veteran nurse was injured. She forgot to step away from the door to an isolation cell before turning her back on an inmate. One moment of distraction and the inmate reached through the service opening of the door, grabbed her neck, and squeezed. Two officers had difficulty getting him to release her. The bruises were visible when she returned to work two weeks later.

I made the mistake of telling Aimee about that particular incident, which caused her to worry every time I was a few minutes late, or didn't wake her to let her know I was home after an evening shift. She started having bad dreams.

I knew it was time for a change. I would miss some of the adrenaline that comes from working where anything could happen at any time, and I would miss being a light in those dark hallways, but if an inmate could recite the make and model of my car and my license plate number, some unsavory individual could predict my work schedule and when my children would be home alone. I limited my hours to part-time and started looking for another employment opportunity.

With my new job as a dialysis nurse came the most difficult orientation I've experienced to date. I'd failed only two quizzes in nursing school. One was in psychology, and the other in nephrology (the study of the kidneys), so landing a job doing dialysis on the sickest of the sick was intimidating. I studied every handout provided to me and pulled old textbooks off the shelves to review everything I possibly could.

Working with a respected group of doctors and nurses made the middle-of-the-night call-ins tolerable. I enjoyed dialysis nursing enough to study for and earn a certification in nephrology, but I kept some part-time hours at the prison. With three college educations to pay for and little in my savings account, the extra income would help.

My full-time and part-time jobs collided one day when I was called to assist a nephrologist who would be inserting a patient's first dialysis access catheter. Familiar correctional officers watched from a few feet away as we placed the dialysis catheter, and as I performed the inmate's first dialysis treatment. The inmate was shackled to the hospital bed, and I had no cause for fear until he asked, "So how is that Mazda holding up?" My last name was engraved on my medical center identification badge.

I drafted a letter of resignation and hand-delivered it to the prison medical director the next day. God offered grace in my hasty decision.

That grace made me realize something was lacking. As long as my children were healthy and happy, the bills were paid, my job was secure, and I wasn't looking for a man, I didn't seek God's direction or approval. I went for weeks at a time without opening my Bible or praying anything but mandatory, impersonal prayers.

There was a void in my life, but until I stumbled over the extra hours for lack of my part-time job, I hadn't noticed. My lifelong friend, Jesus, had become one of those friends I talked to at church and on special occasions, but we spent little time together. He wasn't pushy. He allowed that sort of relationship.

God continued to be gracious, and I continued to let the void go unfilled—or to find other ways to fill it. I came up with a plan and expected God to follow with a blessing. This time, I dragged Paula and Aimee to Houston, considering a move that would place me close to a university offering a master's degree for parish nurses. Rob was away at college, so it was a girls-only vacation. We had fun with some sightseeing stops and enjoyed traveling through parts of the country we hadn't seen before, but everything to do with the school was a bust. I was not impressed with Texas, the campus, or the school's nursing department, and no one at the university seemed impressed with my willingness to drive through several states and use precious vacation days in order to visit their fine institution.

God blessed, in spite of my wandering. We spent a couple days in Galveston, swimming in the gulf (technically we waded and splashed), before we headed home. The trip made it clear, for all three of us, that living near Grandma and Grandpa was best. If there was any regret, it was gone after one Sunday dinner at Grandma's house.

I pursued other ideas and projects, hoping to bring meaning to my life. None of them involved travel or extravagance. They filled my head with distractions and consumed much of my time, but they did little to fill the void I felt. Everything had become all about me, my needs, my entertainment, and my feelings. Sure, God had a plan for me, but when would it start, and how could I ensure it wouldn't be dull and boring?

The testimony of how I had come to faith was ordinary when compared to others. My friend Bob, for instance, had lived a rough and tumble life, leaving him with an attitude that nearly got him kicked out of the army. A two-star general—did you catch that?—a two-star general saw his potential, called him aside, and told him he needed to change his life. Before the conversation was over, Bob was led to believe in Jesus Christ. The change in his life and attitude was night-and-day, black-and-white evident.

Not so with me. Evidence suggested I was a believer, but despite the times I had shared with patients or inmates, or neighbors, I wasn't a confident witness. People listen intently to victims of abuse, to drug addicts, or prostitutes who turn their lives around, but who wants to hear about a little girl whose parents loved her into a decision for Jesus? The only chapter in my life of interest to anyone was complex, and no venue provided for more than a tiny vignette per conversation. Few people knew the real me.

I had tired of brushing off sympathy with comments about how it was God who held our family together and spouting clichés about mercy and grace. My words were true, but my delivery was uninspired. My story wasn't easily wrapped up in a few sentences. Sympathy, often expressed more like pity, typically interrupted when I shared even a portion of what had become a full-length novel.

To my ears, any glory to God sounded like a mandatory tag or the announcement of a summary. I would be talking about how the kids and I had survived because of our faith and our family support when, whether it was there or not, I could see on listener's faces that they were stuck on the question of how I had become widowed.

I wanted a new story, or at least a better ending to the story I was in.

Was God tired of my lame testimony? Whatever had happened to magnificence? Would the miracle surrounding Aimee's birth be the last event of positive significance I would experience this side of heaven? Would God bring us this far so he could claim glory in our survival and leave us there? Surely not. But it felt that way.

I considered moving my church membership. Maybe worshipping with new people was the change I needed. But where would I go? All my peers who had grown up in church with me had moved away or were no longer attending.

An old friend, who had moved away after high school, came home for a visit. He acted surprised to see me in church, "So you're *still* here."

Whether or not he meant to imply I should have outgrown the building and those people, that's what I heard.

My resolve to be content as a single mom was problematic. The effort to convince myself and others of my happiness wore me out, and I found myself, ten years after Jack's death, cycling again through the stages of grief.

Philippians 4:11 says, "Not that I speak in regard to need, for I have learned in whatever state I am, to be content."

I'd memorized that verse and knew the verses preceding it talked of rejoicing and keeping our minds focused on good as the way to learn contentment, but I couldn't quite get there. It takes a lifestyle of rejoicing to learn to be content. I'd been blessed, and I had reason to rejoice, but I continued to want for more. And I wanted it soon.

It was more than wanting to be in love and married again. It was more than rest from the single mother lifestyle. But if anyone had asked, I wouldn't have been able to clearly state exactly what it was.

One Sunday, I saw myself and my attitude in a story being told from the pulpit. We heard about a rich young man who had followed all the rules since he was a child (or so he claimed), but was aware he lacked something—eternal life. When he asked Jesus what he needed to do to have it, the answer was for him to sell all his belongings and give the proceeds to the poor. He walked away, choosing to keep doing life his way, because he was extremely wealthy.

No, I wasn't wealthy. Nor had I followed all the rules. And yes, I already had eternal life. But on those days when I did approach Jesus, it was to ask him to return the joy that had once been a part of my everyday life. And when I didn't like his answer, I walked away—disappointed and sad, like the rich young man in the Bible story. Eventually, I quit asking and went about doing life my way.

A coworker asked me to go with her to a Christian singles group. I went. The same coworker asked me to go to a not-specifically-Christian singles dance. I went. Absolutely nothing was wrong with my going to either of those events. But I was going in rebellion. I'd declared that if God wouldn't satisfy the desire of my heart, I would do it myself. God listened to my repeated requests, and answered. I pretended not to hear.

I adopted a criterion for a date-worthy man and repeated it often to my friends: "He can be a little bit ugly if he is really rich, or he can be a little bit poor if he is really good-looking, but I refuse to have ugly and poor in the same package."

My declaration got a few laughs, but it didn't help me find a man of quality.

My coworker friend had her own criteria. "I want a man who'll say those three magic words."

"What? I love you?"

"No. Go part-time."

She'd been a single mom for a long time. A lot of single mothers want for a helpmate, or a day off work, more than they want a husband or someone to love. I understood.

Some of the "singles" at the Christian singles party weren't yet single, or had only been single a short time. The only man who spent any time getting to know me had a tan line on his left ring finger. I gave him my number and he called, inviting me to a movie. The movie he wanted to see would have made me uncomfortable. I suggested another. Our conversation ended politely, and he never called again.

At least the sixties music at the dance was familiar. I'd been busy working and raising kids through the eighties and hadn't noticed much of the current music. The singles dance was a monthly activity for my friend, and she took me to her regular table.

Unlike high school, the invitations were plentiful. I danced. A couple of the men asked for my phone number. When one of them asked, I purposely recited it so fast he shouldn't have been able to repeat it, let alone remember it. He called me the next day, and we talked for over an hour. He was charming, but certainly not a prince. Maybe it was his stereotypical ponytailed, motorcycle-riding, Vietnam veteran image that caused my kids to protest. Especially Aimee. She didn't trust me when I promised he would never be her stepfather. He didn't talk about himself much, but he was entertaining, and he didn't mind wasting away an evening with me.

Rob protested. "Mom, don't you see the way he looks at you?"

I saw, but we were friends by then. He respected me and came to church with me. There were four divorces in his past, which gave him reason to tease and call me "Number Five." I looked beyond the flaming red warning flags and saw his good qualities.

A year and a half later, I met another man. He was hardworking and kind. Aimee liked him, in part, because she was glad to see me part ways with the other guy. He was divorced, with two teenaged kids, which might explain why he communicated better with Aimee than with me.

I brought up the subject of church. He said, "I went to church when I was young, and I don't need that."

If he didn't want to discuss church, he certainly wouldn't make it easy to talk about Jesus, so I didn't. He hinted of his willingness to walk away before coming between me and my "religion."

We kept dating. I talked to a friend about it. She told me, "Some men are like that. They don't oppose your faith, as long as you don't impose it on them. It doesn't mean he doesn't love you."

Her husband didn't attend church, and she seemed okay with that. Her husband and my boyfriend were the kind of men that if you're already married to, you stay married, but if you're not married yet, then don't do it. Or at least that's what I understood as right. I didn't want a mismatched relationship like that, and my friend knew it, but how could she warn me without admitting her own situation was less than ideal?

Some men avoid relationships with "religious" women altogether, for fear of facing their own spiritual need, or worse, having to share their Sundays. My boyfriend was like that, and I knew it. So I minimized my faith. I became the one to share my Sundays.

I prayed for him to have a change of heart and simultaneously attached my emotional well-being to him. He would have been a good stepfather, a wonderful provider, a good friend, and an attentive husband for me. He possessed all the attributes on my list of must-haves except the most important thing. Friends encouraged the relationship, telling me it was about time I met a man who loved me the way I deserved to be loved.

I knew the meaning behind their comments, but I also knew this man deserved honesty from me. Marriage to me was not an option as long as he chose to leave his faith in the distant past. It wasn't as simple as church attendance. It was about his core beliefs and his lack of understanding mine. We would have had a great honeymoon and probably a good life after that, but I wanted a partner and a spiritual companion, not merely a "good life."

We didn't talk specifically about marriage or a commitment, but he was "the marrying kind," and the assumption was there. I dreaded the inevitable discussion and loss of his companionship. Opening the conversation and trusting God to take it from there? That sounded good. I knew it on Sunday mornings, but on Friday nights I would open my mouth, and the words I needed to say, the words I'd rehearsed—clumped together in my throat, rendering me silent.

When the doorbell rang one afternoon, I wanted to pretend no one was home. The kids would be home from school soon, and I was about four loads of laundry behind. The kitchen was clean and the living room de-cluttered, but other than my teeth, no part of my personal hygiene had been addressed all day. My typical day off.

I opened the door and blinked. In shock? In surprise? He looked the same. His smile was the same. The man who'd taken five prime years from me, before refusing my ultimatum, was looking for an invitation into my home, and back into my life.

"Come on in."

"You look good."

"You look great. I'm a mess." I pointed to the basket of unfolded towels.

We exchanged a mutual hug, the kind you would expect between reuniting friends, but it was less than either of us wanted. We glanced at one another's ring fingers. His ring couldn't have been gone for more than a day or two. We hugged again.

I pushed him away, interrupting our reunion, in order to manage a moment of ethical conflict. "Wait. Why are you here? What are we doing?"

I knew what I was doing. My old love was apologizing and expressing regret. That's all I needed to bring my plans for a break-up into focus. Except for that frank discussion, my current relationship was over.

"No," I told him. "I'm not dating anyone right now."

True. I hadn't been on a date in five days.

We started talking. It felt like progress. We both admitted past mistakes and apologized. Old wounds were opened and fresh forgiveness applied.

"I never stopped loving you." I don't know which of us said it first.

He made promises. I cried, and we hugged again.

Why couldn't he have promised those things before now? I listened and encouraged him, knowing another man's name was still on next week's calendar. I resisted his attempt to kiss me when we said goodbye, but I couldn't stop the memories or the light-headedness as I watched him walk down my driveway to his car.

Two men wanted my affection. Two men were feeding my ego with words of affirmation. Both had qualities I appreciated and admired. Both were good men. It wasn't a question of love. I loved them both for different reasons. Both were Mr. Right. Neither was right for me.

My boyfriend had tickets and was expecting me. I didn't make the call to cancel the next week's date. *I need to tell him in person. He deserves that much.*

I knew the right thing to do was talk to them both and tell them the truth. On television, these situations were written by professionals who knew how to weave and tangle a story, then have everyone satisfied and smiling before the credits roll. I wanted a screenwriter. A good one.

I went on the date, and the break-up didn't happen. Two dates later, and I hadn't confessed my lapse in ethics to either man. Every week that went by made confessing to either man seven days messier and seven times more complicated. I was terrible at juggling lies and no better at covering my tracks. This was a goliath-sized calamity of my own making, yet I continued with the flirting.

The days passed. God thumped me in the conscience and told me precisely how to change this path to disaster. I promised (several times) to do the right thing—tomorrow. Those were definitely not my finest days.

A month or two into this mess, the two men in my life introduced themselves by way of telephone. One man was in the house, waiting for me to finish getting ready for a date, when I picked up the phone without noticing the other man's number on the caller ID.

"Hello. I thought you had plans tonight," he said.

My heart sank. "I do."

"What kind of plans?" Pause. "Never mind. Let me talk to him."

"Talk to who?"

"The man whose truck is parked in your driveway."

I swallowed. Slowly. The man on the phone had spent a few days thinking about this conversation. He didn't wait for me to formulate another lie.

"You can hand him the phone, or I can be ringing your doorbell within a few minutes."

He was serious, not one to make idle threats, but I begged, "No. You can't do that. Please. Don't."

"I can. And I will."

"Please. Can we talk later?"

"I've got nothing to say to you. Give him the phone."

Even though it wasn't a collision in the usual sense, they both walked away injured. I was humiliated and ashamed. I'd known better than to invite another goliath into my life, or into theirs.

My apologies bounced off closed minds. The churchgoing Christian in this trio was me. God forgave me, but my witness had been destroyed with two men I cared for deeply. Everything I claimed to represent made me a liar.

Being released from that trap gave me an odd sense of relief. I felt punished by God for a while. Then I knew I was loved. I knew the collision hadn't happened by fate or happenstance. God had warned me (like a parent warns a child) that he would do something if I didn't, and God keeps his promises.

I knew not to go to that place on Goliath's Mountain, and went there anyway, but there was God's grace—again and still. God is good. All the time.

33

NEVER DONE

They say a woman's work is never done. Do the math. That's doubly true for most single moms. I must have gone up and down the stairs fifty times, but the laundry was done, and the house was as clean as it was going to get for the week. When I chose to mow the lawn on Friday night, it was so I could have some free time on Saturday; maybe watch a movie or shop for some new work shoes and scrubs.

However, this Saturday had been like so many others. All work and no play. Where had I heard that? Oh yeah, that's what I said every Monday morning when anyone asked about my week-end.

At least I had Sundays. Then, I spent three hours in church on Sunday morning, an hour or two having a family dinner at Mom and Dad's, then had an hour or two of *me* time before we headed back to church. On Sunday nights, when friends went out to eat, and . . . well, I don't know what it was that they did, because I was usually too tired to go.

On this particular Saturday night, I was disappointed that my "me time" had been all about work, but happy to be done for the day. I was physically exhausted, yet unable to settle on my pillow. Sleep wouldn't have me.

A minute or two of complaining thoughts turned to a complaining prayer. No greeting or thanking God tonight, I was worn out and needed to get to the point. The point being, that I needed sleep. If

He wouldn't give me much of anything else I asked for, the least He could do, as God of the universe, was help me fall asleep.

God seemed to answer. *Not yet.*

I finished the novel that had been on my nightstand for several weeks. *Not yet.*

Hot chocolate milk. *Not yet.*

Infomercials. *Not yet.*

"God, what do you want with me? Now is not the best time." I scrolled through a list of my good deeds, some of them recent.

I told God what I was willing to do—a new job, more responsibility at church, volunteer work in the community. I made several suggestions, but none of them got a clear response. Surely he wouldn't ask me to do something from my "never" list.

I acknowledged recent *infractions*. There were only a few, I had been too busy to get into any real trouble. Surely, that would make things right with God. I recited some memorized praise. That ought to make God happy.

But God was not moved by my formulaic prayer. *Not yet*, He seemed to be saying.

I was talking to Jesus, as a savior and a friend, asking for favors, and hoping for preferential treatment. That's what my prayer life had become.

A lady I hadn't thought of in years came to my mind. *People Need the Lord* had been the hymn before she went to the platform. Everyone listened as she spoke to our congregation. I remembered her telling about how, for many years, she had been praying for missionaries and for more people to be willing to serve in faraway places.

Then she said, "I would not be able to pray that prayer if I thought God would call one of my children to serve."

She and her husband had worked hard so they could live well, and so their children could have college educations. I thought her testimony sincere. It was, but then she concluded her talk without confessing her haughtiness and unwillingness to trust her children to God's plan. There was no testimony of a changed heart—not even a change in progress. Instead, she left her audience believing she wasn't willing to release her kids to a life of service, especially if sacrifice or danger might be involved.

I was in my teens then, but the expression on her face and the tone of her voice came back as I thought of her. I remembered having an uneasy feeling as she took her seat. I was sad for her. Didn't she know that, in her lack of trust, she was sacrificing her children to a world that would take from them, when to offer them to the Lord would have been to shower them with good?

My pillow was fluffed and turned cool side up. The television was off, and hot chocolate milk warmed me from the inside out.

I wanted sleep, but while examining the speck in another's eye, a plank had created a flood of tears in mine. I saw myself as having the same sort of attitude. Religiously, I'd been asking God for a change, not in my heart, but in His. Bowing my head, closing my eyes, and saying all the right words wasn't even fooling me. I wasn't ready to accept God's will, if that meant being single the rest of my life. That was okay for some people, but not for me.

One thing was for sure. I wouldn't confess my sin publicly. That would make me uneasy, and sad. God was done with this conversation. He allowed me a few hours of sleep.

The pastor read from the book of Jeremiah the next morning. My eyelids were heavy, but I caught the words "captive" and "prosperity." Jeremiah's original message was given to the nation of Israel, but change the names of the places, insert my name here or there, and I had to believe this ancient message was for me. I made a mental note to read the chapters and verses before and after the referenced words. I hadn't read my Bible, searching like that, in quite a while.

A theologian could camp (as my grandma would say) for a month of Sundays in the twenty-ninth chapter of Jeremiah. I only camped there for a couple hours on that Sunday afternoon. But it was enough to keep me thinking.

The captives in Jeremiah's audience were Israelites who had been forced from Jerusalem to Babylon and would not be returned to their homeland for seventy years. They were instructed to build houses, plant gardens, marry, and give their daughters in marriage. They were encouraged to seek and to pray for peace in the place where God had put them. Were those the things a *captive* would do?

I wondered if they considered their prosperity, even in their captivity. How did they know God was still their God? That he cared about them? Were they like me? Did they feel that God was doing nothing?

I had friends who felt captive in their marriages, their jobs, or another sort of life's complicated relationships. I knew plenty of people who anticipated freedom after divorcing or separating from whomever or whatever they were painfully bound to, but after signing the papers or walking away, they were still captive. I could have named a few who had been emotionally captive for longer than the Israelites were.

I felt captive in my single-mom lifestyle. I was living in a place where I didn't want to be. God was still my God, but . . .

I had been widowed for about fifteen years and was tired of being single. Aimee would be leaving for college in a few years and I would be alone, but what I felt was unlike the dread of an empty nest. There was no time in my life I wanted to return to, and no bars or chains were keeping me from moving forward. There was nothing I wanted to cling to and nothing begging me to move.

I don't imagine any of my friends (especially my married friends) recognized how dissatisfied I was with my life circumstance. I put on a believable show. Keeping up with a teenager, work, church, and managing our small household of two wasn't the challenge it had been years earlier. I wore a smile every day.

Some of my friends envied my freedom. How ironic. Could captivity be a matter of perspective?

The writings of Jeremiah stirred my emotion and highlighted my need for change, but for several more weeks, I kept up appearances.

During a small group meeting/Bible study, a friend reminded me, "It's not about you, Rita."

She had borrowed the line from Rick Warren's book, *The Purpose Driven Life*. Our group had used the book as a Bible study guide, and the phrase "It's not about you" had become an easy (and fun) reminder that many of our personal concerns and prayers were inwardly focused and selfishly motivated.

It didn't take writing on a wall or an angelic appearance for me to see I'd been like a toddler with a boo-boo, convinced my pain was of heart-attack proportions. No, I hadn't been captive. I was simply *captivated* by what looked to be the "good life" being lived by those around me. As long as I spent time and energy looking for a shortcut to what I hoped was God's plan for me to prosper, I would remain there—free but living like a prisoner.

My friend did not suspect I felt captive. She wouldn't have guessed I harbored anger in my heart. She couldn't have known I was stubbornly withholding a piece of my heart, soul, and mind as if God would feel the impact of my protest and change the rules of the universe just for me.

I felt captive when I wasn't. I felt poor when I was prosperous. The pain I felt was either common to most everyone or self-inflicted. My feelings were being allowed to rule my brain, and I felt hopelessly hypocritical.

That afternoon I *felt* like praying.

Lord, remember me? I remember you. I remember trusting you with everything, even the hard stuff. I should praise you for releasing me from my most recent trap. That was something, wasn't it! Sorry. Again. I hope you believe me when I say that won't happen again. Not even close. Sorry too, for wanting what you haven't planned for me. It's just that I feel . . . yeah, I know. I don't know what I feel, and I shouldn't trust my feelings.

I know you love me. I remember what it feels (there's that word again!) like to love you back and trust you with my obedience. I remember chasing after you and catching up. Oh, that felt good. You make me feel a kind of good like nothing or no one else can. I can't believe you don't make me wait for all the good stuff until I get to heaven. I don't deserve anything good. I've been chasing after what everyone else seems to be so happy with. Running with the world hasn't brought me prosperity. It has worn me down. I'm tired, Lord. Prosperity is wherever you are, and that's where I want to be. Help me get there. Amen.

Over the next few weeks, one thing after another reminded me that God cherished his relationship with me. God doesn't flirt. He doesn't tease, but he has a way of drawing us to him. Miraculous coincidences. An old friend with a word of encouragement precisely when I needed it. A last-minute home repair recommendation that saved me thousands of dollars. I haven't seen God's image on a piece of toast yet, and I'd be the first skeptic looking for the trail of cash if I did, but it had to be God who turned every traffic light green one day, and then stopped the rain as I pulled into the parking lot where I worked.

Aimee had followed Rob and Paula's footsteps by auditioning and earning a spot in our high school's show choir. The choir practiced hard and was always preparing for the next show. I was in the audience for all three of my kids, cheering them on during local performances, and if my work schedule and my budget permitted, I traveled to out-of-town competitions. By the time Aimee was in her junior year, I could have been a competition judge. It was exciting to watch the group progress from learning the popular music and dance moves to putting it all together, complete with costumes. However, traveling with a crowd of married parents had gotten old. Depressing actually.

I didn't want my girl to be the only one without a parent to bring her flowers at the end of an outstanding performance, so I arranged my priorities and packed the car.

The name of the town is no more important than the name of the hotel chain, and I loved to travel, so it wasn't my accommodations making me wish I were at home in my own bed. I could hear girls giggling in the hallway and a couple laughing in the next room. I was alone (again) in a hotel room.

Rather than throw a pity party because I was the only single parent at this and the past two away competitions, I thought I would watch some TV. A hundred channels, and nothing to watch. I would have read a novel, but I'd forgotten to bring it. That left the Bible.

I almost laughed to realize what I was doing. God had been getting more of my attention recently. There wasn't a man in my life. I had done it again—turned my attention to the one I call "Lord" only when my first three choices weren't handy. How insulted I would be to think someone was my good friend only because I was the only one available.

Sitting cross-legged and propped up by pillows, I was glad a Gideon had been there before me. But first, I had something to say:

Lord, I'm unhappy. I'm trapped. Yes, I know it's just a feeling, but I can't help what I feel. I'm angry again, not for what Jack did, but for what you haven't done. And what's going on between us? I come to you and ask, but you don't answer. Why do I still feel this way?

A page was folded over at the fourth chapter of 1 John. I read through the fourth verse as though it were the introduction to an algebra textbook. (My apologies to any mathematicians.) I read verses 5–16 as though they were explaining simple addition. (Apologies again.)

It wasn't until I got to the seventeenth verse that I gave my full attention to what I was reading. John, the apostle who likely wrote these words, was known as the disciple whom Jesus loved. I needed a tutorial on love. I certainly hadn't been getting it right.

So I read the chapter again, from the beginning. When I arrived at the seventeenth and eighteenth verses this time, the words "perfect" and "love" begged for meditation:

"Love has been perfected among us in this: that we may have boldness in the day of judgment; because as he is, so are we in this world. There is no fear in love; but perfect love casts out fear." (1 John 4:17-18a).

I'd read and heard those verses many times, even heard sermons based on them, so it wasn't for lack of understanding that I had settled for an imperfect kind of romantic love, instead of trusting myself fully to the love of God. What was I afraid of? Sometimes I amaze myself, not because I see deep impactful truths, but because I trample through them on a regular basis without letting them change me.

God had a plan for me to prosper. I was in the way. The person between the desires of my heart and me, was me. I'd been haughty, just like the woman who prayed for missionaries. It was easy to confess my sin—I'd done it a few times. The problem was I just kept going in the same direction, expecting to be excused. Expecting God to wink, pat me on my conscious, and then step aside.

Trusting God's promises when it came to my children, my career, my finances, and my own safety was so much easier than trusting him to arrange my marital status in a way that would satisfy me. One more time, I expressed my desire for companionship, for a partner in life's big deals and little pleasures. A marriage partner. It was a Sunday morning, around noon. I'd had enough of this silly battle, so I went to the front of the church to surrender. I bowed my heart, not just my head. I prayed with my eyes open (thanks for that lesson, Mrs. Curtis) both physically and spiritually. Fully aware that whatever I released to God was his already, I held back nothing. He didn't yell, scold, or pile on punishment. All God wanted from me was obedience—one thing at a time.

I didn't confess publicly or share my transgressions with the congregation. God didn't ask me to, and I won't bother trying to impress anyone with the maturity or spiritual resolve it took to give God the desire of my heart. Knowing it was God's desire for me to experience perfect love as I fell asleep at night was one thing, but remembering to act like that was true the next day (and the days after) was something else. Some mornings, I must have had to restart the repentance process three or four times before getting out of bed.

To repent means to turn away from sin and make a change. Most of the time, it's a process, not a brief experience. True repentance continues after we've asked to be forgiven and walked away from the altar. True repentance isn't proven in a day. I was learning not to follow my feelings first, but I was feeling that my repenting, like woman's work, would never be done.

34

STAINS AND STICKY SPOTS

Jack will never be forgotten. Over thirty years have gone, and I still cry when I think about not being able to say a proper "Good-bye. I love you." Except for a few stains and sticky spots that will not go away, the mess Jack left behind has been scrubbed clean. I can live with that. I can live well with that.

People have asked how I was able to forgive him. Forgive him for what? My parents taught me well: "You discipline a child for throwing the glass of milk across the room, but for the involuntary spilling of milk, you clean up the mess."

Mrs. Curtis was about a decade older than my current age when I caught her with her eyes open during prayer. I may not know who or what caused her stains and sticky spots, but she must have felt what it was like to dream Cinderella dreams in a world full of giants. I like to think she was praying for me that day. If she prayed for God's blessings to fall on me, they have.

Rob, Paula, and Aimee have grown into fine adults who are teaching their own children how to survive, overcome, and thrive in a world where there's bound to be some trouble. All three know what it's like to look a goliath in the eye. All three can put up a good fight, but know better than to fight their battles alone. I pray that they won't be attacked, and for them to choose just the right stone when they are. Does that mean God answers my prayers, the way I want him to? Does that mean we haven't had struggles common to all families? Of course not.

Was Jack right in his thinking that we would be better off without him? Absolutely not! The kids needed him. I needed him. That was most evident during Rob, Paula, and Aimee's teen years. Once the kids grew out of that sweet spot between potty trained and hormones, all of my imperfections were magnified. Some days I was more imperfect than others. Sometimes God took "sides," and it wasn't mine. There were also those times when it seemed I did everything right, and stuff happened anyway.

But the messes and sticky spots that Jack left behind blended so well with the junk of being a teenager, and living with teenagers, that teasing out the root cause of our problems was impossible. It would have been convenient for me, or the kids, to blame things on Jack long after he was gone, but we all knew better. Anything that happened after 1984 was on us.

It's up to Rob, Paula, and Aimee to write the stories of their teen years from their perspective. There were four of us in that household, which means there will be four different sequels to *Goliath's Mountain*. I'm sure to be surprised by the revealing of some antics and anecdotes, but I'm confident all four sequels will end well.

As I write this, I pray my children will treat me and their father kindly in the telling of their stories. I pray, that in hearing our stories, some single mother and her children might appreciate something from my mistakes, and see a better way to fight mean giants.

1 John 5:19-20 says: *We know that we are of God, and the whole world lies under the sway of the wicked one. And we know that the Son of God has come and has given us an understanding, that we may know Him who is true; and we are in Him who is true, in His Son Jesus Christ. This is the true God and eternal life.*

Goliath has a temporary claim on the mountain where we live, and he took from us that which can never be returned or replaced. But this is Our Father's world, and He has done great things for us.

Rob is an officer in the United States Marine Corps. His two sons and his daughter make fathering look easy and fun. He is still a wise and confident advisor, as well as a generous and cheerful tipper.

Paula is busy mothering two boys and two girls. She hasn't lost her passion as a fearless defender and momma bear. She got that from my mother. I think she got her love for music from me, but it was my sister Rhonda and my brother Kevin who showed her what to do with it. She still looks great in pink.

Aimee, a caretaker, a doer, and an encourager, works for a government agency helping people who are about to retire, people with disabilities, and widows with dependent children. Does God know what He is doing—or what! Her little boy, the baby of our family, is the eighth of Jack's and my grandchildren.

Not for anything that I've done, but I'm ridiculously proud, and rightfully so, of Rob, Paula, Aimee, and their children. God is faithful. God is good.

Sounds like your better than average fairytale ending, but there's more.

Roger and I met when both of us (in our mid-forties) submitted to just one more blind date. I had determined this would be the last time I cleaned up, dressed up, and put on make-up, only to be disappointed by a complete stranger. He was ready to give up his pursuit of romance and family.

He seemed like a nice guy when we talked on the phone. He went to church. He had never been married. He had a good job and probably made a decent living. We lived about forty-five minutes from each other, so I had no need to worry about awkward encounters in the grocery store, or at the mall, when this one and only date was over.

When the funeral visitation for a family member conflicted with our date, I suggested we postpone. Roger wanted to go ahead with our dinner plans but move the time back one hour. He didn't say it directly, but he wanted this last blind date to be over as much as I did.

The visitation line was much longer than expected, and I would be late. I called the restaurant and asked the hostess to let him know, almost hoping he wouldn't be willing to wait. I freshened my lipstick in the car and ran toward the restaurant entrance, partly because I was late, but mostly because it was a chilly October evening. The hostess took me right to him.

My evaluation started before I saw his face. His shirt had a collar—a plus. He stood to greet me. Another plus. His handshake was firm, but not crushing. I sensed that his initial evaluation of me was going well. He kept his eyes on me instead of the attractive server, and the conversation volleyed evenly. He was a nondrinker and nonsmoker because it was a lifestyle preference, not because he thought he would die and go to hell if he did that sort of thing.

I told myself, a few bites into the entrée, *"This guy is quite a catch for someone, but probably not for me."* Roger wasn't poor or unattractive, but neither was he exceedingly wealthy or devastatingly handsome. He was cute, interesting, and interested in me. I planned on ordering dessert.

We talked for a least an hour after our plates were cleared, over the last drizzle of chocolate, and then more in the parking lot. The conversation eventually turned to small talk about the cold night air.

The parking lot was clearing, and frost had collected on our car windshields when, finally, he said the words I'd been waiting for.

"Can we do this again? Sometime soon?"

"Why do you think I'm still standing here, with chattering teeth, shivering in the cold? I was hoping you would ask."

He stepped closer and there was some confusion as to whether our good night would be a handshake, a side hug, or a kiss. We turned our cheeks in the same direction, and our faces bumped awkwardly. Our date ended with a good laugh and a verbal "good night."

There was a second date. I heard him say he preferred blondes. Then a third. I mentioned that I wasn't looking for anything serious. By the fourth date, he had heard about how my marriage ended, how I had struggled raising three kids without their father, and about some of my most recent bad choices. He listened. He told me about a goliath or two in his past.

It seemed I was talking to a good and comfortable friend. When I laid down my criteria for a possible husband, with being a believer in Jesus Christ at the top of the list, he didn't blink or stutter. When I added the qualities I knew would be necessary for a God-ordained marriage, and a few of my personal preferences, he told me he was looking for the same things in a woman. I assumed a blonde.

Of course, all the talk of marriage was in a theoretical sense, or to point out the mistakes of some of our friends and acquaintances for entertainment purposes. Neither of us wanted to "rush into anything," although for many years, we'd prayed to find someone like the person sitting on the other side of the table.

I was sick for several days. He sent me flowers. He brought me soup. Not homemade, but he brought me soup. He called me most days, and every evening after work, to see if I needed anything. I liked this guy. I really liked this guy. I didn't deserve this.

I introduced Roger to family and friends on a Sunday morning. They were nodding with approval. I was nodding with doubt.

Roger made a great first impression. One of the greeters at church could be trusted to provide unsolicited opinions of all my church dates. He said, behind Roger's back, "This one's a keeper."

That was in November 1999. Was it time for me to quit chasing after the good and the better, and say yes to God's plan for me to have his best?

The big bomb that's been known to drop and ruin my potential relationships never did explode. I watched and waited, even planned my escape, but there was no bomb. Instead, everything Roger said and did made me love him more.

But I wasn't going to be the first to say it.

He *treated* me like he loved me. We talked every day. He became my go-to person for everything from auto maintenance and home repair, to raising teenagers. He was confident in all things automotive and willing to dive into all things related to home repair. When it came to raising teenagers, all he had was random ideals—thoughts he'd put together from what his parents used to say, lessons from lunchroom chatter at work, or a rare article from one of his automotive, airplane, or scuba diving magazines. He wasn't a know-it-all, but neither was he shy about sharing his opinion, and he was usually right.

Roger was the best friend I'd been hoping for.

I was the only girlfriend he'd ever invited to share a meal with his mother and brother. That was a bit of trivia I learned while helping his mother load the dishwasher. I was invited again for a Thanksgiving meal, and then a family wedding. During the hour and a half ride home, I hoped to hear the words I was waiting for. With only fifteen minutes to my driveway, I asked, "Do you think your mom and brother liked me?"

"I'm sure they did."

"Well, I'm not Lutheran. I hope that's not a problem?"

No answer.

Roger's lack of response was better than what I feared.

Either the bomb was going to drop, or this night would end with me hearing "I love you."

"Roger, do you still wish I were a blonde?" I braced for his answer.

"I never wished you were a blonde."

"But shortly after we met, you told me you preferred blondes."

"Preferred. That's past tense, Rita."

Our hands met on the console. *Patience, Rita. Talk about something else.*

"Roger?"

"Yes."

"Can we get something awkward out of the way?"

"Sure."

"Christmas is a few weeks away, and we haven't talked about exchanging gifts. I haven't bought you anything yet, and I won't if you'd rather skip the whole gift thing?"

"I already bought you something."

"You did! What?"

Of course, he wouldn't tell me. When Roger has a plan, he sticks to it.

I didn't invite him in because we both had an early morning, but our usual goodnight kiss turned into three, then four, then five. If he didn't tell me he loved me after number six, he would *never* tell me. Aimee blinked the porch light.

One quick peck and he offered his goodnight: "Talk to you tomorrow."

During our next conversation and the ones that followed, he amused himself by mentioning the Christmas present he had for me, without disclosing where he had made the purchase or the size of the package. My anticipation of Christmas Day had me almost giddy, then Roger said "Let's open presents tonight."

"But Roger, it's five days 'til Christmas."

I hoped he'd like the sweater and that it fit. *Would he care, or notice, that I'd used the coordinated wrapping paper, ribbon, and bow instead of the big-roll stuff?*

He liked the sweater.

He pulled out a little box. It scared me. No wrapping. Just a ribbon and tiny bow. *It was way too soon,* I thought. *All I wanted was an I love you.*

Roger stepped back, as if to enjoy my brief moment of agony, before he said, "It's not what you think."

"How do you know what I'm thinking?"

I opened the box with trepidation and breathed a sigh of relief to see a delicate gold necklace. It was pretty and shiny, but left me wondering.

"You know what giving a girl a heart means, don't you?" I asked.

"Yes."

I waited.

"I love you, Rita."

"I knew it. I love you too."

We continued to date, eating out and going to movies mostly. I visited his church a time or two, but by Christmas, he had been attending regularly with me. The theme of VBS the next summer had to do with things under the sea. He wore his scuba gear for my fifth and sixth graders to see. What a guy! He invited me to a family reunion. It was fun—being the mystery woman on the arm of their family's most eligible bachelor.

But neither of us wanted to "rush into anything."

By Thanksgiving of 2001, our talk about marriage was a little less theoretical. We were talking every day, seeing each other two or three time a week, in church together every Sunday. When Christmas came, I don't remember the gifts we exchanged, but one of them wasn't an engagement ring. I remember feeling disappointed.

The Sunday after Valentine's Day 2002, I had a new ring to show everyone. No one was surprised, but everyone was pleased to hear we were engaged to be married. That same greeter saw mine and Roger's smiles and looked to my ring finger. He shook Roger's hand and gripped his shoulder. "Roger. It's a good thing you believe in the Trinity. Because you're about to be a husband, a father, *and* a grandfather."

I found it difficult to take my eyes off the ring. Amber-colored windows filtered the sunlight in our church's sanctuary, but the diamond was still able to catch a stream of light and forward it to the back of the pew in front of us. During the prayer that morning, I was mesmerized by the way light danced with the slightest movement of my ring finger. I looked up at Roger. He had his eyes wide open, looking down at my new diamond.

The conversation over Sunday dinner that afternoon was already lively, so I didn't tattle to my family that Roger had his eyes open during a prayer.

We were married in August of 2002. Our honeymoon was perfect, but it wasn't long before I discovered that Roger wasn't. He claims to have known all along that I'm no Cinderella, and life with me would be no fairytale.

We had been married less than a year when I missed one of the onyx earrings that belonged to the set my mom gave me. I mourned briefly, but the clock was ticking, so I selected another necklace and earrings for wherever I was going that required me to leave the house wearing jewelry.

For days, I was in denial. The earring must have fallen behind my dresser, or into an open drawer. There was no immediate need to search. It had to be somewhere in our bedroom. Weeks later, it was still missing. The earring came to mind every time I cleaned. I listened for clicking and checked the vacuum. I cleaned along baseboards and straightened drawers looking for the earring. I started bargaining. I prayed over it.

Dear Lord, help me not to be upset over an earring. It's silly, but it is one of the earrings Mom gave me right after Jack died. It means a lot. I hope you know how much it means to me. Never mind. Of course you know. Amen.

God didn't find it in his will (I didn't think he looked) to show me where my earring had landed. He wouldn't remind me when or where I had worn it last. He wasn't helping me to help myself. The anger stage—again.

This time it was Roger living with me in my anger, and he wasn't interested in being my verbal punching bag. He had vacuumed the living room and dumped the collection of fuzzy dirt in the garage trash. And everyone knows, or they ought to know, that once it's in *that* garbage can, it's gone. Well, not everyone knew that. Roger didn't.

We had words. He suggested I dive into the thirty-gallon container to look for an earring that, by now, had been missing for six months. He wasn't aware that I was still sifting for my earring every time I cleaned.

I didn't dive. I apologized for venting my anger on him, thanked him for helping with the housework, and counted Roger as the huge blessing he was. The acceptance phase? Almost.

I try not to listen when people compare someone's period of mourning or stages of grief to some elusive expectation. To minimize another's loss is unkind and ignorant. To think someone hasn't mourned strongly enough or long enough is judgmental. Just because I put on another pair doesn't mean I wouldn't drive across the country to retrieve my missing earring.

It was something as small as an earring that was taking me back to where I'd been in 1984—back to Goliath's Mountain. The earring was officially lost. I had been through denial, bargaining, and anger. It's fair to assume I'd skip through depression to accept that I still had a beautiful onyx necklace and a single earring that could be crafted into a ring or some other interesting piece of jewelry. Fair, but not so. I chose to be depressed about my lost earring.

After about a month of pouting and whining, some words I had printed and framed caught my eye. They were the words Roger and I spoke at our wedding. We vowed:

> *To be companions and friends.*
> *To be partners in life's big deals and trivial pursuits.*
> *To be each other's biggest fan and greatest ally.*
> *To be comrades in adventure and accomplices in mischief.*
> *To be a voice of consolation in disappointments.*
> *To be a trusted confidant and counselor.*
> *And to be a brother/sister in Christ as we seek God's will.*

Acceptance.

Another giant will come along soon enough. Until then, and even then, God is faithful. God is good. God is so perfectly good. All the time.

Printed in the United States
By Bookmasters